Margery Kempe and Translations of the Flesh

University of Pennsylvania Press
NEW CULTURAL STUDIES SERIES

Joan DeJean, Carroll Smith-Rosenberg, and Peter Stallybrass, Editors

A complete listing of the books in this series appears at the back of the book.

Margery Kempe and Translations of the Flesh

By Karma Lochrie

University of Pennsylvania Press

Philadelphia

Library of Congress Cataloging-in-Publication Data

Lochrie, Karma.
    Margery Kempe and translations of the flesh / by Karma Lochrie.
        p.   cm. — (New cultural studies series)
    Includes bibliographical references and index.
    ISBN 0-8122-3107-4 (cloth); 0-8122-1557-5 (pbk)
    1. Kempe, Margery, b. ca 1373. Book of Margery Kempe.
2. Christian literature, English (Middle)—History and criticism.
3. Mysticism—England—History—Middle Ages, 600–1500. 4. Women,
Christian—England—Religious life—History. 5. Flesh (Theology) in
literature. I. Title. II. Series.
PR2007.K4Z77   1991
248.2'2'092—dc20
[B]   91-26069
                                                              CIP

Contents

Acknowledgments

I am grateful to my colleagues at the University of Hawaii who inspired me to pursue this project in its initial stages, particularly Nell Altizer, Kathleen Falvey, Jay Kastely, and Judith Kellogg. Many scholars have contributed to this effort with their knowledge, suggestions, and comments, including Gail McMurray Gibson, Margot H. King, Valerie Lagorio, Clare A. Lees, and Gillian R. Overing. I am particularly indebted to Allen J. Frantzen at Loyola University of Chicago for his encouragement and support of my research and for his generous readings of this manuscript. Others who read all or part of the manuscript, including Elizabeth Robertson and Willemien Otten, are deserving of my gratitude. For help in preparing the manuscript, I thank Gordon Sellers, who assisted with proofreading and compiling of the index, and Mary Dye, who transfered a draft of the manuscript to a new computer system.

I wish to thank the National Endowment for the Humanities for a Summer Stipend, and Loyola University of Chicago and the University of Hawaii for their grant support. At the University of Pennsylvania Press, I am indebted to my editor, Jerome E. Singerman, for his direction and encouragement, and to Alison Anderson, for her guidance through the final stages of the book. I am also grateful for the assistance of the librarians at Trinity College, Cambridge, and for the enthusiasm and camaraderie of the medievalists at the Newberry Library in Chicago.

Part of Chapter 1 originally appeared in "The Language of Transgression: Body, Flesh, and Word in Mystical Discourse," in *Speaking Two Languages: Traditional Disciplines and Contemporary Theory in Medieval Studies,* ed. Allen J. Frantzen (Albany: State University of New York Press, 1991). Portions of Chapter 3 appeared in *"The Book of Margery Kempe*: the Marginal Woman's Quest for Literary Authority," *Journal of Medieval and Renaissance Studies* 16 (1986): 33–56. Chapter 4 began as a conference paper which was subsequently published, "Margery Kempe and the Rhetoric of Laughter," *Vox Benedictina* 3 (1986). I thank the publishers of these journals and the essay collection for permission to reprint this material in revised form. I also thank the Council of the Early English Text Society for permission to quote from Sanford B. Meech and Hope Emily Allen, *The Book of Margery Kempe,* EETS, o.s. 212 (1940; rpt. 1961).

Finally, I would like to give special thanks to Huma Ibrahim, whose friendship and intellectual vitality have benefited me immeasurably. To my parents, I will always owe a debt of thanks for their continued support.

Introduction

> There is hardly any other calamity more apt to do harm or that is more incurable [than the unbridled speech of women]. If its only consequence were the immense loss of time, this would already be sufficient for the devil. But you must know that there is something else to it: the insatiable itch to see and to speak, not to mention . . . the itch to touch.[1]

In 1415, Jean Gerson, chancellor of the University of Paris, wrote a treatise in response to the alarming claims of St. Bridget and other women to mystical revelation and prophecy. *De probatione spirituum* represents Gerson's attempt to provide guidelines for the Church by which it could identify true mystical inspiration and condemn false religious fervor. In this treatise, Gerson warns against the religious appetites of women and adolescents (whom he lumps together) which make them prone to unbridled speech and passions.[2] In the quotation above, Gerson specifically addresses the problem of woman's speech in conjunction with the appetitive faculties, of sight and touch, in particular. The excessive quality of woman's speech is linked implicitly with that "insatiable itch to touch," and with bodiliness. Behind the visions and speech of women mystics, Gerson senses that "something else" which renders it calamitous, that is, the woman's body. The word he chooses to describe her mystical desire, "itch," is a telling one because it imparts some of Gerson's own horror and disgust at the insufficiently mortified female flesh.[3]

This book begins with Gerson's insatiable itch not in order to draw attention to his misogyny or to make light of his point; rather, I take it as the starting point for my study of one of the most controversial of late medieval mystics, Margery Kempe, in order to highlight what is at stake in any discussion of her. The intersection of woman's body and her speech is a crucial problem in any analysis of late medieval piety. We cannot begin to discuss what Gerson means by his critique until we ask questions about medieval culture's understanding of the female body and about women's speech and writing. In turn, issues surrounding Margery Kempe's mystical practices, her autobiographical mystical treatise, and her methods as an author dictating her work to a scribe await a theoretical investigation of the insatiable itch, including what it means for women to speak and write the body in their mystical visions and treatises.

"Writing the body" is a phrase I borrow from contemporary feminist theory.[4] In using the phrase, however, I am not adopting contemporary understandings of what it means for a woman to "write her body." Instead, I want to argue that Gerson is objecting to a kind of *écriture féminine* in the Middle Ages, that is, a feminine writing of the body. This writing of women mystics, continental as well as English, must be viewed, in turn, against the suppression of the female body in language. While all such suppression exists within—and in the service of—patriarchal culture, it varies through languages and cultures and across time. One of the central purposes of this book is to describe the repression of the female body in the context of medieval culture, rather than solely through contemporary theoretical analysis. Repression of the female body, as we shall see, takes a different form in the Middle Ages than it does in contemporary culture, and therefore the woman writer's task of adopting a language must be viewed specifically within her historical and cultural context. *The Book of Margery Kempe* is positioned within this twin cultural and theoretical focus.

Contemporary discussion of the female body in language is particularly relevant to the study of Margery Kempe and late medieval mysticism because of the presence in both of an emergent concern with the body in mystical imagery and language which so alarmed Gerson. Carolyn Walker Bynum has abundantly discussed and documented the figuration of the female body in late medieval mysticism.[5] Both the medieval idea of the imitation of Christ as an imitation of his humanity—his bodiliness—and the increasingly graphic representations of that bodiliness are defining features of late medieval mysticism and of women's mystical experiences in particular.

The answer to the question of why this is so has changed considerably since 1924 when Huizinga invoked Gerson himself to explain what happened in the late Middle Ages:

> Mysticism is brought into the streets. Many people take to it, without suitable direction, and indulge in too rigid fasts, too protracted vigils, and too abundant tears, all of which disturb their brains. . . . There is nothing more dangerous, says Gerson, than ignorant devotion.[6]

When mysticism takes to the streets, it becomes "common," with all the earmarks of class, social conditioning, and historical corruption. Its mystery is clearly in danger, according to this way of thinking. Furthermore, ignorance and women's excessive emotionalism are blamed by Gerson in the fifteenth century and Huizinga in the twentieth century for the literalism of mystical language, the physicality of its images and practices, and its emphasis on Christ's suffering.

Recent interest in the ecstatic practices of fifteenth-century mystics has contributed to revising our understanding of their mysticism. André Vauchez in particular has argued that the attraction of late medieval piety to women, with its emphasis on the physical aspects of mystical experience, is due in part to its providing them with a "privileged communication" with God and an access to religious mystery otherwise denied them.[7] Vauchez recognizes that feminine mysticism in the late Middle Ages was "profoundly subversive" because of the extent to which it drew attention to the rupture between divine love and intellectual understanding.[8] Bynum likewise emphasizes the way in which late medieval spirituality provided women with a new access to divine love. She characterizes the rationale behind some of the more disturbing late medieval mystical practices with the idea that "bodiliness provides access to the sacred."[9]

This is the point where a feminist interrogation of the body and writing, or language, in medieval culture is helpful, for we cannot understand what "bodily access to the sacred" actually means for the Middle Ages without first determining what and whose body we are talking about, and how that body is situated in patriarchal culture. My point is that the body is not something we can take as a "given," nor something which is the same for the Middle Ages as it is for us in the 1990s. The body, particularly the female body, is itself a construct of science, medicine, theology, literature, education, the clothing industry, advertising, and fitness centers. Except for the last two industries, the same is true for the Middle Ages. The female body, simply put, has a history, and that history is determined by social and religious values, institutions, and patriarchal power structures. As Susan Rubin Suleiman has argued, "The cultural significance of the female body is not only (not even first and foremost) that of a flesh-and-blood entity, but that of a *symbolic construct*."[10]

Scholars have already addressed the Aristotelian and theological identification of the female with the physical, or bodily, in contrast to the male, who is identified with the spirit. In chapter 1 I contend something quite different: that woman was identified not with the body but with the flesh, which stood for all the heaving powers allied against the spirit. The flesh was not synonymous with the body, as we usually take it to be today. This distinction makes a difference in how the Middle Ages might have construed woman not as a passive, corruptible, physical body, but as that principle of disruption in the human psyche, the flesh.

Woman's position as flesh carries over into medieval ideas about the female body and character as pervious, excessive, and susceptible. Instructions for pious living and for chastity are informed by this construction. The identification of woman with flesh, and hence with excess, permeability, and disruption, produces a different model for chastity than that invoked for men. Integrity, viewed as a repairing of the natural but dangerous accessibility of the female body, becomes the spiritual and moral standard for religious women in the Middle Ages. The natural grotesqueness of the woman's body is thus corrected through moral and physical enclosure.[11]

Bodily access to the sacred, however, threatens this ideology of the woman's body by privileging excess, unbridled passion, and that "privileged communication" of the body which Vauchez spoke of. It gives free reign to woman's position as flesh with all the potential for disruption contained therein. If a woman writer chooses to exploit this bodily access through fleshly excess, she exploits the same ideology, and threatens the very structures of power that ideology is meant to reinforce. By occupying and exploiting her position as flesh, the woman writer has recourse to a power derived from the taboo which defines her and which she breaks with her speech.

I want to stress that this position is available to women mystics, but I am not claiming that they all adopt it. Nor is my analysis of the construction of the female body in chapter 1 meant to represent "the whole picture" of female mysticism or medieval culture. I propose it as only one in a collection of constructions useful for reading Margery Kempe, as well as other English and continental mystics. I would like to consider also how this particular symbolic construct differentiates the mystical practices, however bodily, of male and female mystics, and more importantly, how it offers some women, such as Margery Kempe, a position from which to speak and write.

This study of the body carries additional significance for our understanding of medieval culture beyond its importance to the situation of women writing. In *The Politics and Poetics of Transgression*, Peter Stallybrass and Allon White have argued that the cultural category of the body becomes the domain upon which other symbolic constructions rest, such as aesthetic and social hierarchies. Relying upon Bakhtin's investigation of the relationship between carnival and official cultures, Stallybrass and White are interested in how "body-images 'speak' social relations and values with particular force."[12] I will be concerned not so much with how the medieval female body "speaks" social relations as with how it speaks mystical, linguistic, and even contemporary scholarly categories of investigation. As a "taboo-laden" construct, the female body becomes the site of both the medieval Church's strategy of control and the modern mystical scholar's categories of legitimate mystical experience.[13]

Before looking at *The Book of Margery Kempe* to see how she might exploit the position of woman as flesh in her own narrative, I want to contextualize Kempe in another way. As primarily a scholar of literature, I am interested in the ways in which mystical narrative works: how does it begin? what are its conventions? where is the speaker positioned? These kinds of questions are rarely addressed in historical or theological studies of medieval mysticism. The purpose of addressing them here is that if we are to examine how Margery Kempe might have engaged in a medieval practice of "writing the body," we need to know something about the medium in which she worked. Instead of focusing on themes, images, and typologies of mystical revelation, I will be concerned with the crucial relations within a mystic text between the mystic and desire, desire and utterance, utterance and written text, and between mystic and reader. Chapter 2 is aimed at producing a description of the process by which mystical narratives are generated and the difference between these narratives and literary or theological narratives.

In chapter 2 and throughout the rest of the book, I have explicitly avoided placing Kempe in the tradition of the Middle English mystics. While I do draw upon the works of Julian of Norwich, Richard Rolle, Walter Hilton, and the author of *The Cloud of Unknowing*, I am not interested in drawing lines of influence as a way of establishing Kempe's context. In the past, such historical studies have too often succeeded chiefly in marginalizing Kempe rather than contextualizing her. Mystical filiations tend still to be linked to issues of mystical legitimacy, in much the same way that Gerson attempts to measure mystical experience according to a code of legitimate signs of spiritual inspiration. Thus, the English mystics are both defined by a contemporary scholarly code of legitimacy and used to reinforce this code. Except, of course, when they do not, as is the case with Kempe. One example of what I mean is the use of sensual language in the writings of Richard Rolle. Rolle's description of mystical experience in terms of the three-fold way of fire, sweetness, and song has recently been defended by scholars as metaphorical language. Therefore, Rolle is not guilty of corporeal mystical experience or of being seduced by the carnal pleasures of language. This defense is a response to earlier criticism of Rolle's failure to ascend to the higher reaches of contemplation.[14] Insistence on the metaphoricity of Rolle's language is used, in turn, to criticize Kempe and all who use sensual language too literally as *misreaders* of Rolle.

The self-perpetuating nature of such an argument is due to the unquestioned assumptions of the superiority of one kind of language and mystical experience over another. It is, too, an example of what I mean by the way in which the "taboo-laden" category of the female body becomes the basis for the mystical scholar's categories of mystical experience. The medieval taboo governing the female body and the feminine flesh also governs medieval and modern hierarchies of mystical experience and language. One cannot even engage in the study of medieval mysticism without encountering the taboo of the female body transformed into arguments about metaphorical versus literal sensual language. My own aim is to find other more fruitful theoretical and cultural contexts for understanding Margery Kempe. I will not be ignoring this framework of discussion completely; rather, I will set up a theoretical context designed to challenge it.

By viewing the mystic text as a practice through which the body is translated into a written *corpus*, the first two chapters frame the study of Margery Kempe which follows. This practice, as I have already indicated, occurs within the cultural construction of both the body and woman. If woman is identified with the flesh, and specifically, fissured flesh, then the woman writer potentially occupies the site of rupture, where excess and unbridled affections threaten the masculine idea of the integrity of the body. A woman writer such as Kempe brings this fissure into language— into the text—thereby destabilizing it and at the same time offering a place for access to the sacred. The textual fissure which mirrors the psychic one occurs between oral and written texts in Kempe's narrative. At the same time, the mystic's body is engaged in this process of translation whereby the mystic text "reads," in a sense, her own body.

Chapter 3 charts this process of translation and fissuring to the text in the context of Kempe's search for authority in her life and book, the interaction between her dictating voice and written text, her use of English and Latin authorities, and her argument for her own voice. I argue that Kempe demonstrates a knowledge of Latin texts at the same time that she privileges her own voice, and in so doing, I reopen the case of her illiteracy. I use the word "interdiction" here to describe the practice by which Kempe fissures the written text in order to authorize her voice over the scribe's text.[15] In effect, Kempe exploits the instability of the mystic text caused by the incongruity between the oral dialogues of the mystic soul and God and the uncomprehending written text. Her strategy can be understood somewhat in Hélène Cixous's terms as an attempt to "steal into language" and medieval culture. Merely knowing or learning Latin does not guarantee this ability to steal into language, certainly not the language of the Church where women who were literate in Latin or the vernacular, such as Christine de Pizan, were doomed to read their own exclusion.[16] I want to argue that Kempe transgresses the nexus of medieval taboos governing the female body, literate culture, and the authority of written culture by means of her interdiction.

Chapter 4 takes this idea further by exploring how Kempe uses laughter and "good game," as she calls it, to unsettle both her culture and her text. Once again, Kempe tampers with the "taboo-laden" values and concepts of her time. Her laughter is seemingly inconsistent with the seriousness of her own calling and of her book. Yet there is evidence in the text to suggest that she laughs and employs laughter both as a way of combating her detractors and as a rhetoric for her book. The inversive potential of laughter has been argued already by Bakhtin and Stallybrass and White.[17] Kempe's laughter is the means by which she overcomes the challenges to her authority as a mystic. She also uses merriment as a sign of redemption. Both uses are monstrous in the sense that they violate the high seriousness of mystical revelation and her predicament. Yet it is through laughter that she makes a place for her own voice and her body by crossing the taboo which brackets the spiritual away from the material. Laughter always implicates the body and the material, as Bakhtin reminds us, and when this body is female, culture risks two of its sacred taboos.[18] Kempe's own laughter— and the reader's as well—are crucial to her discourse because they bring the female body into language and spirituality.

Although few readers have paid much attention to Kempe's laughter, most are forced to contend with her tears, along with the roars and writhing that accompany them. One way of understanding her weeping has been to situate it within the tradition of holy tears. However, I suggest that her tears are not only signs of the stirring of the Holy Ghost within her soul, as Julian of Norwich describes it. What was first described by scholars as a "terrible hysteria" is actually quite close to fifteenth-century representations of the Virgin at the Crucifixion. Kempe follows a model of compassion found in medieval dramatic depictions of the Virgin and Mary Magdalene and debated by medieval theology. This model is found in conjunction with the image of Christ's suffering body as a book that was read by the Virgin and others who had compassion for him. Through her tears, then, Kempe makes a spectacle of her reading of the body of Christ, a reading which she herself embodies and translates into *The Book of Margery Kempe*. It is ultimately Christ's body which authorizes and embodies her own speech.

The last chapter is less a continuation of the arguments of the rest of the book than it is a study of how culture revises books for its own purposes. At the same time, this chapter offers a critique of the assumptions behind the methods of modern scholarship in its approach to Kempe—assumptions which are based on the history of her book. Scholarship has tended to isolate Kempe's book by maintaining its failure to influence anyone. Yet the surviving manuscript of her *Book* offers evidence of a readership which some might find surprising: Carthusian monks. Copious marginal notes by four different hands and well-thumbed folios suggest a very active readership in the fifteenth- and sixteenth-century community of Mount Grace Priory in Yorkshire, England. At the same time, her book was edited by Wynkyn de Worde and later by Henry Pepwell in the sixteenth century. These editions, which reached a much wider lay audience, excised most of the more controversial aspects of Kempe's mysticism that I have described in the rest of my book. The sixteenth-century excisions have eliminated any trace of Kempe's voice or her boisterous, bodily practices. Her voice is displaced and replaced by that of Christ, while she is reduced to a humble, quiet, listening woman.

This is the Margery Kempe that scholarship knew and compared with Julian of Norwich until the full length manuscript was found in 1934. This is also the Kempe that everyone expected to make great contributions to the history of medieval mysticism, and to be "of the very greatest importance for the history of English literature."[19] After scholars began to read the Middle English edition, they were terribly disappointed. It is this disappointment, rather than any full understanding of Kempe's place in mystical history, which has shaped contemporary evaluations of her. The old taboos that had been successfully restored in the revised printed editions of Kempe's book once more pose problems for her readers, for it is her body and voice which are once again at issue.

My argument in this chapter is not only that scholars have participated in the marginalization of Margery Kempe; I am arguing for a re-examination of our critical categories for understanding late medieval mysticism, mystical language, and mystical texts. I am also proposing that the model of influence as a determiner of a mystic's importance is loaded against the female mystics, just as the modern idea of the "anxiety of influence" is stacked against female authors. In Kempe's case, we cannot say that she influenced later mystics, but we can demonstrate a wide circulation of her work (in revised form) and a very serious acceptance of her book among the English Carthusian community at Mount Grace. This in itself offers interesting possibilities for future study of Kempe and Carthusian spirituality, not in an attempt to prove her influence, but in an effort to read her in terms of the reading communities of her own culture and time. In this way, we might learn something as readers of her *Book*, as my brief look at the similarities between her experiences and those of the Carthusian monk, Richard Methley, demonstrates.

As a scholar whose interest and training are in literature and not mysticism, I have always had medieval literature in the back of my mind as I have written this book. Some of the theoretical discussions I have brought to *The Book of Margery Kempe* are pertinent to our study of medieval literature as well. The representation of the body, male and female, and practice of fissuring a text, for example, are both concepts which might be interestingly explored in Chaucer. The way in which the ideology of the sealed body or the disruptive flesh intersects other domains of material culture, too, needs to be formulated.

Finally, this book indirectly addresses the dilemma of teaching Margery Kempe in the context of a literature survey or graduate course. My own experience at both levels is that we have no way of talking about her book to students who might have read Chaucer and *Sir Gawain and the Green Knight*. She is interesting, yes, but how does one talk about her as an author? My own study of her authorship, the mystic text, her use of laughter, and the theological and gender issues which make up her narrative offers some possible grounds for discussing her in the context of literary culture in the Middle Ages as well as in that of mystical movements.

The intention and emphasis of this book is the raising of such issues and the re-contextualization of Margery Kempe. It is not my purpose to rehabilitate Margery Kempe nor to claim her as a feminist.[20] My feminist project is not, finally, to legitimize or valorize Kempe. In fact, my approach is more to account for her illegitimacy in a new way without judging her to be naive or misguided. Nevertheless, I find Kempe's behavior undesirable as a feminist practice in the twentieth century, and I certainly would not want to argue for her championship of women. At the same time, I think our reactions of alarm, pity, and patronizing acceptance are also misplaced. Although I would not argue for Kempe's calculated and deliberate self-fashioning as it emerges from this analysis, I would maintain that her life and book should not be isolated from the ideological pressures to which both were subject. Further, I think she exhibits an awareness of those pressures, and that her negotiation of them constitutes a feminist problem for scholarship. My analysis represents only one feminist approach to Margery Kempe which begins with the medieval body and ends with medieval scholarship today. It thus joins in the complicity of bodies with books and books with bodies that it attempts to describe in medieval culture and modern scholarship.

Notes

1. Jean Gerson, *De probatione spirituum*, in *Oeuvres complètes*, vol. 9, 177ff. Quoted by Barbara Obrist, "The Swedish Visionary Saint Bridget," in *Medieval Women Writers*, ed. Katharina M. Wilson (Athens: University of Georgia Press, 1984), 236.

2. J. A. Burrow has shown how male youth was identified with some of the same excesses associated with women in *The Ages of Man: A Study in Medieval Writing and Thought* (Oxford: Clarendon Press, 1986), 95–134. I would like to thank Alistair Minnis for bringing to my attention the fact that Gerson's pairing of adolescents and women derives from similar warnings to young men against excessive corporeality in their spiritual pursuits.

3. Carolyn Dinshaw finds in Gerson's comment a simultaneous fascination and repulsion similar to exegetical treatment of the carnal (and feminine) letter of the text, *Chaucer's Sexual Poetics* (Madison: University of Wisconsin Press, 1989), 20–25.

4. The classic discussion of this idea is that of Hélène Cixous, "The Laugh of the Medusa," *New French Feminisms*, ed. Elaine Marks and Isabelle de Courtivron (New York: Schocken Books, 1981), 245–64. Although Cixous states that it "is impossible to *define* a feminine practice of writing," elsewhere in the essay she describes such a practice. See also her essay in Hélène Cixous and Catherine Clément, *The Newly Born Woman*, trans. Betsy Wing (Minneapolis: University of Minnesota Press, 1986), 63–132. Luce Irigaray, too, argues for a feminine writing in *This Sex Which Is Not One*, trans. Catherine Porter (Ithaca, NY: Cornell University Press, 1985), 205–18. Julia Kristeva recognizes a language allied with the mother's body in her use of the term "semiotic," although she ultimately rejects the possibility of a feminine writing, *Desire in Language: A Semiotic Approach to Literature and Art*, ed. Leon S. Roudiez, trans. Thomas Gora, Alice Jardine, and Leon S. Roudiez (New York: Columbia University Press, 1980), 124–47. Jane Gallop writes a series of critical essays on the body in Western thinking and writing, in *Thinking Through the Body* (New York: Columbia University Press, 1988). A range of issues relating to the representation of the female body and writing is addressed in Susan Rubin Suleiman, ed., *The Female Body in Western Culture: Contemporary Perspectives* (Cambridge, MA: Harvard University Press, 1986). The representation and appropriation of the female body in scientific discourse is the subject of the collection of

essays, Mary Jacobus, Evelyn Fox Keller, and Sally Shuttleworth, eds., *Body/Politics: Women and the Discourses of Science* (New York and London: Routledge, 1990).

5. *Holy Feast and Holy Fast: The Religious Significance of Food to Medieval Women* (Berkeley: University of California Press, 1987). Bynum's recent collection of essays also addresses the body in religious symbolism and in the theology of the resurrection, *Fragmentation and Redemption: Essays on Gender and the Human Body in Medieval Religion* (New York: Urzone, 1991).

6. J. Huizinga, *The Waning of the Middle Ages* (New York: Doubleday, 1954), 193.

7. Vauchez, *Les laïcs au Moyen Âge: Pratiques et expériences religieuses* (Paris: Éditions du Cerf, 1987), 202.

8. *Les laïcs*, 247: "Enfin la mystique féminine de la fin du Moyen Âge est profondément subversive dans la mesure où elle souligne le divorce entre l'amour et la connaissance intellectuelle." According to Vauchez, this rupture accompanies the nominalist undermining of the philosophical marriage between faith and reason established by the tradition stretching from Anselm to St. Thomas Aquinas.

9. "The Female Body in Religious Practice," in *Fragments for a History of the Human Body*, ed. Michel Feher, Ramona Naddaff, and Nadia Tazi (New York: Urzone, 1989), Part 1, 164. This idea is not new to this essay of Bynum's; it is a working thesis in her study of the significance of food to women mystics, *Holy Feast and Holy Fast*.

10. *The Female Body in Western Culture*, 2. Jacobus, Keller, and Shuttleworth make a similar claim in their introduction to *Body/Politics*, 4.

11. Peter Stallybrass has argued that in the sixteenth century the woman's body was viewed as "naturally grotesque" owing to its lack of boundaries and its tendency to transgress its own limits, "Patriarchal Territories: The Body Enclosed," in *Rewriting the Renaissance: The Discourses of Sexual Difference in Early Modern Europe*, ed. Margaret W. Ferguson, Maureen Quilligan, and Nancy J. Vickers (Chicago: University of Chicago Press, 1986), 123–42.

12. Peter Stallybrass and Allon White, *The Politics and Poetics of Transgression* (Ithaca, NY: Cornell University Press, 1986), 10. They are drawing upon Mikhail Bakhtin's idea of the bodily in grotesque realism and of carnival in his *Rabelais and His World*, trans. Helene Iswolsky (Bloomington: Indiana Univ. Press, 1984), 1–58. Stallybrass and White delineate four symbolic domains—the human body, psychic forms, geographical space, and social order—by which they maintain that cultures "think themselves . . . through the combined symbolisms of these four hierarchies" (3). Stallybrass and White do not, however, take gender into account in their understanding of the "grotesque body" as it is allied with carnival, except where they acknowledge that carnival is complicit with official culture in its abuse of women and ethnic minorities (19). Their study also begins with early modern Europe, while mine will be confined to the Middle Ages. Nevertheless, their work is a fascinating and wide-ranging study of how these four symbolic systems "are intrinsic to the dialectics of social classification as such" (26).

13. I am borrowing a term from Stallybrass and White akin to Edmund Leach's concept of the "taboo-loaded category"; see *The Politics and Poetics of Transgression*, 24.

14. David Knowles regards Rolle's mystical experiences as those of a beginner who "fails altogether . . . to reckon with the higher degrees of the mystical life," *The English Mystical Tradition* (London: Burns and Oates, 1961), 52. His judgment is based primarily on the sensuality of Rolle's language and experience. Hope Emily Allen, who edited and wrote extensively on Rolle's work, also finds Rolle's mystical development to have been stunted, *Writings Ascribed to Richard Rolle, Hermit of Hampole and Materials for His Biography*, Modern Language Association of America, Monograph Series 3 (New York: D. C. Heath, 1927), 335. Other mystical texts, such as *The Cloud of Unknowing* and Hilton's *Scale of Perfection*, are also viewed as critiques of Rolle's sensual language. Recently, however, scholars have stressed that Rolle's language is not literal, that the experience he describes through vivid language is meant metaphorically. See for example, Wolfgang Riehle, *The Middle English Mystics*, trans. Bernard Standring (London: Routledge and Kegan Paul, 1981), 6–7, 9–10. Riehle's use of the words "metaphor" and "imagery" throughout his study resolves the problem by assuming Rolle's language to be figurative. Rosamund Allen, too, argues for the metaphoricity of Rolle's language: *Richard Rolle: The English Writings* (New York: Paulist Press, 1988), 30–31. See my discussion of this problem, Chapter 2.

15. See Chapter 3 for my explanation of this term as distinguished from David Lawton's use in "The Voice of Margery Kempe's Book," paper presented at the Modern Language Association Convention, 1988. As I have noted elsewhere, Lawton also argues for this privileging of Kempe's voice over the written text.

16. I am referring, of course, to Christine's disastrous reading of *The Book of the Lamentations of Matheolus*, probably in French translation, which initiates her despair and the subsequent search to know the truth about women, Earl Jeffrey Richards, trans., *The Book of the City of Ladies* (New York: Persea Books, 1982), I.1.1–I.2.2, pp. 3–8.

17. Bakhtin, *Rabelais and His World*, 17–38. Stallybrass and White, *The Politics and Poetics of Transgression*, 8–9.

18. "Laughter degrades and materializes," says Bakhtin, *Rabelais and His World*, 20. By "degrade," Bakhtin means that laughter brings down to earth and back to the body, particularly the lower part of the body (21).

19. R. W. Chambers writes this in his introduction to William Butler-Bowdon's translation of *The Book of Margery Kempe* (New York, 1944), xv.

20. I am here defining my purpose in distinction from that described by Sheila Delaney, "'Mothers to Think Back Through': Who Are They? The Ambiguous Example of Christine de Pizan," in *Medieval Texts and Contemporary Readers*, ed. Laurie A. Finke and Martin B. Shichtman (Ithaca, NY: Cornell University Press, 1987), 177–97. Delaney rightly cautions feminist scholars against adopting women writers as role models simply because they were writers.

1. The Body as Text and the Semiotics of Suffering

Clare of Montefalco's (d. 1308) persistent meditation on Christ's Passion in thought and in action was rewarded with a physical cross implanted in her heart. She was said to have felt the *insigne* of His Passion continually until her death. Her sisters so believed in the sign that when she died they tore open her body to find not only the Cross but the complete *insignia* of His Passion, from crown of thorns to the vinegar-soaked sponge offered to slake His thirst on Calvary.[1] Although her Franciscan confessor denounced the story as a fraud, it carries its own important *insignia* of late medieval hagiography and mysticism.[2] Devotion to the Passion, particularly to Christ's suffering humanity, and bodily imitations of Christ's suffering such as Clare's characterize saints' *vitae* and mysticism from the thirteenth to the fifteenth centuries. Women saints and mystics in particular discovered a new source of power and sanctity through bodily manifestations of lives dedicated to Christ's Passion.

The cult of saints had always considered the body of the saint to be one of the "places of sanctification." Relics, like the eucharist itself, often drew their power from the miraculous bodies of saints and bestowed those powers on geographical places, social communities, and individuals.[3] The idea of the *corps glorieux* in hagiography is based on the transformation of the saint's body which supposedly occurred at death, including irradiation, levitation, emission of miraculous odors and fluids, and the preservation of the body from decay or corruption.[4]

The difference between this postmortem glorification of the saint's body and the paramystical phenomena of late medieval hagiography and mysticism is that in the latter the bodily *insignia* are incorporated into spiritual experience. The corporeal effects of meditation on Christ's Passion—such as the inscription of the Passion *insignia* in Claire's heart or the reception of stigmata—become the signs of mystical union and sanctification. Unlike the *corps glorieux*, the living body is the site of the marvelous, and as in Clare's vision, its manifestations are often interior, rather than external.[5] The body's capacity for amazing transformations marks and measures the soul's capacity for imitating Christ's Passion.

Not all these corporeal imitations inspire suffering in the mystic or saint who experiences them. As much rapture as mortification attends these miraculous alterations of the body. In either case, the bodily component of mystical experience manifests a physiological and often literal conformity to Christ's humanity. For many female and some male mystics, the corporeal aspect of mystical meditation was neither metaphorical nor symbolic. For critics of this spirituality, the sheer physicality was suspect and in need of refinement.[6]

Compared to many of the saints and mystics who followed her, Clare of Montefalco is not unusual. However, her sanctification was one of the first to be based on paraphysical phenomena.[7] Her canonization can be seen as part of the larger movement of affective spirituality which thrived during the thirteenth through the fifteenth centuries. Scholars agree on the importance of the body and *imitatio Christi* to this movement. They further attribute this importance to the influence of Franciscan and Cistercian spirituality, as well as to the later Carthusian translation and circulation of mystical texts.[8]

The two identifying features of affective spirituality—its corporeality and the imitation of Christ's suffering humanity—are rarely disputed. What has been considered problematic is not the terms themselves but the antipathy of modern sensibilities to them. In her fascinating study of the religious significance of food to medieval women, Carolyn Walker Bynum has succeeded in drawing attention to this problem and in recovering the "essential strangeness of medieval religious experience."[9]

Even feminist scholarship accepts these categories of affective spirituality as unproblematic in themselves. The difficulty some feminists have with affective spirituality is women's attraction to it. The distinction between body and soul in medieval medicine and theology was analogized to the difference between female and male, an analogy which carried with it the hierarchy of sexual difference. The feminization of the body of Christ in medieval devotional texts further problematizes the woman mystic's *imitatio Christi* because it seems merely to reinforce her subjection to repressive social, sexual, and theological hierarchies. After all, what is it which she embraces in her *imitatio*? The old "equation of victimisation, passivity, subjection with femininity" under the guise of newly gained access to transcendence.[10] Still, the twin *foci* of affective spirituality—the body and imitation of Christ—go unexamined. In accepting these categories, feminist scholarship is forced to operate from within their boundaries and the tiered system those boundaries define, including body/soul, flesh/spirit, literal/figurative language, all of which are constructed on the female/male binarism. Feminist critiques of feminine spirituality adopt positions ironically adjacent to medieval patriarchy, which has both scripted and exploited the binarisms relegating woman to the realm of the body, the flesh, and the literal.

The feminist project of evaluating women's participation in and contribution to this affective mysticism in the late Middle Ages must begin by problematizing its two main terms, the body and the *imitatio Christi*. We must begin by looking at the body itself as an historical construction. As Michel Feher has recently argued, the body is often confused with the "real body," which is without history. Natural science, medicine, even psychology all assume a unity called "the body" that is exempt from historical or cultural construction.[11] It must also be seen as a gendered construction distinguishing female from male, but even this is subject to historical and cultural formulation. We cannot assume even that we know what the Middle Ages meant by the analogy that "Woman is to man as body is to soul." What biological and sexual differences are being brought to bear on this analogy in the first place? In order to understand this analogy, we must ask what may seem to be two obvious questions: whose body is it? and how is this "thing" the Middle Ages called "the body" constructed? One further question helps us to remove ourselves from the medieval hierarchy: where is this body (or these bodies) located? By problematizing the body with these questions, we do not endeavor to make it deliver up its mysteries, as did the overzealous sisters of Clare of Montefalco. We are like them in that we are attempting to read it, but we do not need it for its *insignia*; instead, we are reading it for some of the traces of its construction.

Medieval notions about the body intersect the theological function of the *imitatio Christi*. Conformity to Christ's life and suffering is perhaps the broadest definition of this practice. Yet, like the medieval notion of the body, the concept of imitating Christ is not quite so simple. For both the male and female religious, imitation of Christ's suffering could take many forms, including fasting, self-flagellation, and self-defilement. In addition to these seemingly self-generated forms of *imitatio Christi*, others were involuntary, such as bodily effusions and elongations, stigmata, tears, and seizures. Finally, a third kind of imitation, most familiarly demonstrated in the life of St. Francis, was subsumed by those interior models of devotion associated with Christ's Passion during the late Middle Ages.[12]

From these few examples, we can begin to see that imitation covers a spectrum of meanings, from "following the example of" or "taking as one's model," in the third kind of practice, to "forging a resemblance," as in the mortification of the flesh in the first kind. The second type—involuntary bodily transformations such as Clare of Montefalco's—do not readily fit into most definitions of imitation. Since this form of imitation is, according to Bynum, found almost exclusively among the female religious, the concept already becomes problematic.[13] For a culture in which the body itself seems to be fully gendered, what does it mean for the female religious to imitate Christ? In what sense are what we now call paramystical phenomena an *imitatio Christi*? The variety of forms this second kind of imitation takes suggests that even within this category, *imitatio Christi* functions in more than one way. While stigmata represent the most obvious type of bodily imitation of Christ, Clare's reception of the *insignia* of Christ's Passion clearly functions in this same category but entirely differently. As with my study of the body in the Middle Ages, my investigation into the practice of imitating Christ in female spirituality will aim at determining how it is constructed, rather than how it is characteristic. Neither study is intended to be exhaustive; instead, each is aimed at problematizing the concepts for the purposes of a feminist analysis. These constructs will help, in turn, to contextualize a mystic who is already problematic, Margery Kempe.

The Anatomical Mirror

Medieval science and medicine differentiated between the male and female bodies primarily in terms of the sexual anatomies. Galen's *De usu partium corporis* and Aristotle's *De generatione animalium* provided the basic ideas about sexual anatomy which were transmitted to medieval medicine often through Arabic texts.[14] As Danielle Jacquart and Claude Thomasset have shown in their analysis of *Sexuality and Medicine in the Middle Ages*, medieval medical texts constructed a model of female sexual physiology which was based on male physiology. The relationship was a specular one in that the female anatomy was thought to represent an inverse variation on the male anatomy. Female anatomy was made to duplicate male anatomy, while medicine located sexual difference on an internal-external axis. The female sexual anatomy thus bore an "inverse similarity" or a specularity with respect to male sexual physiology.[15]

This specularity did not suggest either a "fluidity" of sexual identity or an equivalence of sexual make-up.[16] Drawing a one-to-one correspondence between male and female sexual organs allowed medieval medical texts to assert the inferiority of the female apparatus. For example, the female "testicles," or ovaries, were judged to be smaller, less round, and less "fertile" than men's.[17] Not only was the female anatomy deficient in its "comparable" organs, but it proved lacking, as we might expect, wherever it was not similar. The failed one-to-one correspondence proved the inadequacy of the female anatomy rather than of the construction of inverse similarity.

The most crucial aspect of this construction is not the similarity but the location of difference. The construction of similarity allows the fundamental distinction between male and female to be based on the opposition between internal and external, as a passage from the thirteenth-century treatise, *Anatomia vivorum*, indicates through a telling analogy:

> One can compare the relation which exists between the instrument of reproduction in the man and the instrument of reproduction in the woman to the relation which exists between the seal which leaves its imprint and the impression of the seal in the wax. The woman's instrument has an inverted structure, fixed on the inside, where the man's instrument has an [everted] structure extending outwards.[18]

Woman's sexual construction is clearly secondary. The analogy of male and female instruments of reproduction to the seal and wax impressions also constructs difference in terms of activity/passivity and exteriority/ interiority. Even more importantly, the *Anatomia vivorum* establishes the female reproductive system as a pale image of the male anatomy. Like a wax impression, it is always recalling its seal and the seal's symbolized identity.

The analogy between activity and passivity in the *Anatomia vivorum* may be traced to Galenic and Aristotelian theories of conception. Both theories consider the woman's contribution to the fetus to be a material one, that is, the woman provides the matter or flesh to the developing human being, while the man provides the form.[19] The *materia* is characterized by its passivity and its function of feeding the developing embryo. Both the theories of conception and the anatomies of male and female sexual organs rely on the opposition between internal and external, and activity and passivity. The medical theory of the humors, in turn, is used to explain the distinction and further privilege the male physiology. The superior humors of heat and dryness in the male are responsible for external organs, while the inferior qualities of coldness and dampness insure the female's interior sexual structure. The explanation is interesting. The sexual organs in both sexes are internal in the early stages of development, but the heat and dryness of the male succeed in thrusting his organs outward, while the female's humors are powerless to do so.[20]

Sexuality in the Middle Ages was merely one aspect of the bodily. The two terms—body and sexuality—are not equivalent even though modern scholars of medieval religious practices and female spirituality implicitly make this association.[21] A brief summary of medieval medical theories about sexuality, then, cannot claim to provide us with a neat overview of "the medieval bodily." What it can do is suggest that the bodily does not exist as a single concept embracing men and women. Medieval theory about sexual structure distinguishes between the external and internal bodies, the seal and the impressed wax, the male and female. Medieval science constructed sexual physiology using the male as its model and the female as the inverse of the male, resembling it, but only imperfectly, because of its faltering symmetry.

Sexual difference, as it was defined in medieval medicine, was constructed along this internal/external axis with resemblance being the active principle linking the two terms. Turning to medieval theology and devotional works, we can see further how the body is constructed to carry implications not simply for biology but also for gender. Although there are a number of works I could draw upon to examine gender in medieval theology, I will be using Augustine and Bernard of Clairvaux. My reason for choosing these two is that Augustine develops a crucial distinction between the body and the flesh which has important consequences for gender in the Middle Ages, and Bernard adopts Augustine's notion of the flesh, developing it in a way that helps us to understand some of the medical views about the female body we have already surveyed.[22] Both men are, of course, also very important to the development of Christian ideas in the Middle Ages. Bernard of Clairvaux is especially relevant to this study because of his enormous influence on affective spirituality of the late Middle Ages.[23]

The following overview is clearly neither exhaustive nor representative; rather, I aim to sketch a theology which I will argue is gendered and which supports other medieval ideas about woman's chastity, her virtue, and her body. I want to state, too, that I do not present this ideology as a representative one, that is, as the only one which existed in the Middle Ages. I merely want to claim that it was one ideology and that it was a very important one, intersecting as it did other domains of medieval culture. The models for female devotion and imitation of Christ constitute only two such domains.

The Fissured Flesh

Peter Brown traces the changing perception of the body in early Christianity from the frontier between nature and the city to Augustine's notion of the "fissured flesh," which put body at odds with soul, city, and God.[24] The key to this change was Augustine's insistence on the Pauline distinction between the flesh and the body.[25] As Augustine points out in *De civitate Dei*, Paul often used the term "flesh" as a synecdoche for the entire human being.[26] In addition, Paul locates the source of man's evil in the flesh, rather than in the body. The body's role in human sin is merely that of a sort of lackey to the restless, rebellious, and intransigent flesh.[27] The primary human conflict is one of flesh against spirit, or rather, the life of the flesh against the life of the spirit.[28]

For Augustine, the flesh represents "all that led the self to prefer its own will to that of God."[29] The Fall of Man signifies a corruption of flesh and of soul which are no longer directed toward the will of God. Augustine is careful to point out that this corruption was caused not by the flesh, but by the soul, else how could one explain evil committed by the serpent who has no flesh?[30] Neither is the rupture enacted by the soul and flesh together necessarily bodily in nature, for some vices—such as anger, jealousy, and idolatry—are not aimed at bodily gratification.[31]

Fleshly concupiscence is the result of the rebellion of the human will against God's will by drawing all human faculties to the service of its own private purposes.[32] Hence the concupiscence which irrevocably fissured the flesh from the soul, will, and God included the sum of dark forces or drives which caused discord in the soul and in the city of man. The "urge of the flesh" could be controlled but not necessarily by reviling the body: the "law of the mind" must exert pressure to bring the flesh back in conformity with the will.[33] Augustine uses a gendered analogy to explain how the concupiscence is to be monitored:

> caro tumquam coniux est. . . . Concupiscit adversus te, tumquam coniux tua; ama et castiga, donec fiat in una reformatione una concordia.[34]

> (Your flesh is like your wife. . . . It rebels against you, just as your wife does. Love it, rebuke it, until it is made into one harmony, one bond [of flesh and spirit.])

Because the flesh implicates both body and soul, it must be mastered by the "law of the mind" just as the wife should be mastered by the husband. The flesh, like the wife, is not by its nature evil unless it is unmastered. Yet it is the site of disruption, the fissure which estranged the human will from the divine will, human beings from each other, and the law of the mind from the goadings of the senses. Through his analogy, Augustine places the wife not at the site of the body but at the fissure of the flesh where concupiscence forever agitates against the will, the gap through which the self fell from God and from itself.

Bernard of Clairvaux constructs his mysticism of affectivity on the Augustinian distinction between flesh and body and on the vulnerability of the will due to the Fall. The body, for Bernard, is not evil, but it is subjected to the raging of the will in conjunction with the senses. In an interesting twist on Augustine's analogy of the relationship of soul to flesh to body, Bernard focuses on the will as woman in collusion with the flesh to eviscerate the soul:

> Mitiga efferos motus voluntatis, et crudelem bestiam mansuescere cura. Ligatus es: solvere studeas quod rumpere omnino non possis. Eva tua est. Vim facere, aut eatenus offendere eam nullo modo praevalebis.

> (Check the wild motions of the will and take care to tame the wild beast. You are in bonds. Strive to untie what you can never break. The will is your Eve. You will not prevail against her by using force.)[35]

Bernard identifies the corrupted will as that which has been seized by the desires of the flesh, making less distinction between flesh and will than Augustine does. Eve is the perverse will which runs riot with the senses. In his powerful treatise "On Conversion," Bernard dramatizes the resistance of the will to reason and the divine will. Bernard personifies the will as a little old woman whose hair stands on end, scratching her foul ulcers, grinding her teeth in fury, and infecting the very air with her foul breath. In her argument against the soul's remorse, she summons all the fleshly senses to her aid, reminding the soul of the threefold ulcer—voluptuousness, curiosity, and ambition—which afflicts her:

> 'Siquidem voluptuosa sum, curiosa sum, ambitiosa sum, et ab hoc triplici ulcere non est in me sanitas a planta pedis usque ad verticem.' Itaque fauces, et quae obscena sunt corporis, assignata sunt voluptati, quandoquidem velut de novo necesse est singula recenseri. Nam curiositati pes vagus, et indisciplinatus oculus famulantur. At vanitati quidem auris et lingua serviunt, dum per illam impinguat caput meum oleum peccatoris; per hanc ipsa suppleo quod in laudibus meis alii minus fecisse videntur.

("I am voluptuous, I am curious, I am ambitious, and there is not part of me which is free from this threefold ulcer, from the soles of my feet to the top of my head [Is 1:6]. My gullet and the shameful parts of my body are given up to pleasure; we must name them afresh, one by one. The wandering foot and the undisciplined eye are slaves to curiosity, ear and tongue serve vanity, while the sinner's oil pours in to make my head greasy [Ps. 140:5]. With my tongue I myself supply whatever others seem to have omitted in my praise.)[36]

The will's resistance to reason is maintained through the senses, which, though they are not evil in themselves, infect the soul and the flesh. In fact, the senses and the flesh have been perverted by the will, with its threefold ulcer that befouls and defiles them.[37] The "wild motions of the will"—our Eve—are the urges of curiosity, ambition, and pleasure which enlist the senses in their satisfaction. The state of "living in the flesh" is one in which the body is abducted by the appetites and the ulcerous soul. Bernard construes the relationship of body to spirit to flesh in a key analogy:

Sic enim est corpus nostrum inter spiritum, cui servire debet, et carnalia desideria, quae militant adversus animam, sive potestates tenebrarum, ac si iumentum constituas inter raptorem et rusticum.

(Our body finds itself located between the spirit it must serve, and the desires of the flesh or the powers of darkness, which wage war on the soul, as a cow might be between the peasant and the thief.)[38]

The will, the old woman who rages and picks at her ulcers, the Eve of St. Bernard, resembles Augustine's Eve who represents the sensual or the lower reason.[39] In both cases, woman is associated with the perviousness of the flesh which began with a fissure as a result of the Fall and which has festered into ulcers since. Bernard's bovine body merely finds itself caught in the middle of the war between flesh and spirit.

Woman, then, occupies the border between body and soul, the fissure through which a constant assault on the body may be conducted. She is a painful reminder of influx alienating body from soul. In fact, woman in Bernard and Augustine represents the principle of influx itself by means of which the boundaries of body and soul are continually erased. The influx is not, however, primarily induced from the outside; rather, it is the foul little woman scratching her ulcers which produces the perviousness of the senses. While she is in command, "a mass of bloody pus is flowing every-where."[40] Thus the soul finds itself contaminated from within and without and vexed by a kind of spiritual vertigo.

Bernard's theory of affectivity, which underlies his discourse on mystical love, is dependent on the same bond between the will and the senses found in his psychology of sin and conversion. The crux of his idea of love is his concept of affect. While this term is difficult to define in Bernard's work, it is not difficult to identify. Every human soul consists of four affects, love, joy, fear, and sadness. These affects are dependent both on the senses and on the will for their expression.[41] Whether these four affections bring glory or shame depends on how they are ordered and maintained in the soul. The concupiscence of the flesh is an ever-present evil affect because it is ungoverned. Under the watchful eye of reason, the soul pursues its carnal affection in the contemplation of Christ's Passion.

As an attribute of the soul, the affect is a complex interaction of external and internal promptings, very much as sin is. As Bernard contends, "Affects, simply called, are found in us naturally, it seems as though they emanate from our own being, what completes them comes from grace; it is indeed quite certain that grace regulates only what creation has given us, so that virtues are nothing but regulated affects."[42] Love is the purified affect which is regulated by grace and guarded by reason. It is, as Kristeva notes, crucial to Bernard's emphasis on the importance of Christ's humanity: "Thus for the Christian, a human being imprisoned in his flesh, the affect of the flesh is already significant; even though it might be the zero degree of our love for the Other, the affect is already dwelled in by Christ."[43] Christ's indwelling in the affect offers the Christian a perviousness which accedes to glory rather than to shame because it is regulated internally by reason and externally by divine grace.

One logic informs the doctrines both of sin and of mystical love. The bundle of drives unleashed in the Fall when reason abdicated its regulatory role becomes the means by which man is restored to God.[44] The perviousness of the flesh, which is the mark of its perversion, also offers the possibility of redemption.

I do not want to suggest here that Bernard offers a liberating theology for women, nor that he is even aware of the possibilities for redemption I have discussed above. Bernard's scabrous woman resides securely within the gendered ideology of the medieval Church. It is as misogynist as anything we might read from Jerome or medieval sermons. My point is not to make a feminist of Bernard. What I am suggesting is that this very misogynist ideology of woman as flesh offered a possible position of disruption for women, even if neither Bernard nor the authors of devotional treatises for women were aware of this possibility.

It remains to be seen how this ideology became inscribed in devotional treatises for women, making their ideals of chastity and spiritual perfection fundamentally different from those for men. This association of woman with flesh also puts their desire to imitate Christ in a different position from the equivalent male desire. In other words, although women and men both entered the religious life and strove to imitate Christ often through similar physical practices, the gendered ideology I have described rendered those equivalent actions fundamentally different. Even if men adopted a "feminized" ideal of religious perfection, this adoption cannot be seen as equivalent to women's adopting the same ideal. Men begin from a position of the spirit, and this makes all the difference.[45]

If in Bernard's works, a woman occupies the position of the pervious flesh, its fissure, vile affect, what does it mean for the woman religious to imitate Christ? One possibility, the more radical one, is that the woman mystic insists upon that dissimilarity, upon the ambiguous, heterogeneous flesh in her imitation of Christ. From and through a place of disruption, she seeks spiritual perfection. However, this is not how this configuration of body, flesh, spirit and *imitatio* becomes scripted for the female religious. Devotional works written for women do, in fact, assume Bernard's anthropology, but they do so by sublimating it in a theory of the female body. This theory, in turn, serves to suppress the radical possibilities of Bernard's theory of the affections. Such works seek, in effect, to apply a bandage to the fissure of flesh with the doctrine of the enclosed female body.

The Sealed Body

Medieval theology constructs its theory of the female body in conjunction with medieval science. According to the physiological model, woman is identified "with breaches in boundaries."[46] The convergence of the two is seen in the telling justification by Heloise for allowing nuns to drink wine. On the basis of the medieval theory of the humors, Heloise appeals to the "nature" of woman as humid and fumy to argue that women are less apt to become inebriated than men are. She cites the physician Macrobius Theodosius:

> Aristoteles mulieres inquit raro ebriantur crebro senes . . . Mulier humectissimo est corpore; . . . docent praecipue assiduae purgationes superfluo exonerantes corpus humore . . . Muliebre corpus crebris purgationibus deputatum pluribus consertum [est] foraminibus ut pateat in meatus et vias praebeat humori in egestionis exitum confluenti; per haec foramina vapor vini celeriter evanescit.

(Aristotle says that women are rarely inebriated while old men are often. . . . Woman has a very humid body, . . . as is proven daily by her continual purgations which empty the body of superfluous moisture. . . . A woman's body which is visited with frequent purgations is fit with several holes so that it opens into passages and supplies outlets for the excess moisture to be dispersed; through these holes the fume of the wine is quickly discharged.)[47]

While this fumosity allows for purgation of toxins such as wine, it is dangerous in its suggestion of susceptibility to external influences.[48] Women are given to a suspicious superfluity which makes them prone to sickness and which also helps to make up for their humoral deficiency. Cold and moist, they lack the energy, heat, and consistency of men, who are hot and dry.

This physiological susceptibility to external influences finds its theological equivalent in the moral breaches in boundaries associated with woman's nature. It is no coincidence that chastity is defined for woman as a physical and spiritual *integritas*, or intactness.[49] The religious life for women consists primarily in adopting boundaries and maintaining an unbroken body. The thirteenth-century devotional manual for women, *Hali Meidenhad*, provides a good example of how medieval physical and moral categories were conflated for women. The author of *Hali Meidenhad* warns his female reader to guard the sign of her chastity: "Ant tu þenne eadi meiden, þet art iloten to him wið mei[ð]hades merke, ne brec þu nawt þet seil þet seileð inc togederes."[50] (And you then, blessed maiden, who are assigned to him with the sign of virginity, break not thou that seal which seals you together.) This warning refers both to the seal which binds the virgin to Christ and that which signifies her virginity "without breach."[51] As the sweet balm guards the body from rotting, so virginity preserves the living flesh from defilement.[52]

The *Meidenhad* author urges the virgin to preserve her likeness to heavenly nature during her habitation in the postlapsarian "land of unlikeness," where man and woman have lost their original resemblance to God. Yet her unlikeness is clearly more precarious than man's, since her very nature is already situated in the flesh. In a revealing departure from his source, the *Hali Meidenhad* author invites the virgin to savor a special victory over the devil, since he is ashamed to be overcome by a thing "as feeble as flesh is, and especially [by] woman. . . ."[53] Woman represents the frailty of the flesh, concupiscence, a condition she derived from Eve.[54]

The female body—with all its perviousness to external and internal influences—is the signifier of the frailty of the flesh, including the "fleshly will" and the faculties of sight, speech, kiss, and affections.[55] The sealed body, then, becomes the sign not only of virginity but of the *integritas* of all the senses, particularly speech and sight. When virgins are then instructed not to break that which seals them together with God and with themselves, they are being called to enclosure at many levels. The unbroken flesh ultimately means bodily closure and silence. It is no coincidence that female sanctity during the late Middle Ages was often manifested though miraculous closure of the body.[56] The seal is both boundary and suture to the consequences of the breached flesh.

The English Cistercian Aelred of Rievaulx (1110–1167) likewise interprets female chastity in terms of bodily enclosure in his instruction for anchoresses, *De Institutione Inclusarum* (1160–62). The middle fifteenth-century English translation of this work, MS. Bodley 423, defines chastity as a state of being above "the conuersacion of the worlde." The metaphor of conversation here works at the levels of speech and sexuality which Aelred collapses. Condemning the anchoress who thinks it sufficient to "shutte her body betwene too walles," Aelred warns that the intercourse of her thoughts and speech with the world turns her cell into a brothel.[57] The windows of the cell reflect the perviousness of the flesh, while speech in particular betrays the promiscuity of body and soul. Silence is as much a condition for chastity as is sexual renunciation. For Aelred of Rievaulx, as for Ambrose much earlier, female chastity preserves the "invisible frontier" between body and world, a sacred space which resists the condition of abjection posed by the "heaving powers of the flesh."[58]

The thirteenth-century rule for anchoresses, the *Ancrene Wisse*, similarly locates the female body at the frontier of the flesh in its justification to anchoresses for fleeing the world.[59] Like the *De Institutione Inclusarum*, the *Wisse* advocates a sealing of the borders, particularly the border of speech:

> Just as you see water, when it has been firmly stopped and dammed so that it cannot flow downwards, forced to go back and climb upwards, in just this way you should dam up your speech and your thoughts, if you want them to climb and rise up towards heaven instead of falling downwards and being scattered about the world as much idle talk is.[60]

Conversation with the world in thought and speech as well as through sight, habit, and daily contact diffuses one's relationship with God. As a practice of damming up speech and thought, the *Ancrene Wisse* author recommends meditating on Christ's suffering. In particular, he advocates that the recluse imitate Christ's suffering in the five senses on Calvary. For example, just as Christ's mouth was closed by the blows of the Jews, so "you, for love of Him and for your own great good, close up your chattering mouth with your own lips."[61] Eyes and ears should likewise be enclosed, while the anchoress should take example from the nails of Christ's hands to keep her own hands safe within the boundaries of her cell.[62] In this way *imitatio Christi* for the female religious is incongruously identified with the unbroken flesh and the sealed female body. Christ's wounds, far from signifying the perviousness of the female body, serve to remind women of the need to dam up their own vulnerable bodies. Instead of glorifying the feminine, imitation of Christ forces the recluse to internalize the association of the feminine with the breached flesh. The sealed body finds its spiritual complement in seclusion and silence.

Woman's implicit association not only with the senses but with the will, as we saw in Bernard's allegory, is made explicit in another thirteenth-century devotional sermon for women, "Sawles Warde," "The Guardian of the Soul." Based on a Latin sermon of St. Anselm's, this treatise provides its own version of the female will by drawing upon a domestic analogy. According to this analogy, the self is a house which is ruled by Lord Wit. The lord's wife is the unruly Will, who threatens to bring chaos to the entire household "unless Wit as lord chastised her and kept from her much of what she wished to have."[63] She is in league with the dangerous servants, the senses, who follow her whims. Like Bernard's Will, the wife is the principle of misrule in the human psyche, but unlike Bernard's Will, she is safely checked by the domestic economy of the soul.

Bernard's theory of the flesh and the body has important consequences for the female religious. The identification of the feminine with the fissured flesh, the dark drives in complicity with the senses, and ultimately, the loss of boundaries leads to the emphasis on the sealed body in the rules for nuns and anchoresses. The logic of the *imitatio Christi* is thus a logic of renunciation, of enclosure, of finding in Christ's suffering not an image of women's own suffering humanity, but a remonstrance to woman as frail flesh. As such, the female religious's imitation of Christ was not scripted to allow her to transcend or to celebrate the "frail flesh" without a certain masochism.

The psychology of sin, in the theologies of both Bernard and Augustine, is thus a gendered one. "Real" women and men were already implicated differently both in their capacity to sin and in their capacity not to sin. This difference has implications for holiness, too, since models for holiness must take these very capacities into account. The Aristotelian analogy that "spirit is to flesh as man is to woman" must be viewed in the context of the Christian distinction between flesh and body, as evidenced in the works of Bernard and Augustine. Their psychologies of sin and perfection rest upon the association of woman not with the body, which is passive and really neutral in the Fall, but with the flesh and the recalcitrant will. Man, of course, is allied with the higher faculties of the spirit. Woman is the "heaving powers of the flesh," the place of disruption, the breach in the harmonious unity of man and God and the flesh and spirit. Represented in physiological terms, she is windy, susceptible to influences which roamed freely throughout her body; theologically, she is Bernard's ulcerous Will who defies the prompting of God and Reason by giving reign to the heaving powers of the flesh. She is also that perviousness which consists in the heaving powers, the will, and the senses together. Any potential for subversion is effectively controlled and repressed in the concept of the sealed body, as we have seen in spiritual guides for women.

Yet, within the same logic of perfection for the female religious is inscribed a logic of perversion, a potential for disruption. The flesh in its Augustinian and Bernardian senses is neither spiritual nor corporeal, but heterogeneous. It is that which cannot be divided, but neither is it unified or harmonious. It is already impure. The possibility for enlisting the broken flesh into the service of perfection is therefore always present, even in the imitation of Christ. The double logic of the flesh offers the female mystic something different from merely the spectacle of subjection and victimization with which she can identify. It suggests a possible strategy for breaking the seal and transgressing those boundaries that she is supposed to represent and protect.

Whether the female mystic is able to act on this possibility remains to be seen in the medieval practice of imitating Christ.

Imitatio Christi

As I pointed out above, the *imitatio Christi* was not a single concept to which all affective mystics adhered uniformly. It was defined in various ways and practiced even more diversely. In the mid-fifteenth-century devotional treatise, *The Imitation of Christ*, Thomas à Kempis reveals the multiple ways in which imitation of Christ should be considered. He argues in the beginning of the treatise, "Whoever desires to understand and take delight in the words of Christ must strive to conform his whole life to Him."[64] Humility, patience, and scorn for the world are among the signs of a life in proper conformity to Christ's. This imitation through conformity to the virtues of Christ's life is not the goal of the mystical or religious life, but the means to enlightenment, to understanding and delight in the words of Christ. Later on in his counsels on the spiritual life, he invokes imitation of Christ as a model for religious discipline.[65]

For the lay or religious person, pilgrimage to the Holy Land offered yet another way of imitating Christ's life. By visiting the places in which Christ lived and suffered, the pilgrim was expected to relive and participate in the major events of his life. The Holy Sepulcher, Mount Zion, Bethlehem, the room of the Last Supper, and Mount Calvary were all part of the sacred geography which allowed the pilgrim a kind of imitation through inhabitation. The locations were meant not only to inspire remembrance of Christ's suffering, death, and resurrection, but to provide a mental geography for meditation. Imaginary reconstruction of the locations, including their topography, architecture, vegetation, and inhabitants, was the goal of pilgrimage, as guidebooks to the Holy Land reveal. The German monk Theoderich offers his famous twelfth-century *Guide to the Holy Land* to "those who are unable to proceed there in person." His purpose is to rouse his readers through description to remembrance, love, pity, and longing, as he suggests in the conclusion to his book:

> This account of the holy places, wherein our Lord Jesus Christ appeared in bodily presence, . . . we have put together . . . in the hope that the minds of those who read or hear it may be roused to love him through their knowledge of the places that are described here. [66]

Theoderich's account of holy places is meant as a locative sign to enact a transference of geographical site to memory system. The affections are stirred or roused to love through their situation-in-effect in the topography of Christ's bodily presence. For both pilgrim and reader of Theoderich's *Guide*, Christ's bodily presence is translated "through their knowledge of the places" which occurs in the act of remembering.

The two faculties involved in this remembrance, the imagination and memory, are distinct but closely coordinated. In fact, they often overlap. John Trevisa's late fourteenth-century English translation of *De proprietatibus* suggests that the imagination possesses a rudimentary capacity for remembering sense experience as well as a creative power of constructing images of things never experienced. The memory then stores the images and intentions and refers them to the Intellectual Soul, which consists of reason, understanding, and the will.[67]

Theoderich's notion of meditation through mental pilgrimage accords with Ciceronian rhetorical theory as well as with medieval poetics.[68] Geoffrey de Vinsauf's *Poetria nova* suggests the theory behind Theoderich's practice:

> When I wish to recall things I have seen, or heard, or memorized before, or engaged in before, I ponder thus: I say, I heard, I considered, I acted in such or such a way, either at that time or in that place: places, times, images or other similar signposts are for me a sure path which leads me to the things themselves. Through these signs I arrive at active knowledge. Such and such a thing was so, and I picture to myself such and such a thing. . . . Fashion signs for yourself, whatever kind your own inclination suggests.[69]

The critical distinction to be made between Geoffrey's account of the semiotic pilgrimage of memory and Theoderich's is that knowledge functions in the latter as a stimulus for the affections, and by implication for meditation. The signs fashioned by pilgrimage offer a narrative repository for imitation first through the stirring of the affections. The signposts along the way provide a "sure path" not only to the "things themselves," but to the bodily presence which these things signify: the Thing itself to which even things are signs.[70]

This very process of remembering is a kind of *imitatio Christi*. Medieval psychology and aesthetics defined images in terms of their twin capacities for *likeness* and *intention*.[71] Umberto Eco reveals how Aquinas's aesthetics depends on the idea that Christ was Himself an image of God. His similitude represents the very property of beauty.[72] The human faculty of remembrance constructs a region of images or similitudes and, in so doing, enacts an imitation of Christ. However, the imagination may be deceived by images when the intention is misdirected. John the Carpenter in *The Miller's Tale*, for example, is easily tricked into believing the scheme of his wife's lover to delude him. The Miller comments on the inversion which occurs when the affections are diseased, causing them to rule the imagination:

> Lo, which a greet thyng is affeccioun!
> Men may dyen of ymaginacioun,
> So depe may impressioun be take.[73]

John's misdirected intention and affections lead the imagination to run riot and to produce vain images, rather than similitudes. John's belief that he is a second Noah who is chosen to be saved with his wife from the second flood is the incongruous result.

Similitude and intention together determine the power of images to move the affections toward ethical or pious "things." The intention of Theodrich's images is the love of Christ, while the similitude of the images recalls Christ's own resemblance to God. Consideration of images, whether received through reading, visitation, or meditation, constitutes an imitation of Christ by which "spiritual intentions" are linked to "corporeal similitudes."[74] This type of cognition reenacts the incarnation by which, too, spiritual intentions were linked to corporeal similitudes.

This form of imitation, then, might be found in literary production and enjoyment, as well as in mystical activity. As it relates to mystical contemplation, however, this type of imitation is limited to affective spirituality, rather than Pseudo-Dionysian mysticism. It is the production of images and the incorporation of images into memory that constitutes mystical imitation of Christ. Where images are discouraged, remembrance as a mode of *imitatio Christi* is absent. Forgetfulness of all creation and resemblances, including the images which the imagination preserves as signposts for recollection, becomes the method of true contemplation. The "cloud of unknowing" is conceived out of this forgetfulness. As the author of the *Cloud of Unknowing* advises, this forgetfulness must be active and vigilant against the powers of the imagination to forge similitudes and hence, remembrance: "The intense activity, therefore, of your understanding, which will always press upon you when you set yourself to this dark contemplation, must always be put down. For if you do not put it down it will put you down."[75] Pseudo-Dionysian spirituality, like that of the *Cloud* author, privileges forgetfulness over remembrance, the power of loving over and against the power of knowing. Imitation of Christ through image-making and sign-posting has little power to repair the condition of dissimilitude which resulted from the Fall. Such attempts to know God are little more than "proud imaginings."

The fourteenth-century Engish mystic Walter Hilton defends the use of images to inspire recollection and affective devotion, although he considers this type of contemplation inferior to the kind described by the *Cloud* author:

> Inter que signa statuit ecclesia ymagines Domini nostri crucifixi . . . ut per inspeccionem ymaginum revocaretur ad memoriam passio Domini nostri Iesu Christi et aliorum sanctorum passiones, et sic ad compunccionem et devocionem mentes pigre et carnales excitarentur. . . .

(Amongst which signs the Church sets up images of Our Lord crucified. . . in order that the Passion of Our Lord Jesus Christ and also the martyrdoms of other saints may be recalled to the memory by looking at these images; and thus slow and carnal minds may be stirred to compunction and devotion.)[76]

The use of memory and images described above occupies the second stage of contemplative ascent and is not the ultimate goal of contemplation.[77]

In a similar way, Hugh of St. Victor distinguishes among the soul's three ways of seeing: thinking, meditation, and contemplation. The first two stages apprehend through images, while contemplation is a "piercing and spontaneous intuition of the soul." Thinking represents a stage similar to that which we have been calling remembrance or recollection "when the mind becomes aware of things passing through it, when the image of some real thing, entering through the senses or rising up out of the memory is suddenly presented to it."[78] Like Hilton, Hugh regards thinking and meditation on images as inferior to contemplation, because while the first has to do with obscure things, the latter signifies an "entire comprehension."

Affective spirituality, or positive mysticism, differs from Pseudo-Dionysian—or negative—mysticism chiefly in this respect: it perceives a profound relationship between human cognition through the semiotics of the imagination and the life of Christ. Reading, pilgrimage, and meditation are all forms of imitation because they depend on the imaginative capacity for fashioning images and signs which recall the divinity, as does Christ in his Incarnation. The key to both Christ's Incarnation and imaginative cognition is that spiritual intention becomes wedded to corporeal similitude. The power of images to move us makes the faculty of memory essential to the exercise of prudence, as Aquinas explains:

It is necessary in this way to invent similitudes and images because simple and spiritual intentions slip easily from the soul unless they are as it were linked to some corporeal similitudes, because human cognition is stronger in regard to the sensibilia.[79]

Not coincidentally, this argument for the investment of spiritual intention in images and the process of remembering duplicates Bernard's explanation of the Incarnation:

I think this is the principal reason why the invisible God willed to be seen in the flesh and to converse with men as a man. He wanted to recapture the affection of carnal men who were unable to love in any other way, by first drawing them to the salutary love of his own humanity.[80]

The joining of human spiritual intentions with likeness in order to move the affections was the purpose of the Incarnation and is the function of the imagination and memory in aesthetic and mystical practice.

The way in which this activation of memory and imagination works as a meditative practice is elaborated in the fifteenth-century treatise on the ten commandments, *Dives and Pauper*. In response to the Lollard critique of images used in medieval drama, the *Dives and Pauper* considers the function of images in devotion:

> Þey [images] seruyn of thre thyngys. For þey been ordeynyd to steryn manys mende to thynkyn of Cristys incarnacioun and of his passioun and of holye seyntys lyuys. Also þey been ordeynyd to steryn mannys affeccioun and his herte to deuocioun, for often man is more steryd be syghte þan be heryng or redyngge. Also þey been ordeynyd to been a tokene and a book to þe lewed peple, þat þey moun redyn in ymagerye and peynture þat clerkys redyn in boke, . . .[81]

> (They [images] serve three things. They are ordained to stir man's mind to think of Christ's incarnation and of his passion and of holy saints' lives. Also they are ordained to stir man's affection and his heart to devotion, for often man is more stirred by sight than by hearing or reading. Also they are ordained to be a token and a book to the lay people, that they might be able to read in images and paintings what clerks read in books, . . .)

Just as Geoffrey de Vinsauf constructed a narrative of signs as a path which he could follow to active knowledge, Pauper describes a series of "tokens" which recall Christ's life and passion, stirring man's affections to devotion. The analogy between the lay person's book and the clerk's may be extended to the memory as well, which must "read" both the likeness and the intention of the images.[82]

As *imitatio*, reading images allows the one who reads and remembers to dwell temporarily and imperfectly in the region of similitude. The three-fold function of images elaborated by Pauper designates a progression as well, a path of signposts leading from the stirring of memory to the affections, to a construction of tokens by which future *imitatio imaginativa* is insured. It is the likeness which impresses itself on the memory and the affections and which ultimately becomes inscribed in the memory. The circuit of similitude begins in imaginative imitation and ends in reading of tokens, bringing spiritual intentions full circle to join with the human will.

While reading the Crucifixion, as Pauper describes it, requires an understanding of a complex system of correspondences between tokens and significances, the assumption underlying meditative *imitatio* is simple: "All attraction and desire and love come from that which is like, because all things are attracted by and love what is like them."[83] This assumption is made explicit in the writings of Richard Rolle. For the fourteenth-century English mystic, imitation is the desire and the effect of love. It is equivalent to the transformation of the mystical lover into the object of his/her love. Richard Misyn's fifteenth-century English translation of Rolle's *Incendium Amoris* describes meditation on Christ's life and passion as a form of imitation:

> Qwhat is lufe bott transfourmynge of desire In to þe þinge lufyd? Or lufe is grete desire of fayre gude & lufely, with continuance of þoghtis goand in to þat þinge þat it lufys; þe whylk when it has it, þen it ioys, for ioy is not causyd bot of lufe. All lufand to þer lufe treuly ar likkynd, & lufe makis hym like þat lufys to þat þat is lufyd.[84]

> (What is love but the transformation of desire into the thing loved? Or love is great desire of fair and lovely good, with thoughts continually directed unto that thing that it loves; the which, when the lover has it, he joys, for joy is caused only by love. All lovers are likened truly to their love, and love makes him who loves like that which is loved.)

The lover becomes an *imago* herself through the direction of her thoughts. Desire for the loved one leads to mystical union or, in Rolle's words, transformation into the loved one. In the region of unlikeness, the *regio dissimilitudinis* of St. Bernard, the mystic longs to recover that resemblance lost because of the Fall. Imitation is less a prescriptive for mystical union than the measure of the mystic's love and joy. While Rolle elsewhere prescribes a conforming of one's life to Christ's, the *imitatio Christi* described here is a meditational practice, an exercise in desire.[85] According to Rolle, it leads to the wounding of the mind described in the *Song of Songs* and the setting of Christ as a token or sign in one's heart. This token signifies a forgetfulness of everything else except Christ. Through a "continuous direction of one's thoughts," then, the mystic experiences this "recording" of Christ in the mystic's mind and heart.[86] Imitation in this sense is a kind of inscription—of tokens, in Rolle's usage and of *insignia* in the *vita* of Clare of Montefalco—in the mystic's heart. Meditative *imitatio* is a kind of abundant remembrance preserved in the tokens and signs of one's heart.

In fact, such imitation through remembrance was specifically called a *recordatio* (remembrance). Thomas of Cantimpre's *vita* of Margaret of

Ypres (d. 1237) describes her extreme practice of self-flagellation as a *recordatio* which is aimed at uniting her with Christ.[87] In this type of imitation, Margaret's body becomes the written record of Christ's suffering, and spectacle to the act of recollection itself. By making a spectacle of her body, Margaret joins Christ as image, as corporeal similitude in harmony with spiritual intentions. There is no disjunction, in this example, between the act of remembering and the bodily recording of the spiritual recollection.[88]

The purpose of mystical recollection and of imaginative *imitatio* is the experience of suffering. The detailing of Christ's suffering encouraged in meditational treatises and practiced in mystical meditations serves to recall Christ's suffering. The fourteenth-century English mystic Julian of Norwich requests a vision of Christ's suffering so that she might suffer with him as if she were present at the event:

> . . . I desyrede a bodylye syght, whare yn y myght have more knawynge of bodelye paynes of oure lorde oure savyoure, and of the compassyonn of oure ladye and of alle his trewe loveres that were be levande his paynes that tyme and sythene; for I wolde have beene one of thame and suffrede with thame.

> (. . . I desired a bodily sight, through which I might have more knowledge of our Lord and saviour's bodily pains, and of the compassion of our Lady and of all his true lovers who were living at that time and saw his pains, for I would have been one of them and have suffered with them.)[89]

Like the *Meditations on the Life of Christ*, which advocates thinking about the events of Christ's life "as though you were present," Julian desires the suffering of a witness.[90] Her remembrance is keyed to a configuration of five tokens: the bleeding head, the discoloration of the face, the copious bleeding of the body from scourging, the shriveling of the flesh, and finally, the joy and bliss of the Passion.[91] Other memory systems designed for imaginative participation in Christ's suffering are constructed around the instruments of His Passion including the pillar and scourges, crown of thorns, cross and nails.[92] The signs recall Christ's pain and suffering, and so are the means by which Julian and other mystics become spectators to the events.

However, Julian's request for knowledge suggests another capacity in which imaginative *imitatio* induces suffering. The mystic's desire for remembrance of Christ's Passion is not a purely imaginative or spiritual exercise. Julian of Norwich equates her desire for knowledge with the desire that "my body might be filled full of recollection and feeling of his blessed Passion, . . . for I wished that his pains might be my pains, . . ."[93] Mystical recollection renders the body as well as the affections receptive to the suffering of Christ's Passion. A certain physical and affective reenactment of the Passion attends mystical recollection.

The dual nature of suffering—through remembrance and through the affection—is articulated later in Julian of Norwich's *Showings*. She locates this suffering in the two parts of the soul: the higher part, or "substantial nature" and the lower part, or "sensual nature." Christ possessed both parts, but it was sensuality which suffered in His Passion. Both parts participate in Julian's revelation "in which my body was filled full of feeling and memory of Christ's Passion and his dying."[94] Because the sensual nature is joined to Christ through the flesh, this is also where remembrance take place. In contrast to the substantial nature which is always full, the sensual nature is always lacking.[95] Out of this lack comes the desire for the bodily feeling and remembrance which Julian requests at the beginning of her book.

Such corporeal effects of spiritual remembrance are most often associated with *imitatio Christi* as it was understood in the late fifteenth century. The tokens of remembrance themselves become internalized in the mystic's body. Clare of Montefalco's meditation on the images and tokens of Christ's suffering causes her to feel a physical cross in her heart.[96] Whether the tokens are inscribed outwardly on the mystic's body or inwardly on her heart and mind, the activity of meditation and particularly remembrance produces the physical effects of the Passion image, rendering the mystic's body itself a kind of mnemonic of that suffering. From meditation on images comes the translation of the mystic's own body into image of suffering and yet another sign of remembrance.

The Middle English redaction of the life of Elizabeth of Spalbeck (d. 1266) reveals how both the saint's body and the text of her *vita* bear tokens of Christ's life and suffering. The English compiler recounts Elizabeth's extravagant imitation of Christ's suffering, including her self-violence, weeping, and reenactment of the twelve stages of the Cross. Elizabeth's stigmata bleed freshly every Friday, by which Christ "schewiþ in a merueylous manere þe representacyone of his blyssed passyone in þe persone of the same virgyne, . . ."[97] In his conclusion, the Middle English compiler suggests a three-fold representation to be found in the text, body, and life of Elizabeth of Spalbeck:

> Wherfore this virgyne, whos lyfe is alle mirakil, 3e moor-ouer alle hir-selfe is but myrakil, as hit schewiþ by the abouen writynge, figures and expounes not allonly Cryste, but Cryste crucifyed, in hir body, and also þe figuratif body of Cryste, þat is holy chirche.[98]

(Wherefore this virgin, whose life is miraculous, yea morever, she herself is a miracle, as is shown by the above writing, figures and expounds not only Christ, but Christ crucified, in her body, and also the figurative body of Christ, which is the holy church.)

While the writing, figures, and "interpretations" of the text are tokens of the miracle of Christ, the saint's body records "Christ crucified." The text, which so carefully traces the saint's practice of imitating Christ's suffering according to the canonical hours, inscribes her body into the text of remembrance. The body is both sight of the marvelous and spectacle of that remembrance through which the saint achieves mystical union.

Though the spectacle of such *imitatio* is quite dramatic, it is merely the side-effect of the true suffering the mystic experiences in the act of remembering. Julian of Norwich expressly says that her desire for bodily remembrance is aimed at knowledge of Christ and his pain. According to the Monk of Farne, it is the memory itself which suffers in its efforts to know Christ. Drawing upon the angel's instruction to John in Apoc. 10:9–10 to eat the book, the Monk of Farne warns that this knowledge,

> in your mouth and understanding shall be sweet, but . . . shall make your belly bitter, that is to say your memory, because he that increases knowledge increases sorrow too, and hardship gives understanding to the hearing of one who through his compassion with Christ crucified fills up in his flesh the sufferings which are wanting.[99]

The knowledge which brings bitterness to the memory likewise fills the flesh with ineffable suffering. The two kinds of *imitatio*—the one which is a function of the imagination and memory, and the other, of the body—are not distinct in the Monk of Farne's theology. The tokens of suffering in the body commemorate what the memory, imagination, and flesh know. From the signposts of memory are produced the stigmata of the body, but the suffering is never located in either place since the transference of knowledge is never complete. It is endlessly repeated, circulated, and succeeded by intervals of want and repletion.

Imitatio Christi in the Middle Ages, then, is not simply a doctrine of suffering or mortification of the flesh. It is a semiotics of suffering, a complex system of signposts and tokens that do not always observe the boundaries of the physical, imaginary, and symbolic. Nor is the knowledge produced by imitating the magisterial knowledge which accrues to the seeker. Rather, it is more of an "ongoing unsettling process."[100] While the practitioner of imitation dwells in the region of similitudes, his or her suffering fares across the borders of mind, flesh, and spirit like an infusion or contagion. A system of images and signs induce this suffering, while the suffering itself produces its own *insignia* in the body, thereby perpetuating a semiotic system of remembrance. The mystic's body itself is translated into *imago*, into sign of Christ's suffering and God's intentions.

Returning again to Clare of Montefalco and the female mystic, we may now consider where she is located within this semiotic system. Given the gendered distinctions between flesh and spirit, the mystic's *imitatio* is already situated and proceeding in different directions. If the woman mystic/saint's imitation begins already from a different location than the male mystic's, in what direction does she proceed? Toward masochism or assimilation? Or perhaps toward disruption? More importantly, how does the mystic's imitation affect or alter her relationship to language? What gets translated from this imitation onto bodies and into language and texts—the spectacle—will provide us with some clues.

Imaginary Zones and the Broken Seal

Understanding the female mystic's imitation of Christ in the context of medieval culture requires a paradigm of how cultural repression works. In "The Guilty One" Catherine Clément analyzes the workings of culture's repressive structures. In particular, she explores cultural myth-making about what it represses, what it refuses to situate in the culture's symbolic systems: "Somewhere every culture has an imaginary zone for what it excludes, and it is that zone we must try to remember."[101] These imaginary zones are situated in the interstices between symbolic systems and are dangerously mobile rather than fixed.[102] Those who occupy these zones—hysterics and sorceresses in Clément's study—constantly remind the culture of the slippage between its symbolic systems, of the "incompatible synthesis" and impossible transitions which run like "fault lines" beneath the culture.[103]

We have seen how woman in medieval culture occupied the imaginary zone of the flesh, of that which was excluded because it threatened the integrity of the body. Like the scabrous old Will of Bernard's formulation or Ambrose's "heaving powers," woman is situated at the place of "impossible transition" or more exactly, of impossible transgression. In league with the senses, she constantly circulates between the inside and outside, the pure and the impure. She emits foul and fetid breath as she welcomes the filth which pours freely into the memory through the senses. The ulcers on her body mark the infection bred by the "three-fold malignity" that she never tires of proclaiming: "I am voluptuous. I am curious. I am ambitious." The moral infection signified by the ulcers is itself marked by *aggression* of the will and *ingression* of the senses. The three-fold malignity represents a configuration of sexual, epistemological, and social agression which resists divine law and human reason. The flesh is the imaginary zone of medieval culture which it excludes in its doctrine of female chastity and its law of the sealed body.

The female mystic's imitation of Christ resists the medieval law of the sealed body by exploiting woman's situation in the heaving powers of the flesh. Her *imitatio* recalls this imaginary zone through the practice of defilement. Occupying the fissured flesh, woman threatens the cultural value attached to the integrity of the body. When the female mystic imitates Christ, she activates this potential for risking the culture's self-definition through defilement. Mary Douglas explains how such defilement assaults those boundaries most crucial to a culture's identity:

> Each culture has its risks and its specific problems. It attributes a power to some image or another of the body, according to the situation of which the body is the mirror. . . . The things that defile are always wrong one way or another, they are not in their place or else they have crossed a line they never should have crossed and from this shift a danger for someone results.[104]

We have seen how, according to Bernard of Clairvaux's theology, the soul is defiled through the corruption of the will and the unchecked infusion of sense experience. The perviousness of the flesh places the cultural value of the integrity of body and soul continually at risk. Woman defiles by crossing these boundaries and, hence, the larger cultural demarcations which depend upon them.

Julia Kristeva calls this practice of defilement "abjection," and she traces its evolution in Judaeo-Christian tradition.[105] According to her analysis, the abject is that which "does not respect borders, positions, rules. The in-between, the ambiguous, the composite." Abjection is a straying into unstable territories where the limits of the self are not clearly defined.[106] An example of abjection is food loathing which causes retching, a protest of the body. This experience of abjection comes from the awareness of the internal and external threats to the border of the self. Corpses, festering wounds, the smell of decay all have the power to invade the subject/object and inside/outside borders, making those borders pervious and identity problematic.[107]

Abjection is bound to the sacred in the form of taboo. That is, the taboo serves to exclude something—say, a food substance or sexuality—in order to secure the borders of the subject. At the same time, then, the sacred calls into being transgression, since it is transgression of the taboo, rule, or law which gives rise to abjection. The taboos of Judaism and Christianity attempt to prohibit the threat of the abject by protecting the boundaries of the body. The main difference between the two, according to Kristeva, is that Jewish law seeks to protect the pure body from external defilement while Christian law internalizes abjection by making defilement interior.[108] "Not that which goeth into the mouth defileth a man; but that which cometh out of the mouth, this defileth a man" (Matt. 15:11). Christian subjectivity, then, depends on the crucial division of inside/outside (rather than pure/impure of Judaic law).

We can see how abjection is relevant to Ambrose's fear of the "heaving powers of the flesh," Augustine's attention to the "fissured flesh," and Bernard's analogy of the Will to Eve who permits the "wild motions of the soul." Abjection is the result of the Fall whence the boundaries of the body and soul were violated. Because the flesh is heterogeneous—neither body nor soul, but carnal and spiritual at the same time—abjection poses a continual threat to the Christian subject. Yet it also offers a radical notion of perfection. The excess of drives—those heaving powers of the flesh— topple over into love of God. The same interior flux or perviousness of the flesh which leads to sin likewise leads to perfection. According to Kristeva, self-abjection requires of the mystic continual avowal of her impurity, yet is not necessarily masochistic in the usual sense of the word:

> The mystic's familiarity with abjection is a fount of infinite jouissance. One may stress the masochistic economy of the jouissance only if one points out at once that the Christian mystic, far from using it to the benefit of a symbolic or institutional power, displaces it indefinitely . . . within a discourse where the subject is resorbed . . . into communication with the Other and with others.[109]

Such abjection exploits by overturning the medieval effort to exclude abjection and with it, the feminine, from religious experience. The sealed body represents a taboo against that abjection which threatens the boundaries of the soul. If the female mystic chooses to occupy those borders, to confound them by transgressing them, she exploits the medieval association of flesh and feminine. Like Bernard's thief who steals the bovine body from the peasant-spirit in order to sin, the flesh transgresses the spirit's domain continually in the experience of abjection. If the woman mystic's ordeal of abjection is masochistic, it is not in the service of the self-loathing that the

Ancrene Wisse encourages. The mystic who insists on that which has been excluded in medieval Christianity, namely, the feminine, the pervious flesh, and defilement, takes abjection for the sublime.

Imitatio Christi and abjection join in their effects, that is, the signs of transgression. Blood, odors, wounds, tears, and other kinds of bodily effluvia are not only tokens of a body "filled full of recollection and feeling of his Blessed Passion," in Julian of Norwich's words. They are also tokens of that imaginary zone which the mystic recalls, of the crossing of boundaries which separate the pure and whole body from its effects. Unlike relics, which derive power from detached bodily parts, these tokens of mystical imitation are powerful in their *relationship* to the body. They remind us that the body is not an integrated whole, that it may not be separated from its effects, that it is not charmed by the relics which achieve their power through their very detachment. They are signs of mystical desire in action, of the excess which produces them, rather than tokens of uncorrupt bodies capable of conferring power on those communities who hold them sacred.[110]

Abjection is experienced by the mystic through two different but related processes. While bodily emissions are produced by the mystic's desire, bodily closure or blockage results from the mystic's revulsion. The two, in fact, are complementary gestures of abjection. As Carolyn Bynum points out, miraculous effusions were "predicated on extraordinary closure."[111] From extraordinary disgust to craving, female saints and mystics often seek holiness in gestures of abjection which horrify in their disregard for the inside/outside boundaries of the self. Catherine of Siena's disgust for food was exhibited in her severe fasting which eventually led to her death. Yet this disgust was inseparable from her craving for the eucharist, as her biographer, Raymond of Capua, comments:

> The habit of receiving communion practically every day struck root in her and became part of her life . . . Her longing for more and more frequent communion was so intense that when she could not receive it her very body felt the deprivation, and her forces seemed to droop. . . . [W]henever she received Holy Communion, a very torrent of heavenly graces and consolations flooded her soul. These were so abundant that their efforts brimmed over upon her body also, checking the natural flow of its vital juices, and so altering the action of her stomach that it could no longer assimilate food. Indeed, the taking of food became to her not merely unnecessary but actually impossible, except to the accompaniment of great bodily suffering. If food was ever forced down her throat, intense pain followed, no digestion took place, and all that had been violently forced down was violently forced back again.[112]

Catherine's intense longing for the eucharist brings with it the disgust for ordinary food. Her relationship to Christ continually tests the boundaries of the body, as her "ardent love" overcomes the body's "instinctive reflexes" when she drinks the pus of a sick woman.[113] Catherine practices defilement to achieve grace. Catherine of Genoa, who ate lice, and Angela of Foligno, who drank the bathwater of lepers, likewise use defilement to inspire recollection of Christ's suffering and, more importantly, to topple abjection into the sublime.

The model for such abjection is the crucified body of Christ itself. The Long Text of Julian of Norwich's *Showings* begins with a trickle of blood from the crown of thorns in a "living stream" like rain from the eaves: "This vision was living and vivid and hideous and fearful and sweet and lovely."[114] She calls this showing "familiar" and "courteous," words which seem to designate contrary modes of expressing love though intimacy and respectful distance.[115] Another meaning of familiarity is suggested by this vision: that of abjection, of the exposure of the interior of the body, and consequently, the infusion of exterior with interior. The vision is both terrible and sweet in that it "corrupts" the boundaries which define the body; it introduces fissures as tokens of perfection and defilement as its means.

According to Julian, this vision of defilement induces ravishment in the heart. Abjection gives place to compassion, but not without the physical tokens of defilement: tears, stigmata, nosebleeds, smells, lactation, cries, and sometimes speech. This imitation is indicative of a process that leads from rupture to compassion, to heightened sentience, and eventually to transformation. Through excess of desire, the transgression which leads to knowledge and union is produced, but it requires defilement and risks culture. Paradoxically, the mystic's union comes at the cost of fragmentation: "An entire fantastic world, made of bits and pieces, opens up beyond the limit, as soon as the line [of the masculine integrity of the body] is crossed."[116] The bits and pieces comprising the female mystic's *imitatio* are the tokens of the crossing, of the fissuring of the flesh and the rejection of the pure and sealed body.

One of the biblical paradigms for this type of *imitatio* which begins in abject *familiarity* is the story of Thomas's doubt (John 20:24–29). Because Thomas was not with the other disciples when the resurrected Christ appeared to them, he doubted their testimony. He refused to believe in the Resurrection "except I shall see in his hands the print of the nails, and put my finger into the place of the nails, and put my hand into his side " (John 20:25). Christ not only asks him to touch the wounds of his hands, but to place his entire hand in the wound in his side. Although Christ praises those who believe without demanding this evidence, the event establishes a precedent for abjection as a path to belief and mystical union. Christ's familiarity lies in the exposure of the interior of his body, while belief requires an immersion in that interior through a reversal of the principle of the eucharist.[117]

The fissured body of Christ calls for an act of defilement to confirm belief for the doubter as well as the believer. The invitation to immersion in Christ's side is common in the visions of female mystics. In the tenth revelation of her book of *Showings*, Julian of Norwich recounts one such experience:

> Wyth a good chere oure good lorde lokyd in to hys syde and behelde with joy, and with hys swete lokyng he led forth the vnderstandyng of hys creature by the same wound in to hys syd with in; and ther he shewyd a feyer and delectable place, and large jnow for alle mankynde that shalle be savyd and rest in pees and in loue.

> (With a kindly countenance our good Lord looked into his side, and he gazed with joy, and with his sweet regard he drew his creature's understanding into his side by the same wound; and there he revealed a fair and delectable place, large enough for all mankind that will be saved and will rest in peace and in love.)[118]

In a similar vision, the thirteenth-century mystic, Angela of Foligno, interprets her immersion as a gift of profound knowledge. Christ tells her that by drinking the blood from His side, she will be purified. In another vision, Angela learns that the degree of one's immersion in Christ's side signifies different degrees of one's knowledge.[119] Belief for Thomas and knowledge for Julian and Angela are sought in the body's ruptures—those interruptions of the body's integrity which signify cultural risks of perversion on the verge of perfection.

The mystic's union and her perfection, then, come only at the risk of the body. Her perfection in particular exploits the potential of the flesh for excess, and thus perversion, in order to cross the boundaries of her own exclusion. Her imitation of Christ is not indulgence in passive suffering, but a forcing of the Christian paradox which is lodged in the heterogeneity of the flesh—where a woman is also lodged, like some revolting taboo, reminding the body of that imaginary zone it prohibits. Christ's transgression of Old Testament laws governing the flesh, particularly eating, offers the woman mystic the opportunity to place the flesh back into circulation through her imitation. Angela of Foligno provides a startling example of how the mystic enlists the powers of taboo in her *imitatio*. After washing the feet of lepers, she drinks the bathwater in a kind of perverse eucharistic sacrament:

> Et videbatur michi recte quod ego communicassem; quia suavitatem max-
> imam sentiebam, sicut si communicassem. Et quia quedam scarpula illarum
> plagarum erat interposita in gutture, ego conabar ad glutiendum eam, et
> reprehendebat me conscientia expuere sicut si communicassem, quamvis non
> expuerem ad ej[i]ciendum set ad deponendum eam de gutture.[120]

> (It seemed to me truly that I had communicated; indeed, I felt the greatest
> sweetness as if I had received communion. When a scab from the wounds
> remained in my throat, I tried to swallow it. My conscience reproached me to
> spit it out as though I had communicated; however, I would not spit it out in
> order to expel it, but in order to dislodge it from my throat.)

This act of defilement defies medieval taboos against such bodily pollution.[121] The horror of Angela's act lies partly in the transgression of this taboo and partly in the seeming perversion of the eucharist. The mystic's desire forces the line of exclusion separating perversion and perfection, producing a sort of contagion between the two.

In the process of such abjection, the bodily construct which structures the opposition between victimizer and victim breaks down—an opposition which is reinforced at every level of medieval thought. Medieval physiology preserves this opposition in its representation of the female sexual anatomy as the internal mirror of the male anatomy. The seal-and-wax analogy which we observed in the *Anatomia vivorum* operates on the principle of specularity and provides the model for victimization. As the passive surface on which the male anatomy exerts its own impression, the female sexual anatomy is already conceived as victim. Victimization is, in fact, the very essence of it and its reason for existence. The privileged external acting upon the internal and insuring its own impression (and impressiveness) is physiology's endorsement of victimization through its construction of sexual difference.

The sealing of the female body in religious texts endeavors to preserve the boundaries separating the external from the internal, and at the same time, objectifies the internal experience, whether of defilement, wounding, or pain. It creates what Elaine Scarry has called a "language of agency," privileging the agent of pain or suffering with power. The "victim" of this agency thus becomes merely "the passive surface on which the weapon's

power of alteration inscribes itself."[122] The active end of this complicitous
relationship is the powerful, weapon-wielding one; the passive end is a
surface of the weapon's inscription and objectification. The interior of the
body yields itself up to the weapon's exposure of it. The power is located in
the external, and it asserts itself by altering the internal, usually through a
process of externalization and objectification.

Within this linguistic construction of external/internal and active/
passive relationships, language itself is at issue. For the power of victimiz-
ing lies in its ability to "shatter language."[123] Voice or speech acts upon the
body as a weapon, displacing the victimized body's speech with pain. We
can see these categories functioning in the Old Testament, where God's
voice acts upon the human body to effect change, administering the punish-
ments of labor and childbirth as a result of the Fall.[124]

The flesh offers a position of mobility within this economy that is not
subject to the same categories because it is always straying, heterogeneous,
and dangerous. In addition to verging always on sin through its excess of
desire, the flesh also produces a new speech. Both the flesh and woman
conspire in this new speech to recall and circulate that imaginary zone
excluded in institutional and social discourse. Word and flesh are no longer
distinct according to the law derived from the risen Christ's warning to
Mary Magdalene, *Noli me tangere*, "Do not touch me" (John 20:17). The
one touches the other in a violation of the New Testament taboo of the
Godhead (rather than the manhood) of Christ to women, and, by extension, of language to women. Such language insists on the fleshly affections
and on blurring the boundary between *humanus amor* and *divinus amor*, a
distinction which Jean Gerson used to interrogate visions for their truth or
falsehood.[125] Such a language is dangerous in that it threatens to demystify
God's transcendence, and worse, to embarrass it.

One of the most striking examples of how female mystics insist upon a
new language of the flesh is Angela of Foligno's experience of translating
her visions into text by means of her erstwhile scribe, Fra Arnaldo. Her
mystical reception of the Word provides a powerful comment upon her
earlier frustrations with her scribe's efforts to record her visions. This
particular vision begins with her immersion in the crucified body of Christ.
Following this bodily baptism, Angela of Foligno says that Christ then
showed her the Word:

> Et tunc etiam ostendit michi verbum, ita quod modo intelligo, quid est
> verbum, et quid est dicere verbum. Et dixit michi tunc: 'Hoc est verbum quod
> voluit incarnari pro te.' Et tunc etiam transitum fecit per me, et totam me
> tetigit et amplexatus est me.

(And then he showed me the Word, and thus I know what the Word is, and what it is to speak the Word. Then He spoke to me: 'This is the Word which wished to be incarnated for you.' And then the Word passed though me, touched all of me, and embraced me.)[126]

Angela receives the Word like a sacrament in this vision. Elsewhere she compares the incarnate words which speak in her soul with those paltry words which are "exterior to the ineffable divine workings in the soul." Because of the inadequacy of language to convey the incarnate word, she claims that her discourse is blasphemy. Angela's vision reveals the abject in language itself, which is the realm of the flesh.

While she experiences the abject in her vision when her flesh is visited, touched, and embraced by the Word, she recognizes the inadequacy of spoken and written words to articulate this. This mystical incorporation of language contrasts dramatically with the inadequacy of her scribe's efforts to translate into Latin the account Angela dictated in her native Umbrian. Again and again, he listens carefully to her as she is rapt in her visions, records them, and reads them back to her only to find that she cannot understand what he has written. True, she says, the words vaguely recall those she spoke, but she hardly recognizes her experience in his version of it. His account is obscure; it preserves the insignificant and completely ignores the marvelous aspects of the revelation.[127] For his part, the scribe acknowledges that her revelations have been sifted like flour through the sieve of his writing, which manages to preserve only the coarser remnants. The rest is too fine for the *scriptor*'s sieve.[128]

Of course, it is a convention of mystical writings to complain of the inexpressibility of the mystical experience. Language is simply too dull to "get" the riddle of the Word. Angela is bound to blaspheme in her native Umbrian dialect, while her scribe's translation of her visions into Latin obscures even more the mysteries of which she speaks. Each articulation lapses further and further from the truth of the vision. The Word which passes through Angela leaves hardly a trace in the text of her visions, *Le Livre de l'expérience des vrais fidèles*.

Angela's criticism of those words which are exterior to divine mystery is not merely a convention of mystical discourse, however. It is a claim to a privileged language, the Word made flesh and uttered through the flesh. One gains a knowledge of this Word through continuous contemplation of the *liber vitae*, the Book of Life, which is the life and death of the crucified Christ.[129] The Word that speaks through the flesh, through abjection, is manifested through the body—through the trembling of limbs, cries, falling on the ground. Such a language does not deny the "intractable drives" of the flesh, nor does it rest securely on the prohibition of the sealed body. Without the sealed body, the borders between flesh and spirit and letter and spirit are lost. Angela's vision of the Word which touches and embraces her anticipates Hélène Cixous's modern vision of the subversive potential of women's language: "Her flesh speaks true. She lays herself bare. In fact, she physically materializes what she's thinking; she signifies it with her body. In a certain way she *inscribes* what she's saying, because she doesn't deny her drives the intractable and impassioned part they have in speaking."[130]

The female mystic's language begins in transgression, but unlike Eve's transgression, it is not a transgression based on denial. It is more like the affirmative transgression described by Michel Foucault in his vision of an alternative to the Western model of knowledge and language:

> Transgression opens into a scintillating and constantly affirmed world, a world without shadow or twilight, without that serpentine "no" that bites into fruits and lodges their contradictions at their core. It is the solar inversion of satanic denial. It was originally linked to the divine or rather, from this limit marked by the sacred it opens the space where the divine functions.[131]

The serpentine "no" leads to the repression of the feminine and flesh and to a discourse safely ensconced in its tiered system of flesh and spirit, masculine and feminine, literal and figurative, and human and divine, and a religion protected by the ideal of the sealed female body. The woman mystic's transgression functions at the place of the "limit marked by the sacred." Instead of assuming limitations in order to deny them, as medieval theology does, the woman mystic "affirms limited being" in order to transgress, to pass over into divine union and knowledge, which is limitless.[132]

Like Angela's language, which courses through her body, the language of female mystics who insist upon the flesh and the Word, is both intractable and subversive. Considering the exclusion of women from both the oral and written languages of the Church, this claim to a privileged language is an important one. It is accomplished at great cultural and personal risk through the female mystic's *imitatio Christi*. As André Vauchez has argued, the imitation of Christ offers something different to the illiterate lay woman from what it offers to the male religious. It provides her a piety which she often expressed through the body and which she also interpreted—an instrument of power and a privileged communication.[133] The female mystic who speaks from the place of abjection seeks to return language—and words in particular—to Aristotle's definition of words as "symbols of that which suffers in the soul."[134] She does so by implicating the flesh and the medieval construction of woman in that suffering, and thus, in language itself. Here, too, she seeks to transgress the limits of a language which is hopelessly exterior and which excludes the marvelous. From the fissured flesh comes the female mystic's language of suffering, words derived from the wounds of the soul, utterance both intractable and marvelous.

Notes

1. See André Vauchez, *La Sainteté en Occident aux derniers siècles du moyen âge d'après les procès de canonisation et les documents hagiographiques*. Bibliothèque des études françaises d'Athènes et de Rome 241 (Rome: École Française de Rome, 1981), 408, 517. Piero Camporesi also recounts Clare's story as evidence of the medieval fascination with "the behaviour of saintly bodies under post mortem," in *The Incorruptible Flesh: Bodily Mutation and Mortification in Religion and Folklore*, trans. Tania Croft-Murray (Cambridge: Cambridge University Press, 1988), 3–24.
2. Vauchez, *La Sainteté*, 4.
3. See Vauchez, *La Sainteté*, 503. Also Patrick J. Geary's discussion of holy relics, *Furta Sacra: Thefts of Relics in the Central Middle Ages* (Princeton, NJ: Princeton University Press, 1978).
4. Vauchez, *La Sainteté*, see 499–510.
5. See Vauchez, *La Sainteté*, 513–14.
6. For contemporary suspicion of this type of spirituality, particularly as it was practiced by female mystics, see Vauchez, *Les laïcs au Moyen Âge: Pratiques et expériences religieuses* (Paris: Éditions du Cerf, 1987), 273–75; more generally, the author of the *Cloud of Unknowing* and Walter Hilton condemn this spirituality: James Walsh, trans., *The Cloud of Unknowing* (New York: Paulist Press, 1981), 205–36; and M.L. Del Mastro, trans., *The Stairway of Perfection* (New York: Image Books, 1979), 94–95.
7. Vauchez, *La Sainteté*, 515.
8. See Carolyn Walker Bynum, *Holy Feast and Holy Fast: The Religious Significance of Food to Medieval Women* (Berkeley: University of California Press, 1987), 253–59; see also Vauchez's discussion of the Franciscan movement in connection with female spirituality, *Les laïcs au Moyen Âge*, 189–202. For Cistercian influence, see Bynum, *Jesus as Mother: Studies in the Spirituality of the High Middle Ages* (Berkeley: University of California Press, 1982), 129–54.
9. See Bynum, *Holy Feast and Holy Fast*, and "The Female Body and Religious Practice in the Middle Ages" in *Fragments for a History of the Human Body*, Part 1, ed. Michel Feher, Ramona Naddaff and Nadia Tazi (New York: Urzone, 1989), 160–219.
10. See the argument of Sarah Beckwith, "A Very Material Mysticism: The Medieval Mysticism of Margery Kempe," in *Medieval Literature: Criticism, Ideology,*

and History, ed. David Aers (Brighton: Harvester Press, 1986), 34–57. Beckwith warns that feminists should be more critical of women's attraction to this spirituality and less quick merely to celebrate the marginal (54).

11. See Feher's Introduction to Feher et al., eds., *Fragments for a History of the Human Body*, 11–12.

12. See Richard Kieckhefer, *Unquiet Souls: Fourteenth-Century Saints and Their Religious Milieu* (Chicago: University of Chicago Press, 1984), 98; for an account of this shift from the evangelical to the interior models of *imitatio Christi*, see Vauchez, *Les laïcs*, 455–60.

13. Bynum distinguishes between the external and internal, or psychosomatic, manipulation of the body, the former being more predominant in male spirituality and the latter in female piety, "The Female Body," 164–65. I will not be using the same distinctions, but she is the only scholar I know who recognizes differences among the forms that "bodily" imitation takes.

14. Danielle Jacquart and Claude Thomasset, *Sexuality and Medicine in the Middle Ages*, trans. Matthew Adamson (Princeton, NJ: Princeton University Press, 1988), 54–69. For a good overview of medieval attitudes toward the female body, see Elizabeth Robertson, *Early English Devotional Prose and the Female Audience* (Knoxville: University of Tennessee Press, 1990), 32–43.

15. Ian Maclean argues that after 1600 most physicians rejected the Aristotelian view of the inequality of the sexualities of men and women: *The Renaissance Notion of Woman: A Study in the Fortunes of Scholasticism and Medical Science in European Intellectual Life* (Cambridge: Cambridge University Press, 1980), 28–46.

16. Bynum argues for the fluidity of "gender imagery" and the "permeable boundaries" between the sexes, "The Female Body," 185–86. This argument is a dangerous one because it conveniently overlooks the repression of female sexuality in such a construction, as well as the way in which sameness is used here to establish difference and inferiority.

17. Jacquart and Thomasset, *Sexuality and Medicine in the Middle Ages*, 36–37. For a recent discussion of the hierarchical model of medieval sexual physiology, see Thomas Laqueur, *Making Sex: Body and Gender from the Greeks to Freud* (Cambridge: Cambridge University Press, 1990), 1–62.

18. Quoted from *Anatomia vivorum* in Jacquart and Thomasset, *Sexuality and Medicine in the Middle Ages*, 37. Their quotation uses "inverted" to describe the male anatomy. Clearly, this is a mistake which I have corrected with the word "everted."

19. Aristotle attributed matter to the mother and form to the father, while Galen argued that both father and mother provided seeds to the fetus. Yet, like Aristotle, Galen viewed the mother chiefly as a provider of the food, or material, of the body. See Bynum, "The Female Body," 182.

20. Vern L. Bullough, "Medical and Scientific Views of Women," *Viator* 4 (1973): 487–93.

21. Bynum makes this point: "The Female Body," 162.

22. Elaine Pagels has studied the theory and influence of Augustine's account of the Fall in *Adam, Eve, and the Serpent* (New York: Random House, 1988).

23. For Bernard's contribution to medieval piety, see Bynum, *Jesus as Mother*,

125–69; and Clarissa W. Atkinson, *Mystic and Pilgrim: The Book and the World of Margery Kempe* (Ithaca, NY: Cornell University Press, 1983), 137–38; and Kieckhefer, *Unquiet Souls*, 90–91.

24. *The Body and Society: Men, Women, and Sexual Renunciation in Early Christianity* (New York: Columbia University Press, 1988), 341–47.

25. See Augustine, *De Genesi ad litteram*, 10, 12, 20, PL 34, col. 416.

26. *De civitate Dei*, ed. Bernardus Dombart and Alphonsus Kalb, CCSL 48 (Turnhout: Brepols, 1955), 14, 2–3, pp. 414–18.

27. For a good summary of the Pauline view, see Brown, *Body and Society*, 47–49.

28. See Romans 7:18–24 and 8:1–13.

29. Brown, *Body and Society*, 418. For Augustine on this idea, see *De civitate Dei*, 14, 3, pp. 416–18.

30. *De civitate Dei*, 14, 3, p. 417.

31. *De civitate Dei*, 14, 2, p. 416.

32. *De trinitate*, ed. W. J. Mountain and Fr. Glorie, CCSL 50 (Turnhout: Brepols, 1968), 12, 10 and 15, pp. 364–65 and 369–70; and *De civitate Dei*, 14, 27, pp. 450–51.

33. See Brown, *Body and Society*, 424.

34. *Enarrationes in psalmos*, ed. D. Eligius Dekkers and Iohannes Fraipont, CCSL 40 (Turnhout: Brepols, 1956) 16, p. 2037. All translations are my own unless otherwise indicated.

35. *Sermo de conversione ad clericos*, 7, 12, in *S. Bernardi Opera*, vol. IV, ed. J. Leclercq and H. M. Rochais (Rome: Editiones Cistercienses, 1957), 86–87. Translated by G. R. Evans, *Bernard of Clairvaux: Selected Works* (New York: Paulist Press, 1987), 74.

36. *Sermo de conversione ad clericos*, 6, 10, in *S. Bernardi Opera*, vol. IV, p. 83; translated in Evans, *Bernard of Clairvaux*, 74.

37. *Sermo de conversione*, 6, 11, *S. Bernardi Opera*, IV, pp. 84–85.

38. Bernard of Clairvaux, *Sermones de deversis*, Sermo LXXXV, *S. Bernardi Opera*, vol. VI, pt. 1 (Rome: Editiones Cistercienses, 1970), p. 327. Translated in Julia Kristeva, *Tales of Love*, trans. Leon S. Roudiez (New York: Columbia University Press, 1987), 159.

39. For this idea in Augustine, see D. W. Robertson, Jr., *A Preface to Chaucer: Studies in Medieval Perspectives* (Princeton, NJ: Princeton University Press, 1962), 80–81.

40. See Evans, *Bernard of Clairvaux*, 75.

41. See Kristeva's discussion of the relationship between affect, senses, and will, *Tales of Love*, 155. I will be using affections interchangeably with "affect," since Bernard often seems to use the two terms synonymously. Kristeva maintains that Bernard sometimes uses *affectiones* to include "the various feelings, made up of affects, that the soul has for God" (155).

42. Quoted in Kristeva, *Tales of Love*, 156. See her discussion of affects and the will, 155–56.

43. Kristeva, *Tales of Love*, 157.

44. See *Sermones super cantica canticorum*, 20, 6, in *S. Bernardi Opera*, vol. 1, ed.

J. Leclercq, H. M. Rochais, and C. H. Talbot (Rome: Editiones Cistercienses, 1957), 118–19.

45. Bynum has also argued that the use of feminine language and the physical practices of the male religious differ fundamentally from those of the female religious in that reversal is at the heart of the symbols they adopt. A Cistercian who claims maternal qualities or the monk who imitates Christ's nurturing does so by reversing the symbolic binary pairs of male/female, spirit/flesh, authority/nurture, etc. Bynum argues that women, by contrast, adopt the same symbols and imagery, but in continuity with their "social and biological self," *Holy Feast and Holy Fast*, 277–96. I do not agree with Bynum, but I am also arguing for the cultural and ideological differences their actions signify.

46. Bynum, "The Female Body," 186; see also Jacquart and Thomasset, who summarize the medieval medical view that the openings in the female body make it particularly windy and vulnerable to external influence, 66.

47. J. T. Muckle, ed., "The Letter of Heloise on Religious Life and Abelard's First Reply," *Mediaeval Studies* 17 (1955): 246. Heloise cites Macrobius's work, *Saturnalia*, VII, 6.16–17, 18.

48. For a discussion of the problem of windiness in women and its treatment, see Beryl Rowland, ed., *Medieval Woman's Guide to Health: The First English Gynecological Handbook* (Kent, OH: Kent State University Press, 1981), 105–9. Hildegard of Bingen also writes on the windiness of women in her *Causae et curae*; see Barbara Newman, *Sister of Wisdom: St. Hildegard's Theology of the Feminine* (Berkeley: University of California Press, 1987), 127–30.

49. Ambrose was especially concerned that the virgin preserve *integritas* in order to prevent the "polluting 'admixture'" from the outside world; see Brown, *Body and Society*, 354. For a discussion of the ideals of physical and spiritual integrity, see John Bugge, *Virginitas: An Essay in the History of the Medieval Ideal*, Archives internationales d'histoire des idées, series minor 17 (The Hague: Nijhoff, 1975), 115–33. Jane Tibbetts Schulenburg points out how the distinction between physical and spiritual *integritas* becomes problematic for Augustine when he addresses the subject of rape: "The Heroics of Virginity: *Brides of Christ and Sacrificial Mutilation*" in *Women in the Middle Ages and the Renaissance: Literary and Historical Perspectives*, ed. Mary Beth Rose (Syracuse, NY: Syracuse University Press, 1986), 35. It is interesting that Thomas Aquinas's criterion for beauty was also *integritas*, Umberto Eco, *The Aesthetics of Thomas Aquinas*, trans. Hugh Bredin (Cambridge, MA: Harvard University Press, 1988), 98–102.

50. Bella Millett, ed., *Hali Meiðhad*, EETS, o.s. 284 (London: Oxford University Press, 1982), 5. I will be referring to this work by its more common title, *Hali Meidenhad*.

51. *Hali Meiðhad*, 5–6: "Ant hwet is lufsumre þing ant mare to herien bimong eor[ð]lich[e] þing þen þe mihte of meiðhad bute bruche ant cleane, ibrowden on himseoluen, þe make[ð] of eorðlich mon ant wummon heouene engel, . . ." (And what is a more beautiful thing and more praiseworthy among earthly things than the virtue of virginity pure and without breach, modelled on that of Christ himself, who makes a heavenly angel of an earthly man and woman, . . .)

52. *Hali Meiðhad*, 6.

53. *Hali Meiðhad*, 7: "Ant eauer se þu strengeluker stondest a ein him, se he o teone ant o grome wodeluker weorre ; for swa muche þe hokerluker him þuncheð to beon ouercumen, þet þing se feble as flesch is, ant nomeliche of wummon, schal him ouerstihen." (And always as you stand more strongly against him [the devil], so he out of sorrow and out of anger attacks more furiously; because it seems to him so much the more shameful to be overcome, that that thing which is as feeble as flesh is, and especially woman, shall surpass him.) *Nomeliche* here suggests our modern word, "namely," but I am grateful to Bella Millett for reminding me that it does not have the same meaning in Middle English. This passage represents an addition to the source for this passage, Gregory's *Regula Pastoralis*, which implicates both sexes in fleshly frailty, see 33n.

54. For the allegorizing of Eve as flesh, see John Bugge, *Virginitas*, 13–29. Elizabeth Robertson has investigated how the *Meidenhad* author uses the conventional view of woman as morally inferior and physically bound to offer the female religious a means of transcendence, *Early English Devotional Prose and the Female Audience*, 77–93. For Bernard's idea of the "region of unlikeness," see Etienne Gilson, *The Mystical Theology of St. Bernard*, trans. A. H. C. Downes (London, 1940), 33–59.

55. *Hali Meiðhad*, 8. Even the famous description of the disfigurement of the female body caused by marriage and childbirth represents for the *Meidenhad* author a kind of fleshly perversion. See his descriptions, 17–18.

56. For examples of the discussion, see Bynum, *Holy Feast and Holy Fast*, 211, 274; and "The Female Body," 165.

57. *Aelred of Rievaulx's De Institutione Inclusarum*, ed. John Ayto and Alexandra Barratt, EETS, o.s. 287 (London: Oxford University Press, 1984), 9, 2. Ann K. Warren, too, calls Aelred's imagery of the anchoress "genital," and contrasts it with the "anal" imagery of the *Ancrene Wisse*, *Anchorites and Their Patrons in Medieval England* (Berkeley: University of California Press, 1985), 109.

58. See Brown, *Body and Society*, 354 and 349.

59. For a very detailed analysis of how gender is crucial to an understanding of the *Ancrene Wisse*, see Elizabeth Robertson, "The Rule of the Body: The Feminine Spirituality of the *Ancrene Wisse*," in *Seeking the Woman in Late Medieval and Renaissance Writings: Essays in Feminist Contextual Criticism*, ed. Sheila Fisher and Janet E. Halley (Knoxville: University of Tennessee Press, 1989), 109–34. Robertson shows how the male author scripts his instructions for a female audience by emphasizing the bodily aspects of contemplation and by encouraging an internalization of the women's inferiority. See also Robertson, *Early English Devotional Prose*, 44–76.

60. M. B. Salu, trans., *The Ancrene Riwle* (London: Burns and Oates, 1955), 32. For the Middle English, see J.R.R. Tolkien, ed., *Ancrene Wisse: The English Text of the Ancrene Riwle, ed. from MS. Corpus Christi, Cambridge 402*, EETS 249 (London: Oxford University Press, 1962), 39.

61. Salu, *Ancrene Riwle*, 46. Janet Grayson discusses the *Wisse* author's emphasis on the regulation of women's senses and their alliance with them in *Structure*

and Imagery in Ancrene Wisse (Hanover, NH: University Press of New England, 1974), 39 and 54.

62. Salu, *Ancrene Riwle*, 51.

63. Quoted in Robertson, *Early English Devotional Prose*, 135.

64. Thomas à Kempis, *The Imitation of Christ*, trans. Leo Sherley-Price (New York: Penguin, 1952), 27.

65. This position is not unusual. Bynum discusses it in Cistercian writings, specifically those which feminize Christ using maternal imagery. As she points out, the Cistercians adopt this maternal role in an imitation of Christ but they do so "as a way of describing a figure or institution . . . that teaches or exercises authority" (*Jesus as Mother*, 148).

66. Trans. Aubrey Stewart, 2nd. ed. (New York: Italica Press, 1986), 73.

67. See V. A. Kolve's discussion of Trevisa, *Chaucer and the Imagery of Narrative: The First Five Canterbury Tales* (Stanford, CA: Stanford University Press, 1984), 22–23.

68. On the art of memory in Cicero's *Ad Herennium*, see Frances A. Yates, *The Art of Memory* (London: Routledge and Kegan Paul, 1966), 20–26; also Kolve's discussion of images and memory, *Chaucer and the Imagery of Narrative*, 9–58.

69. Quoted in Kolve, *Chaucer and the Imagery of Narrative*, 44.

70. See Eugene Vance's discussion of natural versus conventional signs in Augustine's *On Christian Doctrine* in *Mervelous Signals: Poetics and Sign Theory in the Middle Ages* (Lincoln: University of Nebraska Press, 1986), 13–33.

71. Kolve shows how the memory systems of Albertus Magnus and St. Thomas Aquinas differed from those of classical rhetoric because of this element of intention. It is this intention which makes the image and the faculty of memory indispensable to ethics as well as to aesthetics. See Kolve, *Chaucer and the Imagery of Narrative*, 45–65.

72. *The Aesthetics of Thomas Aquinas*, trans. Hugh Bredin (Cambridge, MA: Harvard University Press, 1988), 123–25.

73. Larry D. Benson, ed., *The Riverside Chaucer* (New York: Riverside, 1987), 1:508–10.

74. I am using Aquinas's justification for images and memory quoted in Kolve, *Chaucer and the Imagery of Narrative*, 46.

75. *The Cloud of Unknowing*, trans. James Walsh, 139.

76. Quoted and translated in Rosemary Woolf, *The English Religious Lyric in the Middle Ages* (Oxford: Clarendon Press, 1968), 184.

77. See M. L. Del Mastro, trans., *The Stairway of Perfection* (New York: Image Books, 1979), 67–68.

78. *Selected Spiritual Writings*, trans. A Religious of CSMV (London: Faber and Faber, 1962), 183.

79. *Summa theologiae*, 2.2.49, I, quoted in Kolve, *Chaucer and the Imagery of Narrative*, 46.

80. *Sermones super cantica canticorum* 20, 6; quoted in Kristeva, *Tales of Love*, 158.

81. Priscilla Heath Barnum, ed., *Dives and Pauper*, EETS, o.s. 275 (London: Oxford University Press, 1976), 82.

82. Rosemary Woolf gives a good account of the dispute over the purpose of images in the fifteenth century in *The English Mystery Plays* (Berkeley: University of California Press, 1972), 77–92.

83. I am quoting Meister Eckhart although he does not agree with Rolle and other positive mystics on the function of images. See *Meister Eckhart: The Essential Sermons, Commentaries, Treatises and Defense*, trans. Edmund Colledge and Bernard McGinn (New York: Paulist Press, 1981), 214.

84. Richard Rolle, *The Fire of Love and The Mending of Life or The Rule of Living*, trans. Richard Misyn, ed. Rev. Ralph Harvey, EETS, o.s. 106 (London, 1896; rpt. 1973), 40.

85. See Misyn, *Fire of Love*, 45 and 105–19.

86. *Fire of Love*, 40. Misyn's translation uses the word "record" in the *Mending of Life* in reference to meditation on Christ's suffering, 119.

87. See Bynum, *Holy Feast and Holy Fast*, 256.

88. Bynum argues (256) that there is a difference, but this is in part because she argues for a kind of absolute physicality in women's spirituality which is somehow separate from acts of cognition. She uses the physical to mean the bodily and fleshly.

89. Julian of Norwich, *The Book of Showings to the Anchoress Julian of Norwich*, Part 1, ed. Edmund College and James Walsh (Toronto: Pontifical Institute of Mediaeval Studies, 1978), 202. Translated by Edmund Colledge and James Walsh, *Showings* (New York: Paulist Press, 1978), 126.

90. Isa Ragusa and Rosalie B. Green, eds., *Meditations on the Life of Christ: An Illustrated MS. of the Fourteenth Century*, trans. Isa Ragusa (Princeton, NJ: Princeton University Press, 1961), 15.

91. *A Book of Showings*, Part 2, ed. Colledge and Walsh, 389–90.

92. See Kolve's discussion, *Chaucer and the Imagery of Narrative*, 49–50; also Douglas Gray, *Themes and Images in the Medieval English Religious Lyric* (London: Routledge and Kegan Paul, 1972), 123–45.

93. Julian of Norwich, *Showings*, trans. Colledge and Walsh, 180.

94. *Showings*, trans. Colledge and Walsh, 288.

95. *Showings*, trans. Colledge and Walsh, 291.

96. Vauchez, *La Sainteté*, 517.

97. C. Horstmann, *Prosalegenden. Die Legenden des MS. Douce 114. Anglia* 8 (1885): 107.

98. *Proslagenden*, 118.

99. Hugh Farmer, ed., *The Monk of Farne: The Meditations of a Fourteenth Century Monk*, trans. by a Benedictine of Stanbrook (London: Darton, Longman and Todd, 1961), 76. This passage recalls Col. 1:24 in which the sufferings which are wanting refer to those which are still to come in Christ's body, that is, the Church and its members.

100. I am following Trinh T. Minh-ha's borrowing of Eastern notions of consciousness here as opposed to the Western separation of body and intellect, which leads to a consciousness based on accumulated knowledge and experience, *Woman, Native, Other: Writing Postcoloniality and Feminism* (Bloomington: Indiana University Press, 1989), 40.

101. Hélène Cixous and Catherine Clément, *The Newly Born Woman*, trans. Betsy Wing (Minneapolis: University of Minnesota Press, 1986), 6.

102. Clément, *Newly Born Woman*, 7.

103. Clément views a woman's place as anomaly as only partially subversive because of the Imaginary's lack of power over the Symbolic and the Real: "caught in the same network of language," according to Clément, hysterics and sorceresses are unable to produce real structural change, *Newly Born Woman*, 9–10.

104. Quoted from *Purity and Danger* in Clément, *Newly Born Woman*, 33.

105. Julia Kristeva, *Powers of Horror: An Essay in Abjection*, trans. Leon S. Roudiez (New York: Columbia University Press, 1982). Clément depicts a similar notion with her term, "contagion." However, because her concept is derived specifically from her analysis of the sorceress, it is less flexible than Kristeva's "abjection."

106. Kristeva, *Powers of Horror*, 4, 11.

107. *Powers of Horror*, 2–3 and 7–8.

108. See Kristeva's analysis of this difference, *Powers of Horror*, 90–132.

109. Kristeva, *Powers of Horror*, 127.

110. Patrick Geary argues that relics are passive, that they depend on cultures to activate their powers; see *Furta Sacra: Thefts of Relics in the Central Middle Ages* (Princeton, NJ: Princeton University Press, 1978), 5–9.

111. See Bynum, *Holy Feast and Holy Fast*, 274, 211.

112. Quoted in Bynum, *Holy Feast and Holy Fast*, 168.

113. Christ appears to Catherine in a vision to thank her for forcing herself to "swallow without qualm a drink from which nature recoiled in disgust"; see Bynum, *Holy Feast and Holy Fast*, 172.

114. Julian of Norwich, *Showings*, trans. Colledge and Walsh, 188; see also 181.

115. For the two terms in Middle English mysticism, see Riehle, *The Middle English Mystics*, 54, 97–98. Riehle points out that *courtesie*, because its semantic field had become generalized, could mean simply "goodness," "generosity," and "favor" (54).

116. Clément, *Newly Born Woman*, 33, in reference to anomalous elements of society, such as sorceresses or witches.

117. My discussion of Thomas's doubt is indebted to the analysis of Elaine Scarry, *The Body in Pain: The Making and Unmaking of the World* (Oxford: Oxford University Press, 1985), 215.

118. Julian of Norwich, *A Book of Showings*, Part 2, ed. Colledge and Walsh, 394–95; translated by Colledge and Walsh, *Showings*, 200.

119. M.J. Ferré and L. Baudry, *Le Livre de l'expérience des vrais fidèles: Texte latin publié d'après le manuscript d'Assise* (Paris: Droz, 1927), par. 17, p. 16; par. 135, p. 294.

120. Ferré and Baudry, *Le Livre de l'expérience des vrais fidèles*, par. 53, p. 106.

121. This taboo is elaborated in *Decretorum libri XX*, bk. 19., ch. 84, PL 140, col. 1002. Jacques Le Goff discusses medieval taboos in *The Medieval Imagination*, trans. Arthur Goldhammer (Chicago: University of Chicago Press, 1988), 94–98.

122. Scarry, *Body in Pain*, 220; see also 15–18 for her analysis of this "language of agency."

123. See Scarry's discussion, *Body in Pain*, 172.

124. See Scarry in the Old Testament construction of the body, voice, and pain, *Body in Pain*, 182–220.

125. Vauchez discusses Gerson's distinction, *Les laïcs*, 273.

126. Ferré and Baudry, *Le Livre de l'expérience des vrais fidèles*, 518.

127. Ferré and Baudry, *Le Livre de l'expérience des vrais fidèles*, par. 34, p. 42.

128. Par. 34, p. 40. Nevertheless, the scribe asserts that the translation is true because Christ himself has approved it (par. 34, p. 42).

129. Angela identifies this as the way to humility, par. 183, p. 428.

130. Cixous, "The Laugh of the Medusa," in *New French Feminisms*, ed. Elaine Marks and Isabelle de Courtivron (New York: Schocken Books, 1980), 251.

131. Foucault, *Language, Counter-Memory, Practice: Selected Essays and Interviews*, trans. Donald F. Bouchard and Sherry Simon (Ithaca, NY: Cornell University Press, 1977), 37.

132. This idea is also from Foucault, *Language*, 35. Foucault's formulation of this new knowledge and language is influenced by Buddhism, according to Uta Liebmann Schaub, "Foucault's Oriental Subtext," *PMLA* 104 (May 1989): 306–16.

133. Vauchez also argues that feminine mysticism was subversive because it contributed to the split between mystical love and intellectual knowledge, between faith and reason, see my Introduction.

134. *Peri Hermenias I*, trans. Harold P. Cooke, Loeb Classical Library (Cambridge, MA: Harvard University Press, 1938), 114–15.

2. The Text as Body and Mystical Discourse

> Would that my longing might imprint its own characters on the hearts of them that hear, just as the hand that writes presents them to the eyes of readers.
>
> The Monk of Farne

The reception of the Word which begins in the imitation of Christ is inscribed through signs in the mystic's own body. As we have seen in the previous chapter, *imitatio Christi* enlists the powers of the flesh, including the mystic's desire and affections, in a practice of abjection. In effect, this practice crosses medieval culture's imaginary zones which preserve the masculine integrity of the body by excluding the perviousness of the flesh, body, and language. Drawing upon the "heaving powers" of the flesh, the female mystic breaks taboos against the female body and defilement. In addition, she places language back into circulation with the flesh, as in Angela of Foligno's marvelous vision. In her speech and practice, she violates the boundaries separating external and internal and the principle of specularity which operates between the two. She does not, then, become victimized by her practice; rather, she unsettles the very terms of victimization.

The translation of practice into discourse and of bodies into texts is the next stage of mystical experience. In some ways, this is the most difficult part of the mystic's *imitatio*. The Monk of Farne wished that the mystic's longing might imprint itself on the hearts of his or her hearers; this wish reveals the intersection of the mystic's *imitatio* and the writing of mystical texts. The *insignia* of mystical desire imprinted in the mystic's memory and on the mystic's body must somehow become transferred to the reader's memory and heart through the act of writing. As the Monk indicates, writing and written texts ensure the transference of words to sight, but not necessarily the translation of longing into understanding. The mystic's desire is not as easily inscribed in the hearts of others as characters are written onto a page. The Monk's comment also points to a feature of mystical discourse, that is, the simultaneity of speaking and writing. The readers are listeners, in effect, endeavoring to hear the mystic's longing through the written text.

The transference of the *insignia* of desire from body to text must first be examined in the context of mystical discourse itself. The suggestion above that mystical discourse assumes a simultaneity of speech and writing already reveals a difference between mystical texts and other kinds of texts. I would like to propose that we determine what a mystical text is before we try to observe the relationship of that text to the mystic's body, memory, and desire. The position which such an examination of mystical discourse would occupy, however, needs to be distinguished from other types of investigations of mysticism. The interrogation of mysticism as a discourse will, as we shall see, disclose a new area for literary and mystical study. It will also reformulate the feminist problem posed by the mystical texts of female mystics. Instead of beginning with the effects of mystical discourse—its physical language and the practices of mystical excess—and asking whether they constitute an already appropriated form of expression for the female mystic, this study will begin with the discourse itself. I will be drawing on a variety of mystical works written by men and women in Latin and the vernacular in order to be able to sketch broadly the features of the discourse.

After identifying features of mystical discourse, I want to narrow my focus to the gendered framework for this discourse in mystical works by women. In order to do this, I have selected a few Middle English mystical writings not usually considered in studies of Middle English mysticism. In this part of the chapter, I intend to broaden the scope of our category of Middle English mysticism while focusing on texts by women. Instead of focusing on Richard Rolle, Walter Hilton, the *Cloud* author, and Julian of Norwich, I will use examples from Middle English translations of the continental works of Bridget of Sweden (1303–73), Catherine of Siena (1347–80), and Mechtild of Hackeborn (1241–99): *The Revelations of St. Birgitta*, *The Orcherd of Syon*, and *The Booke of Gostlye Grace of Mechtild of Hackeborn* respectively. Although these mystical writers come from different countries—Sweden, Italy, and Germany—and different time periods, their works were translated into Middle English and enjoyed a popularity in the fourteenth century.

By using their works, I hope to open up the field of what we call Middle English mysticism to include those works which were widely read in the vernacular, even though they are not technically English works. I would also like to recontextualize the study of Margery Kempe in the next three chapters in order to focus on the gendered and discursive relationships of fourteenth-century mystical texts. I am not interested in comparing Kempe to these mystics nor rescuing her from her comparison to Middle English mystical authors. Rather, I would like to bring new texts to the discussion of Middle English mysticism and to suggest a text-based rather than author-based approach to this discussion. However, I also admit that my selection is based, in part, on the fact that the writer in each case is a woman in order to return the discussion of mystical discourse to the gendered constructions of mystical desire and the body discussed in chapter 1.

These translated texts will provide examples, though not exhaustive ones, of the discourse I am about to describe. In turn, they will provide a context for the remaining discussion of Kempe's articulation of body and text in *The Book of Margery Kempe*.

Covetous Utterance

Many valuable studies have been made of the mystical language of the late Middle Ages, particularly its themes, concepts, and symbolism. Sheer gory detail and sexually explicit metaphors for mystical union lend affective spirituality to such analysis. In addition, attempts to establish the sources and circulation of such language have contributed to the understanding, if not the legitimizing, of the late medieval mystics.[1] Stylistic analyses of mystical prose look beyond the imagery and themes to determine how such rhetorical devices as alliteration, metonymy, and metaphor shape mystical experience and sign divine mystery.[2] In the interests of charting the territory of affective spirituality, however, the nature of mysticism itself has had to stand for the discourse itself. The late medieval preoccupation with continuous and affective meditation on Christ's Passion, for example, has come to dictate our own scholarly discussions of medieval mysticism. The older preference for negative mysticism in scholarly studies has given way to a cataloguing of the language and imagery of positive mysticism, still with an eye toward distinguising true from false mysticism, "devotional decorum" from morbid sensibility.[3]

Apart from merely describing the language and theology of mystical texts, studies of mystical texts often begin with the ecclesiastical and social contexts which gave rise to late medieval spirituality.[4] The changing religious roles for women, the rise of lay spirituality, heretical challenges to Church orthodoxy and authority, and the influence of itinerant preachers on female piety are all factors which account for the phenomenon of late medieval spirituality.[5] Other factors often cited to explain the increase in women's involvement in religious life are demographic pressures and monastic surpluses. In addition, the economic anxieties of a new bourgeoisie are invoked to explain the attraction of a spirituality based on renunciation.[6] Such contextual studies may be very useful in dislodging our own anachronistic modern assumptions about spirituality, but they do not help us to understand mysticism as a discourse. In fact, they tend to minimize text and discourse, both of which are pressed into the service of the context.[7]

A further problem with the study of mystical discourse is that contextual studies as well as thematic studies often do not distinguish between hagiography and mysticism. Saints' lives and hagiographic conventions, such as the conversionary experiences and ordeals of sexual abstinence, are used to explain mystical texts. Similarly, the ideals of sanctity—patience, charity, devotion to the Passion—are applied as models for understanding mystical texts.[8] Although the autobiographical register of mystical and hagiographic texts lends them a certain similarity, generic differences in structure, purpose, and manner of production are ignored. Discontinuities posed by the comparison of Latin and vernacular texts are also neglected. Most importantly for this study, the practice of using hagiography to read mystical texts contributes to the repression of both discourses. What makes a mystical text a mystical text becomes as irrelevant as what makes a *vita* hagiography.

In the case of Margery Kempe, this collapsing of hagiographic and mystical discourses often leads scholars to focus only on her life. Her own specific references to Bridget of Sweden and Marie d'Oignies in her *Book* invite more studied comparative analyses, yet most studies limit themselves to the correspondences between their lives or unusual behavior. Jacques de Vitry's *vita* of Marie d'Oignies is invoked to explain Kempe's practice of weeping frequently and boisterously, but little distinction is made between his text and *The Book of Margery Kempe*. The same is true with Bridget of Sweden. In spite of the fact that Kempe refers explicitly to "Brides book," Bridget's life is favored over her *Revelations* to explain the phenomenon of Margery Kempe. Like other mystical treatises, *The Book of Margery Kempe* labors under this unexamined interchangeability of mystical texts and hagiographic texts.

Nearly all of these studies of mysticism emphasize a taxonomy of mystical devotion without much attention to mysticism as a discourse. The inclusion of Julian of Norwich and Margery Kempe both in the *Norton Anthology of English Literature* and in the *Norton Anthology of Literature by Women* raises the issue of how mysticism is a discursive practice as well as a theology. Among anthologized literary texts, the presence of mystical texts problematizes literary expectations. Medieval ideas about authorship, for example, seem to exclude mystical authorship. A. J. Minnis has shown how scholastic idioms of literary theory influenced literary and exegetical texts, but we have yet to understand how mystical texts may be understood in terms of this literary theory. While we can see how Chaucer exploits the medieval distinction between *compilator* and *auctor* in order to avoid blame in his *Canterbury Tales* and *Troilus*, we have no context for considering the mystical texts in relation to Chaucer's texts or any other literary texts.[9] The mystical text seems to lie outside medieval taxonomies of authorship and textual production.

Mystical texts clearly differ from literary texts in their mode of production. The author of the text is often not the writer of it. Catherine of Siena dictated much of her *Dialogue* to Raymond of Capua, while Mechtild of Hackeborn was unaware that the visions she was revealing to her sisters at Helfta were secretly being compiled into the *Liber Spiritualis Gratiae*.[10] The fourteenth-century Dominican friar, Henry Suso, reported his visions at the encouragement of Elizabeth Stagl, who secretly wrote them down afterwards. When he discovered this "theft," he burned some of her efforts until a heavenly message prevented him from continuing.[11] Angela of Foligno recounted her visions to Fra Arnaldo, who translated them simultaneously into Latin with some difficulty, as we have seen in chapter 1. The scribal authors and mystics who dictate their visions often unwittingly cooperate in the production of mystical texts. Yet because we privilege the writer, scholars often assume that the scribes acted as refiners and revisors of oral mystical texts.

This is especially true of controversial female mystics, whose spirituality is today viewed as aberrant or excessive. Dorothy of Montau, for example, is sometimes considered to have distorted the practice of devotion to Christ's suffering through her extreme ascetic practices and her "pathological fleshly visions."[12] Dorothy's lack of education, along with her mystical practices, leads most scholars to view her dictation of her *Life* as less a collaboration with her scribe, John Marienwerder, than a "filtering" of the mystic's dictation through the scribe.[13] Clearly, this kind of interpretation relies upon a scribe-centered theory of textual production. This theory, in turn, is based on literary and exegetical conventions of production, not on mystical ones. The fundamental orality of mystical texts is subsumed under this literary/exegetical model of textual production.

These scattered examples suggest that our current categories for textual and discursive analysis are inadequate for the study of mystical texts and discourses. Reading mystical texts as literary, exegetical, or even hagiographic texts only confuses the discourses.[14] In turn, our readings of mystical texts become filtered through our expectations of these other kinds of texts. Such readings often reinforce the categories we use more than they do an understanding of how mystical discourse functions or where mystic speech is located in mystical texts. The categories themselves foreclose investigation of mystical texts. This can be seen clearly in the case of *The Book of Margery Kempe*, which is made to serve modern generic expectations of autobiography at the expense of its mystical content, or alternatively, of saints' lives at the expense of much of the narrative.

In order to observe the mystic's translation of body into text, then, we need to look elsewhere than the language, historical and social contexts, and theologies of mystical writings. Michel de Certeau, a French theoretician of sixteenth-and seventeenth-century mysticism, suggests one possible strategy. He urges treating mystical texts as "modes of utterance."[15] He cautions that,

> it is best to limit oneself to the consideration of what goes on in texts whose status is labeled "mystic," instead of wielding a ready-made definition (whether ideological or imaginary) of what it is that was inscribed in those texts by an operation of writing.[16]

I would like to draw upon de Certeau's description in order to describe medieval mystical discourse. Although de Certeau describes sixteenth- and seventeeth-century mysticism, I have tried to select as much of his theory as I think helps in the reading and understanding of medieval mystical texts.

In order to consider "what goes on" in mystical texts, it is necessary first to distinguish their practices from those of other texts. The chief distinction between the mystical mode of utterance and other modes which might be called theological is that the latter depend on the construction of "a particular coherent set of statements organized according to 'truth' criteria," while mystic utterance does not.[17] Before looking at what mystic utterance *does*, I would like to make one further distinction. Unlike the other modes of medieval discourse, mystic discourse does not rely on the textual system of *auctoritas*. In other words, the mystical text does not rely on either textual or institutional authorization of its statements. Thus, the mystical text defines, identifies, and authorizes itself differently than most other kinds of medieval discourse.[18]

Prayer and dialogue are two forms which mystic discourse takes, but both begin with the desire for dialogue, with a void that the communication-to-come will fill. Instead of collecting "true" statements uttered by others, the mystical text sets up a void which inhabits the speaker, the "I" of the mystical narrative. This is the place which conducts the "divine will to speak." The mystic who wishes to make a place of herself for the divine will to speak enters upon a struggle with language itself, the "trouble" from which mystical texts are born.[19] The mode of discourse she seeks is utterance rather than statements "of truth" or objects of knowledge.

Mystic utterance, according to de Certeau, begins in a language contract with the other. The purpose of this contract is to make hearing first, and then speech, possible. The model for this discursive contract is the Annunciation. The Virgin retires from the world of objects, alone and apart, thereby making a space for the divine will to speak. She only wills to hear. The Word is conceived in this speech-hearing act. The mystic's speech begins in a similar kind of willing or desire. The *volo* of the mystic's speech is a desire tied to nothing except the will of God.[20] It is a desire without objects and without the ability to carry out what it wills. Through a kind of exile, the mystic subject establishes her subjectivity on the basis of this desire and this lack. The "I," then, is the empty space from which the Other speaks.

The will to hear is encouraged in a variety of ways in medieval guides for devotion. Clearly, the renunciation of the world and the purification of the soul are prerequisite to receiving the gift of attention to the divine Word. In fact, chastity and worldly renunciation, as we have seen, condition one's reception of the divine Word. In his treatise *Adversus Jovinianum*, one of St. Jerome's distinctions between virgins and spouses is that only virgins may hear the divine Word in their souls.[21] This idea is implied in all the counsels to silence found in rules for anchoresses and holy women.[22] The purification of the soul and renunciation of the world accomplish two things: they repair the soul's unlikeness caused by the Fall, and they attune the "inner ear" of the soul.[23]

The fourteenth-century English mystic Richard Rolle of Hampole is a good example of how mystical desire gives way to receptivity to divine speech. In his *Incendium Amoris*, Rolle asserts the importance of an initial conversion in which the mystic learns "to desire nothing but him."[24] This desire disposes the mystic then to receive the three signs of perfect love: warmth (*calor*), sweetness (*dulcor*), and song (*canor*). The physical sensations of warmth and sweetness transform body and soul in Rolle's threefold system of mystical experience. Finally, divine speech takes the form of divine song, which in turn, transforms God's lovers into "lasting melody."[25]

This is not all, however. The mystic is not merely a passive cipher for God's will, but the center of a different kind of discourse, a discourse which is allocutionary, present, dialogic. The mystical subject desires a colloquy, in Middle English terms, a *dalliance*, and draws attention to the "I" where this desire may be fulfilled. There the domain of mystical speech is the act of speaking and hearing rather than the assemblage of objects of speech and knowledge found in other kinds of theological discourse. Mystical discourse seeks to cut through the language of the world, "replacing the statement of an idea with utterance by an 'I'."[26] It also cuts itself off from institutional and textual authorizations that are external to it. Rolle even distinguishes his *canor* from those "outward cadences of church song" which he flees in order to receive that melody which transforms the entire being into a hymn.[27] Rolle rejects the institutional forum for hymns of divine praise to enjoy divine music in his soul.

This raises a fundamental problem of mystical discourse: how does it authorize its own utterance? The measure of the truth of mystical utterance is its position and presence at the place of the mystical subject. The mystical text claims divine inspiration for its authority, but this alone is not enough. Its authority depends on its being "in the very place at which the Speaker speaks." This leaves quite a bit of room for the mystic's doubts about herself as the true location of divine speech. A more pressing concern is that this location not assume the position of its institutional counterpart, but that it not contradict it either. The mystical text is always, therefore, in a state of quandary about its own position because it cannot resort to the usual authorizations. Michel de Certeau identifies the problematic positioning of mystic utterance which justifies the mystic's doubts:

> . . . divine utterance is both what founds the text, and what it must make manifest. That is why the text is destabilized: it is at the same time *beside* the authorized institution, but outside it and *in* what authorizes that institution, i.e., the Word of God. In such a discourse, which claims to speak on behalf of the Holy Spirit and attempts to impose that convention on the addressee, a particular assertion is at work, affirming that what is said in this *place*, different from the one of magisterium language, is the *same* as what is said in the tradition, or else that these two places amount to the same.[28]

The mystical text doubly affirms its own place *outside* the magisterium language and its own complementarity to that language. The way in which the mystic makes this assertion and the place she assigns to the magisterium language (for it is never out of sight or mind) vary in mystical texts. Yet the nature of this assertion and positioning of the mystic utterance is crucial to the authorization of the mystical text and therefore to our description of mystical discourse. We will look at some examples later to observe this dilemma of the mystical text.

Mystic utterance, then, is not interested in statements of truth but in speech-acts, dialogues which are located at the place of the speaking subject. The question which underlies all mystical utterance is not whether it is true or not but whether the mystic occupies the place of the Other's speech and who that Other which speaks through the mystic is. It begins in the contractual desire, the *volo* which desires nothing and thus hears everything. It is not surprising that the mystical texts are defined by experience, that is, the presence, place, and acts of utterance.[29] The mystic is more interested in the word as event, rather than as textual relic of an ancient truth. The lack which the mystic attempts to occupy constructs the dialogues, dalliances, colloquies, and occasions for communing.[30] These forms of utterance make up the topography of the mystical text.

The "where" of mystical utterance, which is key to the discourse, has still to be located somewhere between the contractual "I desire" and the manifestation of the divine speech. The lack or loss which makes divine speech possible is an alienation from the self, an emptying of the ego, a divestiture of worldly attributes and desires. Such an emptying can occur in many different ways and over a period of time. It might be self-initiated, as is Julian of Norwich's desire for three wounds, or divinely initiated, as are the series of ordeals which lead to Margery Kempe's conversion, including a postpartum madness and business failures.[31] The experience is likewise a mixed one, alternating between pain and pleasure as despair gives way to delight in the loss. During this period of loss, the body may be rejected (or numbed, as through Julian's illness), but it will return later.

This self-voiding is not the same thing as self-denial or self-effacement. The mystic creates a void in the sense of an opening through which she passes, leaving behind the stability of her existence in the world.[32] In her dialogues with God and in her writing, the mystic displaces herself, making of the place where she used to be a "passageway" for her speech. The emptied out space of the self is filled, or re-placed, by the incarnate Word, or by the body and name of Christ. Rolle is well known for his devotion to the

name of Christ as an aid to meditation.[33] Uttering the name of Christ seems
to be the way to "fix firmly in your heart the consciousness of his passion
and of his wounds." It also is a way of increasing the fervor of love and
occupying the heart so that "no evil thing can have any living space" in it.[34]
Not only does he instruct others to fix their attention on the name, but he
practices his own advice in his lyrics. In his "Cantus Amoris," his longing
for Christ gives way (or makes way) for the filling up of his poem and
himself with the name uttered in song:

> Jhesu, my dere and my drewry, delyte ert þou to syng.
> Jhesu, my myrth and melody, when will þow com, my keyng?
> Jhesu, my hele and my hony, my whart and my comfortyng,
> Jhesu, I covayte for to dy when it es þi payng.
>
> (Jesu, my dear and my bounty, delight are you to sing.
> Jesu, my mirth and melody, when will you come, my king?
> Jesu, my help and my honey, my health, my comforting,
> Jesu, I desire to die when it's to you pleasing.)[35]

The name acts as a sign to stir Rolle's ardor and as a refuge from the
soul's sins, turbulence, and lethargy.[36]

The name of Christ is both invocation and vocation, as the fifteenth-
century treatise, *A Pistle of Discrecioun of Stirrings*, suggests. The name is
both a calling and a place of habitation, the starting point of contemplation:

> Seeþ ȝoure cleping, and in þat cleping þat ȝe ben clepid, stondeþ stifly and
> abideþ in þe name of Iesu. Þi cleping is to be verrey contemplatyfe, ensaumplid
> by Mary, Martha sister.[37]
>
> (See your vocation, and in that vocation to which you have been called, stand
> firmly and abide in the name of Jesus. Your vocation should be truly con-
> templative, as exemplified by Mary, Martha's sister.)

Drawing upon Paul's discussion of vocation, the *Discrecioun* author derives
the contemplative vocation from the "cleping" and abiding in the name of
Jesus.

The place which the name occupies is created by the excesses of the
flesh. Before the heaving powers topple into the sublime, there is an
absence which needs to be filled. The name of Jesus in Rolle's poem comes
to create a body where one is lacking. It authorizes speech and the body of

writing produced in the mystic's effort to recall the absent body, Christ's and her own. The absence of the body occurs through the voiding of the self in mystical anticipation of speaking/listening, and it recapitulates the absence mourned by the women at Christ's tomb and the apostles after Christ's death. The body needs to be recreated through mystical discourse, and that is often done through the name.[38]

Although the name differs in mystical texts—sometimes it is Jesus, Lord, Love, Father, or the Trinity—the practice of naming is common to English and continental mystical texts and to negative and positive mysticism. This practice derives from Bernard of Clairvaux's proliferation of names for Jesus in his fifteenth sermon on the Song of Songs. In this sermon, Bernard discusses the invocation of Christ's name as a transfusion of majesty and power into love and mercy.[39] In the scriptural text, "Thy name is as oil poured out" (Song of Songs 1:3), Bernard finds a threefold analogy between the properties of oil and the Name of giving light, nourishing, and anointing. All three properties contribute to the health of the soul. More importantly, once the Name is experienced (not merely heard) by the soul, it leads to an extravagance of expression in the form of praise, of naming anew: the transfusion, then, between flesh and speech. The Name itself is an extravagance which engenders affective outpouring and extravagant speech. Experience of the Name in the soul and the affections produces an extravagant litany of naming, of searching for new words and idioms for God, Christ, and the Trinity. The Name itself permits such extravagance, such expression.

The other function of the naming is a dual one: as a function of *imitatio Christi*, it signs the Passion and suffering of Christ; as a function of mystical discourse, it is a "password," a "principle of travel."[40] The first function is an example of how Christic imitation operates at the level of signs and memory, as was discussed in chapter 1. The second function is a channeling of the affections through the discourse. That is, the heaving powers find the name, the hole in the text, through which to travel, to topple, and to unsettle the stability of the discourse. The name itself exceeds all other words, "everything that we say or write," in the words of Richard Rolle.[41] It provides an entrance and an exit in the text for the mystical excess, since at the same time that the invocation introduces the name, it reduces "all that we may say or write. Mystical rapture cannot remain, then, in the discourse, but passes on elsewhere. It seeks the rupture and the instability at the edge of all language.

If mystic speech thus produces an *efflux* of mystical affection, it is not without the *influx* described earlier. The discourse itself is rendered pervious, like the flesh, through loss. Meditation on Christ's Passion often produces a filling up with Word and body. When the fourteenth-century Italian mystic Angela of Foligno seeks a sign that it is Christ who speaks to her, she immediately feels the cross "corporeally" in conjunction with his love in her soul.[42] The influx of the signs of Christ's speech, his love, and the cross, is a response to the loss which here figures as a question. This influx is only possible through two desires, for knowledge and for memory. Angela desires "to know," in its etymological sense derived from the Latin, *sapientia*, from the Latin verb for "to taste." Both William of St. Thierry in the twelfth century and the mystical writer Rudolph Biberach in the fourteenth defined knowledge in terms of tasting or savoring (*sapere* and *gustare*).[43] More generally in the case of Angela of Foligno, knowledge is a fleshing out of the empty space from which the other speaks, a corporeal tasting. Likewise, memory is invoked to flesh out this space in Julian of Norwich's *Showings*, as we have already seen. After asking God for a sickness, Julian describes how her body became so completely numb that she believed herself to be "at the point of death." Suddenly she realized that she should ask for a second "gift," "that my body might be filled full of recollection and feeling of his blessed Passion." The desire for recollection, like the desire for knowledge, seeks to relieve and insure the loss of self.

The loss of the body which accompanies the influx of the corporeal word should not be confused with a complete rejection of the body. This rejection is merely a preliminary step to the incorporation of the body in the mystical experience. As m. de Certeau argues in *La fable mystique*, the rejection of body and world is preparatory for the task of offering body to spirit in order to incarnate discourse.[44] While the body may be renounced in order for the self to be lost, it is reconstituted in and around the Word. The mystical ecstasy which marks the loss of self relocates into bodily excess, particularly in late medieval mysticism. Still, it is the desire first for nothing, and secondarily for knowledge or recollection, which creates the surplus that redefines the body. The role of the affections in the *imitatio Christi* here is crucial, since they are rooted in that "voraciousness" characterized by Bernard of Clairvaux as the fleshly desire for knowledge.[45] It is this affective surplus that is passed on to the body, incarnating discourse and focusing that discourse on bodily excess.

The Monk of Farne insists that the mystic's love demands a "passion which recognizes no measure," quoting Bernard's famous address to such a love in his sermon on the Song of Songs:

> O love, you are indeed rash, violent, fragrant, impetuous, and brooking
> consideration of naught but yourself, you eschew all else and despise every-
> thing, content with yourself alone. You subvert order, disregard custom,
> recognize no measure. All that propriety, reason, self-respect, deliberation and
> judgement would seem to demand you triumph over, and reduce to captivity
> within your grasp.[46]

In Bernardian language, the voraciousness of this love is most often expressed in the desire for the kiss of the beloved.[47] The *calor*, or warmth, so
crucial to Rolle's theory of love simultaneously infuses both body and
speech. It is caused by the divine speech in the soul. The fire of love,
however, is also fueled by the mystic's excessive love and it overflows into
song. Whichever way it is expressed, it is transgressive of custom, order,
and propriety by its very nature. In fact, the Monk of Farne goes so far as to
call it a covetousness which does not settle for the mean objects prized by
the "merely covetous."[48] The mystic aspires to be the "most covetous," to
disperse the effects of this superlative covetousness in marvelous utterance,
bodily *insignia*, and written texts. From the mystic's marvelous body the
marvelous text is produced. From the mystic's covetous longing and fleshly
abundance, two bodies become inscribed. The text, the *corpus verborum*,
recalls the mystical body and, ultimately, Christ's body in a relationship of
imitatio. Yet this relationship of bodily texts to textual bodies does not
occur without a certain rupture—a fissuring which intersects the flesh and
mystical texts.

The Fissured Text

Bodily excess is merely one of the speech-effects of the divine locution in the
soul and its manifestation. The other is the written text, a different sort of
body which bears a more problematic relationship to the divine word. As
de Certeau maintains in the passage quoted earlier, the mystical text is
always destabilized because "divine utterance is both what founds the text,
and what it must make manifest." It cannot rely upon some body of
arguments or statements to authorize it. The written text is ultimately
incapable of manifesting the divine utterance which founds it. In the
passage by the Monk of Farne in the beginning of this chapter, we can see
the mystic's frustration with the discontinuity of that longing which drives
the dialogic relationship with the divine, and the written text, which presents the physical evidence of this relationship. It is the longing which

represents the true discourse of the mystical text, yet this longing is power-less to leave its visual imprint in the written text. In fact, the Monk of Farne immediately reproaches himself for having desired to be able to imprint his longing on the hearts of his readers in the first place: "I reproach myself for having spoken foolishly, and am not worthy to be heard for my folly." The reason for his folly is that only the Trinity is capable of such stigmata in the hearts of readers. While the mystic endeavors to manifest divine speech in his text, he cannot ultimately transmit it to his readers. The Monk is left with the prayer that "the Lord open the ear of whomsoever he please, and the Spirit breathe where he will."[49]

The instability of the mystical text, then, derives from its authorization in divine speech and from its mode of utterance. A mode of utterance depends on ears willing to hear, not merely on diligent readers. The mystical text is, in fact, a dual text, oral and written, which asserts divine dialogue with the soul as the only true discourse, yet settles for a written discourse powerless to engage its reader in this true discourse. The text often recognizes its own failure to "utter God" at the same time that it asserts its location in God's speech. Meister Eckhart sees failed utterance as the condition of all human production, not only of mystical texts:

> All creatures want to utter God in all their works; they all come close as they can in uttering him, and yet they cannot utter him. Whether they like it or not, they all want to utter God, and yet he remains unuttered.[50]

While mystical texts fail in their utterance, they do provide passage through utterance to something else—through the Name or experience of immer-sion in the body of Christ—which is elsewhere than the utterance. Passage is provided in place of utterance at the cost of the mystical text's own authority. In a sense, mystical texts undermine their own authorization in divine utterance. The oral text which utters is always and continually "unuttered" in the written text.

The mystical text, then, is always fissured at the juncture between its oral and written texts. Utterance slips through the written text in spite of the mystic's efforts to impress it on the hearts of readers. This fissure is also the site of excess of, and access to, the flesh in the sense that it offers the place for mystical rapture. The mystical text is rendered pervious to the promptings of mystical desire and to divine utterance, yet it never captures these things. The text can only circulate desire and utterance without ever settling into them. Like the mystic's body, the text becomes a spectacle of desire and utterance, of bodily and textual memory, and of affective excess.

If the fissured flesh permits the transgression of that imaginary zone of Christianity, the integrity of the body, what is its textual equivalent? The fissured text also permits perviousness, as we have seen, but the effect of this perviousness is a breakdown of a construct which otherwise rests securely on the external/internal demarcation of the body: the distinction between literal and figurative language. For example, Richard Rolle's tripartite description of mystical love in terms of *calor, dulcor,* and *canor,* "fire," "sweetness," and "song," eludes the distinctions between spiritual and physical, and hence, figurative and literal semantic fields. Those who argue for the metaphoricity of Rolle's language tend to treat his description of mystical love and union as so many "concepts" or "stages" of mystical practice.[51] Yet, as we have seen, the mystical text is a practice more than a collection of concepts or truths. Rolle's three-fold description often travels across metaphorical boundaries, contaminating spiritual experience with sensual language. Mystical language itself becomes the spectacle of the mystic's abjection as words stray across semantic hierarchies and the literal is no longer subsumed by the figurative.

Examples of this collapse in the registers of meaning of mystical language abound in English and continental works. While mystical scholars endeavor to distinguish between "spiritual" and "literal," or "physical," mystical terminology, the integrity of these fields, like that of the body, sometimes breaks down. The language of the senses, of tasting, touching, smelling, hearing, and speaking, is one area in which this collapsing of linguistic registers takes place.[52] Even more striking, however, is the practice of immersion in Christ's wound discussed earlier in connection with *imitatio Christi.* As the place of mystical communication and knowledge, the wound of Christ offers the mystic access to mystical union. Yet the "metaphor" for communication is threatened by erotic "materializing" of the mystic experience.[53] In the Franciscan text by James of Milan, the *Stimulus Amoris,* the act of union is described not as immersion, but as a joining of wounds: *vulnus vulneri copulatur.* The Latin *vulnus* summons its homology, *vulva,* inscribing the female sexual anatomy into the wounded body of Christ.[54] As a place of mystical union and knowledge, the wound of Christ is sexualized even when the Latin homology is not present. Whether the wound is *vulva* or breast in women's mystical visions, it is never quite free of erotic associations, for the knowledge itself is invested with the erotic. The coming to know Christ, which *imitatio* strives after, is an erotic act. Language, like imitation, travels across the integrity of the physical and spiritual realms of knowledge and signification.

Another source of the mystical text's instability is the tainted nature of all human speech, making the mystic utterance presumptuous if not blasphemous. In the midst of his meditation on Christ's Passion, Rolle loses confidence in his own speech, which, despite his reverence, rings hollow. "I cannot devise any harmonious syllables for it, but gabble like a parrot with no idea what I am talking about."[55] His babbling is due to his sin. All human speech, therefore, defiles: ". . . [I]f I set my tongue to your name it defiles it, . . ."[56] The Monk of Farne asks God not to be offended by his speech though he is a man of "polluted lips." His awareness of his own pollution reduces him nearly to silence until he is able to ask God to speak through him:

> What am I to say? Shall I keep silence or speak? Hold my peace or give utterance? For what thou showest me is exceedingly profound, and being defiled I dare not speak of such matters. Speak thou then for me, O Lord, this time, and let there be a good word in thy mouth, which may bring grace to those that hear it. Truly I would not restrain my lips, were they not defiled from yesterday and the day before, so that they are not worthy to expound so great a mystery.[57]

The mystic returns again and again to this location between silence and utterance, doubt and presumption. The continual awareness of his own defilement is the source of his dialogue with God, for speech itself pollutes his lips. Every act of speaking, then, defiles him.

Not surprisingly, this location of mystic speech is abjection, according to Kristeva's description of it in *Powers of Horror*. With the double transgressions—of Eve and of Christ—speech itself always risks defilement, one external and the other internal. This is what makes mystic speech problematic and even dangerous. Mystic speech is always located in (or straying into) abjection. It always trangresses and blasphemes because it speaks of divine mysteries through polluted lips. It also transgresses in its association with the excess of the flesh. The same overflow of desire which leads to sin is inseparable from the excess which becomes "completely submersed into (divine) speech in order to become beauty and love," according to Kristeva.[58] The mystic continually traverses the borders between the two fleshes, toppling the sin into love. Unlike official theology, mystic speech is depraved because it comprehends both impulses. The mystic's depravity both conditions and disrupts his/her speech. It is through the defilement of utterance—the betrayal of speech by polluted lips—that a place is made for divine speech in the soul. Because writing avoids the experience of abjection, the mystic's speech always strays from the written text. However, as we will see later, the mystical text attempts to displace abject speech onto reading and meditating on Christ's Passion. Yet the written text always works against abject speech because it maintains the illusion that, according to the Monk of Farne, the hand that writes leaves an imprint of its characters as distinct as the visual evidence. The longing of the mystic, while it leaves its traces in the written text, has no such powers of impression over its readers, who unlike the mystic do not have the faculty of hearing the mystical text.[59]

The mystic's frustration with the incapacity of speech to imprint itself upon the text and ears of readers is compounded by the precariousness of the mystic's own receptivity to divine speech. The same receptivity to divine speech renders the mystic vulnerable to the corrupt speech of other spirits—of the flesh, the world, and the fiend.[60] The fifteenth-century treatise, "A Tretis of Discrescyon of Spirites," warns about the vulnerability of the receptive soul to the speech of all three spirits. The author warns that, after confession, the purified soul is like a "clean paper leaf for its ability to receive that which men write on it." Disposed as it is to consent, the soul must beware whether it consents to evil or good spirits, which write upon its parchment. Good or evil, each thought, the author maintains, smites our hearts. The speech itself is not our own "unless you consent to the thought whatsoever it be, that is evermore our own. Jesus grant us his grace to consent to the good and withstand the evil," prays the author.[61] The mystic's disposition to receive divine speech always calls the text into question. The mystical text, then, is engaged in a continual process of self-verification.

Before looking at how the mystic attempts to inscribe her longing on the hearts of her readers, we must return to the longing itself to see how it functions in her own discourse. The mystic's longing, as we have seen, is a contractual vow with God that founds divine speech in the soul. It is a longing for nothing, for an emptiness. This longing is identified by its lack, not only of the worldly others to which one could direct one's desire but also of God. In this respect, the longing that propels the mystical text is not unlike desire defined by Augustine as *rerum absentium concupiscentia* "concupiscence for absent things." While the mystic's concupiscence always aims at the *unio mystica*, the mystical union with God, it also animates her discourse. Rolle says as much in his *Incendium Amoris*. While every other kind of affection for worldly things practiced in excess is evil, Rolle explains, love for God is always excessive because He is absent:

> No creature can love God too much. In everything else what is practised in
> excess turns to evil, but the virtue of love is such that the more it abounds the

more splendid it becomes. A lover will languish if he does not have the object of his love near him. Which is why the Scripture says, 'Tell my Beloved that I languish for love,' [Song of Songs 5:8] as if it were saying, 'It is because I cannot see him whom I love; my very body is wasting away with the intensity of my devotion!'[62]

We can see from Rolle's account of this desire that it is related to the voiding of the self, that the longing for the absent love leads to a wasting away of body, an emptying of physical resources. Mystical languishing, then, is both an excess and an emptying at the same time—a fullness produced by a lack and producing a loss. Yet how does this conjunction of mystical concupiscence and absence lead to mystical discourse?

A partial answer to this question may be found in the figure of Mary Magdalene in late medieval spirituality.[63] While she was popular for her role as penitent sinner, she was also venerated for her superior love of Christ. Bernard of Clairvaux even names her as the bride in the Song of Songs who desires the kiss of the heavenly Bridegroom, while Anselm marvels over her "burning love" which brought her to weep next to the empty tomb.[64] As a figure of the mystical lover, the Magdalene plays a crucial role, as can be seen from the *Quem quaeritis* trope of liturgical drama to the late medieval Digby play of the Resurrection.[65] The Gospel accounts concerning what happened at the sepulcher of Christ all focus on Mary's distress at the disappearance of Christ's body. In the Gospel of John, this distress is focused upon the dialogue between the Magdalene and Christ. He asks her, "Woman, why weepest thou? Whom seekest thou?" Thinking he is the gardener, she asks him if he has removed the body to tell her where he has placed it (John 20:13–15). She then recognizes Christ when he addresses her by name.

Like Mary Magdalene, the mystic desires a body which is absent, and she suffers as a consequence. Her loss inspires her search for the body of Christ in mystical experience. Echoing the Magdalene's encounter with Christ at the empty sepulcher, for example, Margery Kempe emerges from her despair that Christ has forsaken her when He asks: "Daughter, why do you weep so sorely? I have come to you, Jesus Christ, who died on the Cross suffering bitter pains and passions for you."[66] The loss of the body in mystical discourse, however, is not recovered simply by Christ's assurances to her. The mystic's desire for the absent body seeks solace in the embodying of her discourse, in the creation of a body in language. De Certeau claims that the task of mystics is "to invent in the word a body of love. Hence their quest for 'annunciations,' for words made flesh, for conceptions through the ear."[67] Beginning with Mary Magdalene's vigil at Christ's tomb, the mystic proceeds backwards to the annunciation.

The inventing of a body in discourse may obviously occur in a number of ways. The mystical text itself is a body created from the divine speech of the soul. Mystical meditation and contemplation, however, are also sites for the missing body in the form of sensory events and symbolic signs of divine presence in the soul.[68] Other mystical inventions of the body in discourse assume the form of teaching or communication with the world, charitable works, and public acts of penance. While renunciation of their own bodies may precede such inventions, the body returns elsewhere in all modes of mystic discourse.

The voraciousness described by Bernard as the expression of mystical desire, then, seeks its satisfaction first in meditation on Christ's suffering, by which it knows and savors. It seeks secondly to please both God and listener/readers by investing a "body of love" in its words. The Monk of Farne concludes his meditation on the crucified Christ with a comment on the necessity created by love of restoring the absent body to the word: "A heart on fire cannot but utter burning words, and a heart wounded by love must needs wound others with its words."[69] The affections—here of burning love—"must needs" incarnate mystic discourse and, ultimately, lend utterance the power to burn and words the force to wound.

Yet the mystical text always leaves what it desires to inscribe unuttered. Utterance occupies the fissure between oral and written texts, the one a product of excess desire, the other, a body to take the place of the one which is lacking. The textual body of words also imitates the mystic's body, as the mystic imitates Christ, not as passive suffering, but as a practice of recalling those heaving powers which fissure flesh and text. The written text inscribes the mystic's abjection through blasphemous utterance. Reversing the example of Clare of Montefalco's body, which contained the text of Christ's suffering, the textual body bears the traces of fleshly access—traces which are not so easily inscribed on the hearts of readers. The mystical text, like the mystical body, is engaged in an *imitatio Christi* by incarnating discourse, signifying "that which suffers in the soul" through words and the return of the body through discourse. Mystic and text imitate Christ in an effort to make word flesh and body, utterance.

One last position which needs to be considered in this discussion of mystical discourse is the position of the reader. So far, the reader has emerged at several junctures chiefly to remind the mystic of the failure of his/her desire to produce the spiritual stigmatization necessary to the reader's transformation. Clearly, the reader's experience of reading inspires the kind of imitation through the imagination described in the first chapter. The reader is much like the overzealous sisters of Clare of Montefalco, searching for the *insignia* which are both mnemonic signs of Christ's suffering and instigations to her own recollection and affective response. The insignia, however, are finally not so important as the activity of reading itself, whether it takes the form of bodily dissection, as is the case with Clare's sisters, or something else.

The fissured texts and flesh which rupture the masculine integrity of the body in order to make rapture possible condition reading as well as mystic speech. The reconstitution of the absent body in the written text is, as we have seen, incomplete; yet the written text demands to be read as a body. Readers of mystical texts are expected to be able to read the body, not only the displaced mystical body but the body of Christ. Julian of Norwich's *Showings* begins with the trickle of blood from the pierced forehead of Christ. Her own explications of her visions are themselves readings of the ongoing *insignifying* of Christ's body from the first trickle of blood caused by the crown of thorns to the changing color of Christ's face to the copious bodily bleeding to the shrivelling of the body.[70]

The act of reading the body itself produces the suffering through imaginative recollection and through the failure of language, of eventual utterance. If mystical desire to utter always exceeds the power to utter God, the divine remains unread as well as unuttered. It is the fissure between flesh and word, utterance and desire which initiates the reader's rapture. Reading the body of Christ leads to a crisis, a hiatus between the living presence of the Word and its Resurrection, for, as Kristeva argues, the Crucifixion occupies that "caesura" or rupture at the center of the Passion narrative.[71] The mystical text only reproduces this hiatus in and through language. Utterance is "choked marvelous communication which silences it."[72]

Confronted by this silence in the body of Christ and mystical text, the reader is presented with the possibility of rapture. Unlike exegetical reading, mystical reading does not search for the truth in this silence. In fact, such a hermeneutic forecloses the possibility of mystical rapture since it depends on the integrity of the mystical text and the enclosure of occult truths in external language. Mystical texts traverse this linguistic boundary when they stray across the cultural limits assigned to the body. The rupture displaced from the body of Christ and displayed in language offers the reader access to the marvelous language of mystical rapture. If the Monk of Farne can never finally impress his longing on the hearts of readers, he may at least establish a site for their own longing to be activated.

The fissure in the mystical text obviously offers the female mystic that "access to the sacred" which was usually denied her. The fissured text offers the woman writer an opening through which she might both enter language and find a place for her desire, affections, and disruptions. The mystical text, in fact, bears an affinity to the flesh, in its permeability, its fissure, and its excesses. Given the cultural construction of the feminine in the Middle Ages, the mystical text of this period might be called feminine, not in the sense of the controlled feminine—silent, sealed, and far removed from conversation with the world—such as we found in devotional treatises, but in the sense of that which is feared in medieval culture. Although men may occupy this feminine position, they do so only by leaving temporarily their culturally constructed positions as male. The similarities I have collected among men and women are thus limited by medieval gender. Therefore, I would like to turn now to the mystical writings of women in order to observe how they negotiate the features of mystical discourse that I have described.

Middle English Sites and Practices

We have seen from the examples of mystical texts so far, particularly from the meditations of the Monk of Farne and the works of Richard Rolle, how Latin and Middle English instructions for devotion formulated a discourse which was often enacted in the texts themselves.[73] It remains to be seen how this discourse was practiced specifically in women's mystical texts in medieval England. These will provide a new context for reading *The Book of Margery Kempe*. Instead of comparing Kempe to Julian of Norwich, Richard Rolle, the *Cloud* author, and Walter Hilton, I would like to focus selectively on instances of some of the mystical practices already discussed. Further, we will see how mystical discourse suited the women mystical writers' purpose of developing a language to speak and an authority for that language. This, in turn, will provide a fitting pretext for the study of Kempe's contributions to mystical discourse.

The choice of texts for this study of mystical discourse is necessarily limited and selective—limited, in part, by the availability of edited texts, and selective of works by women mystics who were somehow important to the shape of Middle English mysticism and to Margery Kempe herself. The three translated texts include: *The Booke of Gostlye Grace of Mechtild of Hackeborn*, *The Revelations of St. Birgitta*, and Catherine of Siena's *The Orcherd of Syon*.[74] All three texts belong to the affective spiritual tradition.

All were translated during the fifteenth century and are linked to the Carthusians and to Syon Monastery in England. Mechtild's *Booke* survives in two fifteenth-century manuscript translations of the Latin *Liber Spiritualis Gratiae*.[75] There are seven extant manuscripts of the Middle English translation of the Latin *Revelationes Celestes* by Bridget of Sweden.[76] Catherine of Siena's *Dialogue* became *The Orcherd of Syon* in the three surviving Middle English translations, two of which are believed to have been prepared for the first generation of Birgittine nuns at Syon Abbey.[77] In addition to manuscript versions, the English translation of the *Orcherd* was printed by Wynkyn de Worde in 1519.

The popularity of the treatises is evidenced not only by the number of surviving manuscripts, but by the body of anthologized extracts from these works and specific references to them in other devotional treatises. Among the anthologized mystical codices, excerpts from Bridget of Sweden's *Revelations* and Mechtild of Hackeborn's *Booke of Gostlye Grace* appear together in a British Library collection.[78] Another manuscript contains three prayers from Mechtild's revelations followed by a prayer from St. Birgitta's *Revelations*.[79] Excerpts from all three works by Catherine of Siena, Bridget, and Mechtild, as well as from those of Richard Rolle, also survive in a single codex.[80] In addition, the three treatises appear by way of allusion and quotation in other mystical writings. The Carthusian meditation on the life of Christ, the *Speculum Devotorum*, for example, uses both Bridget's *Revelations* and Catherine's *Orcherd* and alludes to one of Mechtild's visions. Mechtild is also referred to in the English guide to liturgy for the Syon nuns, *The Myroure of Oure Ladye*.[81] Finally, marginal citations to the works of Catherine and Mechtild appear in a manuscript of Henry Suso's *Horologium Diuinae Sapientiae*.[82] Apparently, these works served as authorities as well as glosses with respect to other medieval spiritual texts.

These works are also linked by their relationship to the Brigittine monastery at Syon at Isleworth in England. Both the *Revelations* and the *Orcherd* were probably completed soon after the foundation of Syon in 1415.[83] The Middle English *Revelations* is not listed in the Syon Monastery's catalogue, but there are seven Latin manuscripts of Bridget's works listed in the same catalogue.[84] The library may nevertheless have contained a translation of the work of its founder. The catalogue only lists the holdings of the men's library in the double monastery. While the nun's library is not catalogued, we do know that it included other translations of devotional works from Latin, including *The Myroure of oure Ladye* and *Martilogue*. Therefore, it is possible that the library included a translation of the *Revela-*

tions. Considering the importance of Bridget to the Syon order, it is likely that some translation of her *Revelations* was available to the Birgittine nuns.

Mechtild's *Liber Spiritualis Gratiae* is linked to Syon Monastery through the Carthusians. The Carthusians are generally credited with bringing continental spiritual works to England and translating them. Among the works in their libraries are the revelations of both Mechtild and Catherine of Siena.[85] The Carthusian order at Sheen is thought to have introduced Mechtild's *Liber* to England and to have had it translated, possibly by a Syon monk. The Carthusians at Sheen and the Birgittine Order at Syon Monastery were closely connected, the former supplying the latter with translators, scribes, and book donors. The library catalogue from Syon monastery lists three early sixteenth-century printed copies and four manuscript versions in Engish and Latin.[86]

The Middle English title of Catherine of Siena's work confirms its connection with Syon Monastery. The *Orcherd of Syon* was probably translated for the first generation of nuns at Syon Abbey, including the "Religyous modir & deuoute sustren clepid & chosen bisily to laboure at the hous of Syon."[87] Wynkyn de Worde's printed edition of *The Orchard of Syon* was made from a manuscript copy belonging to Syon Monastery.[88] In fact, the whole "orchard" framework of the Middle English translation places Catherine's *Dialogue* within an allegorical context specifically addressed to the Syon nuns. The title possibly invokes Bridget's vision of the "new vineyard" which inspired her founding of the Birgittine Order.[89] Along with the works of Sts. Bridget and Mechtild, the *Orcherd* was clearly an important text to the Birgittine Order and the Carthusians.

The Syon connection between these two treatises is important contextually for the study of Margery Kempe. Kempe visited Syon Monastery in 1434 for a period of three days. The Middle English works of Bridget and Mechthild were presumably available at the monastery's library at that time. Kempe was already familiar with the works of Saint Bridget, including her life and revelations, for she mentions both in her own mystical treatise. She even visits one of Bridget's "maidens" in Rome.[90] Finally, although Kempe's acquaintance with Mechtild's *Booke of Gostlye Grace* is not confirmed in her treatise, her visit to Syon raises the possibility of her familiarity with it. In addition, her association with a Dominican confessor, her trip to Germany recounted in Book II, and her travels among those who might have been familiar with devotional works such as Mechtild's increase the chance that she knew Mechtild's work.

Kempe's possible familiarity with these treatises, however, is not the main reason for studying them along with her *Book*. I am not interested here in drawing lines of influence between these treatises and Kempe's. Instead, these texts may be considered to circulate with Kempe's along with the texts of other English mystics. Hope Emily Allen first suggested that *The Book of Margery Kempe* "was circulating contemporaneously with the translations" of the works of Bridget, Catherine, and Mechtild.[91] Within this circulation, we can observe the practice of mystical discourse.

The first significant problem posed by each of these texts involves both authority and language. Each mystic experienced anxieties about the authorship of her own text. The main reason for this is that, as Vauchez has argued, women in the Middle Ages were excluded from the discourse of learning and revelation. They occupied a place of *inculture* outside the Latinity which bounded medieval culture in both the Church and in the universities.[92] Alexander Murray has shown that literacy after the mid-thirteenth century came to be defined more rigorously than as a knowledge of Latin: it required knowledge of Latin literature as well.[93] Bridget of Sweden's painful attempts to learn Latin and Catherine of Siena's rudimentary knowledge are the testaments to their exclusion.[94] Mechtild of Hackeborn belonged to the Benedictine monastery at Helfta, which was known for its learning under Gertrude the Great. Therefore she did not suffer as the other two did from exclusion from Latin culture. Nevertheless, she was hesitant to write her revelations down for fear of their reception, and she ended up confiding them to two sisters who recorded them in Latin surreptitiously.[95]

Ironically, though each mystic wrote (or dictated) her revelations in her vernacular, the texts were translated into Latin. Bridget of Sweden's confessors translated her Swedish revelations into Latin, the *Liber Revelationum Celestium S. Birgitta*, which has since become the authoritative text.[96] Catherine of Siena partly wrote and partly dictated her *Dialogue* in her native Italian. It was first circulated in Italian, and later, "to ensure wide circulation," was translated into Latin versions by her confessor, Raymond of Capua, and by one of the scribes of her dictation, Stefano Maconi.[97] Mechtild of Hackeborn's confidants secretly recorded her visions in Latin over a period of eight years without her knowledge. Clearly, their texts did not suffer the same exclusion that they did.

Nevertheless, one of the effects of their exclusion was that their authority as secretaries of God's word was always at risk. Clerical opposition to Bridget and Catherine is documented.[98] The right to speak was nowhere

guaranteed to the female mystic. Even Mechtild feared the disapproval of
Church authorities for the transcription of the revelations by Church authorities. Only reassurances from Christ, that the writing was part of his
plan to edify others, and from her scribes, that the abbess and prelate
approved the writing, finally reconciled Mechtild to the written text of her
revelations. If the treatises on the discernment of spirits had counselled
discretion so that the "clene paper" of the soul resisted the mind's consent
to inscription by evil thoughts, Bridget, Catherine, and Mechtild experienced the caution doubly at the level of written discourse itself. Discretion
for women, as we have seen in chapter 1, meant preserving the blank page of
the soul not only from the eager pens of evil spirits but from the written
records of medieval culture. Just as women were to preserve their bodies
and souls from physical and spiritual assaults, so they felt constrained to
spare the clean paper leaf of culture the imprint of their own indiscretion.

Their exclusion from magisterium language is partly responsible for
the fact that their discourse is primarily dialogic rather than instructive. The
mystical treatises of Walter Hilton, the *Cloud* author, and even Richard
Rolle take up an entirely different mode than do the works of these women
translated into Middle English. Each of the male mystics proposes to
instruct his audience, whether learned or the "boystus & vntaght" (rude
and untaught), as Misyn's translation of Rolle's *Incendium Amoris* calls
them, in the way of perfect love.[99] Mystical texts whose primary intention is
to instruct distinguish between divine and human *auctores*. The human
author is responsible for the literal sense of his text, while God authors the
truth which is transmitted through the literal sense.[100] This distinction
allows the *Cloud* author to declare his own unworthiness and naiveté at the
same time that he attributes to God the power of his treatise to move his
reader to contemplation.[101] The primary transaction of this type of mystical text is between human author and reader, who join to minimize misunderstanding and perversion of divine truth. The *Cloud* author begs his
reader "to make up on your part what is lacking on mine." "Pryde of
connynge" and disputation, which characterize human sciences, are de-
serted for the hermeneutic of the mystical text, which joins divine grace
with human charity and love.[102] This kind of mystical text functions as a
speculum in its medieval sense of an exemplar of understanding to which
both author and reader are raised through love, grace, and devotion.[103] As
exemplary texts, the *specula* of mystical instruction are primarily public
discourses.[104]

The discourse of the three Middle English treatises is fundamentally private. It is a conversation which takes place elsewhere than the written text in spite of the mystic's attempt to make it present. The gap between the dialogue of the soul with God and the written text and again, between the Latin text and the Middle English translation, is a continual source of the text's instability. The privacy and secrecy of the exchange between God and the soul is compromised by its transcription and translation. *The Revelations of St. Birgitto* begins with the private contract between Christ and his "spouse" in which he vows "to shewe the my privey concelles." Even if the exchange of vows serves to authorize the written text, it also calls attention to its own crude circulation of these "privey concelles." The written text always remains just out of earshot of the allocutions between God and the soul.

The Booke of Gostlye Grace is most conscious of the gap between the two texts—the speech of God to the soul and the written text. Partly because the text was composed in secret without Mechtild's knowledge, both the scribes and Mechtild herself express their fears for the integrity of the written text. The scribes attribute any faults in the text to their "unkunnynge," and they make that precarious affirmation discussed earlier that the mystical text speaks from a place both different and the same as that authorized by Christian tradition:

> 3if anye sentence thay fynde whiche maye nought be wittnessede in scripture, so that hitt be nou3t agaynes the gospelle ande holye wrytte, þane schulde þay commytte hitt to the grace of owre lorde."[105]

> (If any sentence they [readers] find which may not be verified in Scripture, as long as it is not against the gospel and holy writ, then they should attribute it to the grace of our lord.)

Mechtild's own doubt about the truth of their writing sends her in despair to ask Christ: "Whareby maye y knowe if itt be alle soyth þat þaye wryte of þis schewynges when I haffe nowht redde þame ande I haffe now3t approuyd þame?" (How may I know if it be all truth that they write of these showings when I have not read them and I have not approved them?) He assures her that He abides in the hearts, ears, mouths, and hands of her scribes. "Ande so alle thynge þat þaye indyte ande wryte in me ande be me which am soythfastnes, itt es soth ande trewe" (And so all things that they compose and write in me and by me, who am very truth, it is veritable and true.)[106]

Though Mechtild is satisfied of her writers' inspiration, she reserves a certain privacy within the text of those heavenly "privitees" which remain unwritten.[107] The written text records only some of the truth, for, as the writers explain, Mechtild kept many revelations to herself. Other revelations were so "spiritual" that language itself was powerless to "schewe itt in wordes." God speaks to Mechtild with "many priuey wordes and sownyges [private conversations]." Within the gesture of "showing" lies the equally strong effort to conceal what written language merely publicizes. Unlike the Church's efforts to institutionalize secrecy in its exegesis of Scriptures, the mystical text of Mechtild does not claim to understand or explain these "privey wordes" which elude the text.[108]

This secret place within the mystical text corresponds to the wound in Christ's body through which the mystic first learns and then inhabits heavenly "privitee." Catherine of Siena describes the ascension of the soul to mystical union using Christ's body as a grid or ladder. The soul begins at Christ's feet, or the affections and desire, through which it is raised to perfect love and the second level of the wound in Christ's side.[109] There the spiritual lovers "come to the great hole in the side of my son, where they may find the privy secrets of the heart." The wound is the location of Christ's "shewing,"

> where I schewide to ȝou þe pryuytees of myn herte, makynge so to be knowen to ȝou þat I loue ȝou moore þan I couþe schewe ȝou wiþ þis fynyte peyne."[110]

> (where I showed to you the secrets of my heart, making it known to you that I love you more than I could show you with this finite pain.)

The secrets which Mechtild receives at Christ's wounds and heart pulse to her in hymns of praise to the Virgin and incantations of love.[111] In an unusual vision, Mechtild places her head on Christ's foot wound and hears the sound of a pot boiling furiously. When she is perplexed, Christ explains that the noise of the pot—"renne, renne, renne"—signifies his restless period on earth. In some cases, such as when she enters His heart, the secrets exceed the powers of language to recount: "sche tastyd ande saw þat none erthelye man maye speke."[112]

The wound of Christ marks the place in his body and in the text where the other speaks and shows. It is also a refuge from the institutional places which have become corrupted, as God tells Catherine of Siena:

> The place þere ȝe schulden stonde is Crist crucified, myn oonli sooþfast sone, Ihesu. Þere schulde ȝe dwelle and hyde ȝou in þe holys of hise woundis, & namely in þe greet wounde of his syde, in þe which wounde by affeccyoun of loue ȝe schulen be ioyful.[113]

(The place where you should stand is the crucified Christ, my only true son, Jesu. There you should dwell and hide yourself in the holes of his wounds, and especially in the great wound of his side, in which you shall be joyful through the affection of love.)

The critiques of the Church and its ministers in the *Revelations* and *Orcherd of Syon* necessitate the creation of this new location from which to speak and hear the unspeakable divine showings.[114]

Yet the mystic always doubts her own speech and her receptivity to divine speech. The problem of her unworthiness continually calls into question the truth of the showings. Mechtild's self-reprimands and despair over her unworthiness can become cloying, but they represent the dual pressures of the mystical text and the culture's taboo against woman's speech. She also worries about the source of the speeches she receives, particularly those which reassure her of her self-doubts. Thus when she hears a voice reason that she will not be excluded from God's grace, she assumes it is the speech of her own soul attempting to quiet its fears. God Himself intervenes to claim the words.[115] Ironically, the mystic often calls attention to her own unlikeliness to receive divine speech and her doubts about the speeches themselves in her vigilant attempt to confirm their truth. The discourse is both plagued and propelled by its own improbability.

Without the recourse to institutional authority, the mystical text must continually renew its claim in divine utterance. Catherine's desire to know how to determine the source of visions, good or evil, elicits from the divine voice the very means by which the reader may judge her text.[116] The same circumspection about the source of her utterances leads Bridget of Sweden wrongly to doubt Christ's speech to her. The true test of divine utterance is that which makes it possible in the first place: the desire for nothing but God:

Þer-fore dowte the notte bot that the good spiritte of God ys than with the whan thu desyryste no þing bot God, and of him thu art all inflamed.[117]

(Therefore doubt not but that the good spirit of God is then with you when you desire nothing but God, and you are all inflamed with him.)

The mystic brings her desire to the utterance, investing that speech with the body of her own passions.

The contractual desire for nothing but God that gives way to mystical annunciations founds the text. It is also what produces the mystic's suffering, as though the words themselves were traces of the suffering of the soul, as Aristotle claimed. Between the mystic's desire and her suffering lies the place of divine speech. Bridget of Sweden experiences this simultaneous desire and suffering as hunger and satiety for God's words:

> O my God mooste swete, how suete bene thy wordis to my soule, which sualwith hem as mete althir suettist. And thei entren with ioye in-to my herte, for whan I here thy wordes, I am bothe full and hungry; fulle, for me delitith no thinge but thi wordes; hungry, for the more I here hem the more feruently I desyre hem.

> (O my God most sweet, how sweet are your words to my soul, which swallows them as the sweetest of all meat. And they enter with joy into my heart, for when I hear your words, I am both full and hungry; full, for I delight in nothing but your words; hungry, for the more I hear them the more fervently I desire them.)[118]

Desire for God's presence in words or other visitations in the soul always produces suffering. Abundance arouses desire and suffering caused by the lack of the Other, and this in turn inspires the mystic's quest for fulfillment. Bernard of Clairvaux suggests that the suffering of desire is what makes a place for divine speech in the first place. In his sermon on the Song of Songs, Bernard places suffering in desire: "Any soul into which he is to enter must anticipate his coming through the *fervor of a desire* that consumes all stains due to vice and makes a clean place for the Lord."[119] Out of the deprivation of God's presence, the mystic "clamors her heart's desire for him," in the words of Bernard, as Bridget does toward the end of her *Revelations*. Divine speech finds its place in Bridget's desire at the same time that its absence elicits the clamoring of the heart's desire. This is how mystical dialogue is instigated, through the clamorings of desire for one who is absent.

For Catherine of Siena, desire clamors for knowledge of oneself and God even though it proves troubling. Reminded of her own sinfulness and the wretchedness of the world, the soul who pursues knowledge through desire is bound to discover pain. God explains to Catherine in the first chapter of her book that "in þe knowynge of me þe soule is chaufid wiþ sich a loue þat for þat brennynge loue þe soule is yn contynuel peyne."[120] Only death brings "hunger and desire" without pain, she learns in one dialogue. She herself experiences this pain and joy associated with mystical desire and knowledge.[121] More importantly, her desire to know leads her to make four petitions which initiate the dialogue with God. Yet her desire always threatens to silence her own speech. The sheer abundance of the one transgresses the limits of language, devours words, and leaves the mystic on the verge of silence. After God's communication to Catherine of Siena of his providence, she attempts to thank him, but is reduced instead to silence or childish babbling:

> O good lord, what schal I seye? What schal I speke? Al my spekyng is to þee no spekyng. Þerfore I schal seye þus as a child dooþ: A, A, A, for I can noon oþire speke. Þe tonge of my body is sich þat it schal haue eende, & þerfore it cannot expresse þe affeccioun of þe soule which desireþ infinytly.

> (O good lord, what shall I say? What shall I speak? All my speaking is to you no speaking. Therefore I shall say thus as a child does: Ah, Ah, Ah, for I can speak nothing else. The tongue of my body is such that it shall have end, and therefore it cannot express the affection of the soul which desires infinitely.)[122]

The infinite desire of the soul teaches the mystic the limits of language which she occupies. Always aware that her speech is no speech to the Other, she observes it exhaust itself and expose itself for what it is, random phonemic outbursts. Catherine is forced to recognize the impossibility of her own speech in view of the "priuytees of God":

> I haue seen þe priuytees of God, which is vnleeful a man to speke. What schal I þanne seye? Certeyne, I may noþing seie worþily, þus abidynge in my boistous bodyly wittis.

> (I have seen the mysteries [secrets] of God, which it is unlawful for a person to speak. What shall I then say? Certainly, I may not say anything worthily, thus inhabiting as I am my crude bodily wits.)

Between infinite desire and God's "preuytees," mystic speech falters. It may now only return, as Catherine's does, to yet another petition for divine speech to fulfill her infinite desire.

The crisis of language experienced by Catherine of Siena is caused by her entrance into the "unleeful" (unlawful) domain of God's mysteries. The mystic transgresses the lawful limits of language only to find her speech overwhelmed by "marvelous communication" and her own desire. Her speech is continually disappearing, but this makes divine speech possible. Her silence is not the silence of discretion advocated for women by such devotional treatises of women as *Hali Meidenhad, Ancrene Wisse,* or *De institutione inclusarum.* It is a silence inspired by "unleeful" knowledge of God's secret showings—those tastings and savorings into which language disappears.

If mystic discourse is always in danger of disappearing completely, it reappears in the body of the mystic, in the burning love, the spiritual drunkenness, even the wounds of bitterness in the heart.[123] Catherine of Siena sweats from the heat of holy desire. Mechtild of Hackeborn feels a "shining of the divinity pierce all the limbs and parts of my body with a fully clear light." Irradiance and the liquefaction of the body are both signs of that "marvelous communication " which chokes off private communication of the soul with God.[124]

Traces of the discourse may be found in the entire *sensorium* of the mystical text, including those "private sounds," tastings and savorings of a holy sweet, kisses redolent of honey, intoxicating smells, and unspeakable sights.[125] The absence of the other who is desired and the faltering of mystic discourse give rise to this other body and other communication, a matrix of sensory utterances. While the *sensoria* of these mystical texts differ in their organization and expression, they serve to celebrate the loss of language in the face of marvelous communication.

If readers remain unmoved by the mystical text, it is because the true act of writing takes place in the heart, as the Monk of Farne laments. Mechtild begs Christ to "wryte [my] name in [thy] herte." This inscription takes place in the heart of the mystic (and reader), but the affections bear the impressions of the inscription. One of the proofs of the truth of Mechtild's book is that a sister received a "luffynge styrrynge" throughout every part of her body just by glancing at the written text.[126] If the soul lacks the burning heat of charity, Christ tells Bridget, his words become like gristle in the cold mouths of his listeners. To those heated by love, his words are as fat grease or tallow which melts as it is savored. The disposition of the heart, rather than the intellect, determines the reader's receptivity to the mystical text and divine speech. For the soul finds "goodly wisdom," according to a Brigittine vision, not only in "letturis," or learning and literature, but in the heart and in good living.[127]

In fact, the mystical text rejects institutional discourse, including learning, letters, and textual authority, whether it explicitly criticizes them or not. It is true that Catherine of Siena and Bridget of Sweden were more outspoken in their critiques of the clergy than was Mechtild of Hackeborn.[128] The *Orcherd of Syon* devotes the better part of a chapter to the faults and sins of priests and ministers of the Church. Christ singles out "the gouernour of the church and hys clerkys" among the five groups He indicts as his enemies in Bridget's *Revelations*.[129] By comparison, Mechtild's *Booke of Gostlye Grace* has little to say about the Church and its ministers and, some would argue, even positions itself as a "staunch ally" of the Church in the face of religious dissent.[130]

Regardless of what the mystical treatise has to say about the Church, the discourse itself rivals it. By claiming the prerogative of hearer and witness to the divine word, the mystical text severs itself from the institutional discourses which are grounded in textual authority.[131] If this is true of mystical texts in general, it is even more true of medieval texts by women, lay or religious. The exclusion of women from the learning and culture of the Church and from the *auctoritas* of textual tradition makes their utterances highly suspicious, if not subversive. Though each of the three women discussed submitted to the spiritual direction or approval of others, their election to receive and transmit divine speech is already a critique of the institution they claim to support. Their insistence upon divine witness infers a failure of the Church.[132] Mechtild of Hackeborn, the least explicitly critical of the Church, makes one of the most audacious claims to her authority as a witness. She is instructed in a vision to make a house of her heart with a window through which God may give His gifts to men. She interprets this as a license to teach others:

> Offe þis sche hadde vnderstondynge þat here mowth schulde be þat oone wyndowe, with þe whiche mowth sche schulde mynystre Goddes worde by doctrine and comforth to hem þat come to here.[133]

> (Of this she understood that her mouth should be that one window, with which she should administer God's word by means of doctrine and comfort to them who came to her.)

Not only does Mechtild reverse the usual interpretation of the mouth as one of the five windows leading to the corruption of the soul—and for woman, her most drafty one—but she authorizes her own speech in the text and in the world.

Their election to hear and minister God's word is in itself a critique which these women continually speak in their texts. Their very claim to be the place where God speaks points to the institution's betrayal of the Word entrusted to it. Although the Middle English mystical texts of Mechtild, Bridget, and Catherine differ in many important ways, they share a discursive practice. This practice is also shared somewhat by other mystics such as Richard Rolle and the Monk of Farne, but the position from which the texts speak is fundamentally different. Women's *inculture* means that the absence from which they speak is not only an absence of self, but of *auctoritas*, textual as well as institutional.

The mystical text is chiefly characterized by its abundance, which cannot be contained in a book, according to Mechtild of Hackeborn.

Mystic discourse always exceeds the boundaries of book, inscription, and margin, as well as the order of rubric and colophon. From the excess of the affections comes this discourse of abundance; from the crossing of the boundaries of the sealed body, this marvelous communication. The body of the text exceeds the prohibitions against the feminine and the flesh. Body and book conspire in the discourse of female mystics to disrupt their enclosures.

Nowhere is this more dramatically enacted than in *The Book of Margery Kempe*. The first autobiography in the English language and the work of an illiterate woman, this mystical treatise has defied (or failed) attempts to place it within the mystical tradition defined by the works of Walter Hilton, Richard Rolle, the author of the *Cloud of Unknowing*, and Julian of Norwich. Kempe's position in the fourteenth and early fifteenth centuries is further complicated by her own worldly connections as a wife of John Kempe, mother of fourteen children, member of the merchant class, and daughter of a respectable burgess and mayor of her hometown of King's Lynn in Norfolk.[134] She never enters a convent or anchorage, but instead insists on traveling widely on pilgrimages, visiting local bishops and archbishops, and causing a disturbance with her "bold speech" wherever she goes. Kempe remains one of the most problematic of mystics, English or continental, because of her very mobility and unbridled mystical practices. Her publicity defies the categories of holiness available to women in her time.[135] Her practices of roaring, writhing on the ground, preaching, and insisting on herself as a bride of Christ all incited controversy in her own time, and continue to incite critical frustration among modern mystical scholars.[136] For this reason, she is an excellent example of the problematic nature of woman's position as flesh in medieval culture. She also provides a troublesome case for the way in which medieval taboos against the flesh and female body might be violated in a lived life and a mystical narrative. We shall observe the way in which she translates body into discourse, its challenge to church authority, and her own struggles with authority as an author and mystic. The trajectory from body to text by way of the fissured and feminine flesh in Margery Kempe's life and book is the subject of the next three chapters.

Notes

1. Most such attempts focus on the works of Bernard of Clairvaux and Anselm and the influence of the Cistercians and Franciscans, see Clarissa W. Atkinson, *Mystic and Pilgrim: The Book and the World of Margery Kempe* (Ithaca, NY: Cornell

University Press), 129–56; also, Carolyn Walker Bynum, *Jesus As Mother: Studies in the Spirituality of the High Middle Ages* (Berkeley: University of California Press, 1987), 110–69.

2. See Robert K. Stone, *Middle English Prose Style: Margery Kempe and Julian of Norwich* (The Hague and Paris: Mouton, 1970). Wolfgang Riehle also examines the style of mystical language mostly in Rolle, Julian, and Kempe in *The Middle English Mystics*, trans. Bernard Standring (London: Routledge and Kegan Paul, 1981).

3. Rosemary Woolf views late medieval spirituality as exceeding devotional and literary decorum, *The English Religious Lyric in the Middle Ages* (Oxford: Clarendon Press, 1968), 245. David Knowles also distinguishes between the two sensibilities in *The Religious Orders in England*, vol. 2 (Cambridge: Cambridge University Press, 1957), 222–23.

4. For example, see Carolyn Walker Bynum, *Holy Feast and Holy Fast: The Religious Significance of Food to Medieval Women* (Berkeley: University of California Press, 1987), 13–69; Richard Kieckhefer, *Unquiet Souls: Fourteenth-Century Saints and Their Religious Milieu* (Chicago: University of Chicago Press, 1982), 1–20; André Vauchez, *La Sainteté en Occident aux derniers siècles du moyen âge d'après les procès de canonisation et les documents hagiographiques*, Bibliothèque des études françaises d'Athènes et de Rome 241 (Rome: École Française de Rome, 1981), 243–49 and 440–45.

5. Bynum, *Holy Feast and Holy Fast*, 16–20.

6. See Bynum's discussion of these factors, *Holy Feast and Holy Fast*, 18–20.

7. Lee Patterson points out the shortcomings of such historicism in *Negotiating the Past: The Historical Understanding of Medieval Literature* (Madison: University of Wisconsin Press, 1987), 42–45.

8. See Kieckhefer, *Unquiet Souls*, 1–15; Bynum, *Holy Feast and Holy Fast*, although Bynum cautions against confusing hagiographical clichés with devotional practice, 87; and Donald Weinstein and Rudolph M. Bell, *Saints and Society: The Two Worlds of Western Christendom, 1000–1700* (Chicago: University of Chicago Press, 1982).

9. See A. J. Minnis's discussion of Chaucer's self-proclaimed role as *compilator*, *Medieval Theory of Authorship: Scholastic Literary Attitudes in the Later Middle Ages* (London: Scolar Press, 1984; 2nd ed. Philadelphia: University of Pennsylvania Press, 1988), 190–210.

10. See Catherine of Siena, *Catherine of Siena: The Dialogue*, trans. Suzanne Noffke (New York: Paulist Press, 1980), 23; see also Theresa M. Halligan's introduction to the Middle English text of German mystic Mechtild of Hackeborn's *Liber Spiritualis Gratiae: The Book of Gostlye Grace of Mechtild of Hackeborn*, ed. Theresa M. Halligan, Studies and Texts 49 (Toronto: Pontifical Institute of Medieval Studies, 1979), 7.

11. Henry Suso, *The Life of the Servant*, trans. James M. Clark (London, 1952), 15–16.

12. Quoted in Ute Stargardt, "The Influence of Dorotea von Mantau on the Mysticism of Margery Kempe" (Dissertation, University of Tennessee, 1981), 13–14.

13. See Kieckhefer, *Unquiet Souls*, who cautions that Marienwerder filtered Dorothy's words, 23; and Stargardt, "The Influence of Dorotea von Mantau," 161–63.

14. I would like to qualify this statement, however, by acknowledging that, indeed, texts were often hybrids of mystical and exegetical discourses, such as Bernard of Clairvaux's commentary on the Song of Songs. Nevertheless, there are distinctions to be made, as Minnis's study of authorship proves. I think one can better understand Bernard's text by making such distinctions in advance without necessarily insisting on their mutual exclusivity.

15. *Heterologies: Discourse on the Other*, trans. Brian Massumi (Minneapolis: University of Minnesota Press, 1986), 80–100. He, too, uses examples from late medieval spirituality in his discussion of the "absent body," in *La fable mystique, XVIᵉ–XVIIᵉ*, Bibliothèque des Histoires (Paris: Éditions Gallimard, 1982). I will return to this problem later.

16. *Heterologies*, 82.

17. De Certeau makes this distinction specifically between theological and mystical discourse, *Heterologies*, 90.

18. See de Certeau, *Heterologies*, 92.

19. De Certeau outlines these two forms of mystic speech and the "trouble" from which mystic texts are born: *Heterologies*, 88.

20. The term *volo* signifies in de Certeau's analysis of mystic speech this function of desire, *Heterologies*, 92.

21. PL 23, cols. 238 and 239.

22. See *Hali Meiðhad*, ed. Bella Millett, EETS, o.s. 284 (London: Oxford University Press, 1982), 8; Aelred of Rievaulx, *De Institutione Inclusarum*, ed. John Ayto and Alexandra Barratt, EETS, o.s. 284 (London: Oxford University Press, 1984), 4–5; *Ancrene Wisse: The English Text of the Ancrene Riwle* EETS 249 (London: Oxford University Press, 1962), 32.

23. The "healing of the inner eye" is the most common idea found in medieval devotional treatises. For example, see Pseudo-Bonaventure, *Meditations on the Life of Christ*, trans. Isa Ragusa, ed. Isa Ragusa and Rosalie Green (Princeton, NJ: Princeton University Press, 1961), 262. Also, "The Privity of the Passion" in MS Thornton, in C. Horstman, ed., *Yorkshire Writers: Richard Rolle of Hampole: An English Father of the Church and His Followers* (London: Swan Sonnenschein, 1895), vol. 1, 198. This last work is not one of the works attributed to Rolle in more recent editions of his work.

24. Rolle, *The Incendium Amoris of Richard Rolle of Hampole*, ed. Margaret Deanesly, Publications of the Univesity of Manchester, Historical Series 26 (London, 1915), 148. He says this elsewhere, particularly in his lyrics, see his "Cantus Amoris" in *Ego Domino* and "A Song of Love-Longing to Jesus" in *English Writings of Richard Rolle, Hermit of Hampole*, ed. Hope Emily Allen (Oxford: Clarendon Press, 1931), 70–72 and 41–43. Cited below as *English Writings*, ed. H. E. Allen.

25. For the three stages, see *Incendium Amoris*, 182–87. Rosamund S. Allen discusses these stages in the introduction to her translation, *Richard Rolle: The English Writings* (New York: Paulist Press, 1988), 38. Cited below as *Richard Rolle*, trans. R. Allen.

26. *Heterologies*, 88.

27. See *Incendium Amoris*, 232–35 and 238–41.

28. *Heterologies*, 92–93.

29. De Certeau, *Heterologies*: "Moreover, the 'experience' by which mystic writings define themselves has as its essential elements the *ego*, the 'center of utterance,' and the *present*, the 'source of time,' the 'presence of the world that the act of utterance alone makes possible' "(90).

30. See Riehle's discussion of these words and their erotic associations for mystical conversation with the divine, *Middle English Mystics*, 102–3.

31. Julian of Norwich, *Showings*, trans. Edmund Colledge and James Walsh (New York: Paulist Press, 1978), 179–81. *The Book of Margery Kempe*, ed. Sanford B. Meech and Hope Emily Allen, EETS 212, o.s. (London: Oxford University Press, 1940; rpt. 1961), 6–11.

32. Trinh T. Minh-ha makes a similar distinction between self-effacement and voiding as a problematic for women writers, *Woman, Native, Other*, 35.

33. See R. S. Allen's introduction, *Richard Rolle*, 40.

34. *Richard Rolle*, trans. R. S. Allen, 149 and 150; for the Middle English, see *English Writings*, ed. H. E. Allen, 80 and 81.

35. *English Writings*, ed. H. E. Allen, 71; *Richard Rolle*, trans. R. S. Allen, 142.

36. See also "The Form of Living" in *English Writings*, ed. H. E. Allen, 108.

37. In *Deonise Hid Diuinite*, ed. Phyllis Hodgson, EETS, o.s. 231 (London: Oxford University Press, 1958), 73. The passage conflates ideas from 1 Corinthians 1:26 and 7:20, and Ephesians 4:1. All translations from Middle English are my own unless otherwise indicated.

38. I am indebted here to de Certeau's analysis of Jean-Joseph Surin's use of the name in "Surin's Melancholy," *Heterologies*, 111–12.

39. *Sermones super cantica canticorum*, in *S. Bernardi Opera*, vol. I, ed. J. Leclercq, H. M. Rochais, and C. H. Talbot (Rome: Editiones Cistercienses, 1957), 82–88. On the devotion to the name in Middle English mysticism, see Riehle, *Middle English Mystics*, 26–28.

40. De Certeau distinguishes between two functions of naming in St. John of the Cross and Surin, *Heterologies*, 112–13. He uses this first function—that of sign of Christ's suffering in John of the Cross. The second function is my own.

41. *English Writings*, ed. H. E. Allen, 108.

42. *Le Livre de l'expérience des vrais fidèles*, ed. Ferré and Baudry, p. 54, par. 35.

43. See Bynum, *Holy Feast and Holy Fast*, 151.

44. *La fable mystique*, 108. De Certeau comments, too, that in the mysticism of the late Middle Ages, "the production of a body plays an essential role," (my translation) 107–8.

45. Kristeva discusses desire and the affections in Bernard, *Tales of Love*, 151–69, particularly, 159–60.

46. *Sermo 89 in Cantica*, trans. in *Monk of Farne*, ed. Farmer, 102.

47. For examples, see *Monk of Farne*, ed. Farmer, 67 and 103; also Rolle, *Incendium Amoris*, ed. Deanesly, 218.

48. *Monk of Farne*, ed. Farmer, 48.

49. *Monk of Farne*, ed. Farmer, 63.

50. Eckhart, *Meister Eckhart: The Essential Sermons, Commentaries, Treatises,*

and Defense, trans. Edmund Colledge and Bernard Mcginn (New York: Paulist Press, 1981), 204.

51. For example, see R. S. Allen's argument in her introduction, *Richard Rolle*, 28–31; also Riehle tries to establish figurative limits particularly on the erotic language of the English mystics, *Middle English Mystics*, 94–103.

52. Here again, Riehle tries to keep separate metaphorical and literal uses of sense experience in mystical language, *Middle English Mystics*, 115–18.

53. I am using Riehle's word, *Middle English Mystics*, 118; he attributes this practice of materializing to the woman mystic whose "imagination knows no restraints."

54. See Riehle, *Middle English Mystics*, 46.

55. *Richard Rolle*, trans. R. S. Allen, 119; this section does not appear in H.E. Allen's Middle English edition of Rolle's writings.

56. *Richard Rolle*, R. S. Allen, 98.

57. *Monk of Farne*, ed. Farmer, 63. See also p. 33 for another instance of this.

58. *Tales of Love*, 124. She comments that the heterogeneity of the flesh makes the impulse to mystical love and sin metonymic to one another. She observes, "one of the insights of Christianity, and not the least one, is to have gathered in a single move perversion and beauty as the lining and cloth of one and the same economy" (125).

59. See Walter J. Ong's interesting discussion of how literate cultures often confuse simple, circumscribed meaning with the segmented, fixed appearance of characters and words on the page. Unlike oral cultures, then, they assume that literal meaning is clear and simple. *The Presence of the Word: Some Prolegomena for Culture in Religious History* (New Haven, CT: Yale University Press, 1967), 46–47.

60. "A Tretis of Discrescyon of Spirites," in Hodgson, ed., *Deonise Hid Diuinite*, 81.

61. Hodgson, ed., *Deonise Hid Diuinite*, 93–94; see also 90–91.

62. Richard Rolle, *The Fire of Love*, trans. Clifton Wolters (New York: Penguin, 1972), 99. See *Incendium Amoris*, ed. Deanesly, 194.

63. See de Certeau's discussion of her role as "cette figure éponymique des mystiques modernes" whose weeping at the tomb of Christ "organise le discours apostolique," *La fable mystique*, 110.

64. Bernard of Clairvaux, *Sermones cantica canticorum*, Ser. 7, VI, 8; also Anselm, *The Prayers and Meditations of St. Anselm*, trans. Benedicta Ward (Middlesex: Penguin, 1973), 201–6. For a discussion of the Magdalene as repentant sinner and mystical lover, see Benedicta Ward, *Harlots of the Desert: A Study of Repentance in Early Monastic Sources* (Kalamazoo, MI: Cistercian Publications Inc., 1987), 10–25.

65. Among the many studies of the *Quem quaeritis* are those of O. B. Hardison, *Christian Rite and Christian Drama in the Middle Ages* (Baltimore, MD: Johns Hopkins University Press, 1965). The Digby play of the Resurrection may be found in Donald C. Baker, John L. Murphy, and Louis B. Hall Jr., *The Late Medieval Religious Plays of Bodleian MSS Digby 133 and E Museo 160*, EETS, o.s. 287 (London: Oxford University Press, 1982).

66. *The Book of Margery Kempe*, ed. Meech and Allen, 16. Unless otherwise noted, all quoted passages are from this edition.

67. *La fable mystique*: "La 'naissance' qu'ils attendent tous, d'une manière ou d'une autre, doit inventer au verbe un corps d'amour. D'où leur quête d' 'annonciations,' de paroles qui fassent corps, d'enfantements par l'oreille" (108).

68. De Certeau constructs mystical discourse along a triangular scheme which places the body in the center of the three poles of the triangle: mystical experience, symbolic discourse, and social practice, *La fable mystique*, 109.

69. Farmer, *Monk of Farne*, 110.

70. These are four of the five ways of contemplating the Passion which Julian enacts in her book. The final way is contemplating the transformation of his suffering into joy and bliss, see Colledge and Walsh, *A Book of Showings*, 389–90.

71. Julia Kristeva, "Holbein's Dead Christ," in *Fragments for a History of the Human Body*, Part 1, ed. Michel Feher, Ramona Naddaff, and Nadia Tazi (New York: Urzone, 1989), 261.

72. I am using Foucault's description of mystical language in *Language, Counter-Memory, Practice*, 48.

73. This is not always true, as may be seen in the works of Richard Rolle. For example, some of his Latin works, such as the *Incendium Amoris*, are more instructional works than mystical dialogues or prayers like the "Meditations on the Passion."

74. Mechtild of Hackeborn, *The Booke of Gostlye Grace of Mechtild of Hackeborn*, ed. Theresa A. Halligan, Studies and Texts 46 (Toronto: Pontifical Institute of Medieval Studies, 1979); Bridget of Sweden, *The Revelations of Saint Birgitta*, ed. William Patterson Cumming, EETS, o.s. 178 (London, 1929; rpt. 1971); Catherine of Siena, *The Orcherd of Syon*, ed. Phyllis Hodgson and Gabriel M. Liegey, EETS, o.s. 258 (London: Oxford University Press, 1966).

75. See Mechtild, *Booke of Gostlye Grace*, 1; Halligan explains that the correct Latin title of Mechtild's work is *Liber Specialis Gratiae*, but the Middle English translation is taken from an edition which uses *Spiritualis* in place of *Specialis*.

76. See *Revelations of Saint Birgitta*, xvi–xxii.

77. *Orcherd of Syon*, vii; British Museum Harleian MS 3432 and MS C 25 (James 75), Cambridge; and MS 162, Pierpont Morgan Library. In addition, twenty-five manuscripts contain Italian editions, sixteen manuscripts include Latin translations, and four printed texts date from 1472.

78. London, British Library, MS Sloane 982, ff. 54r–61v includes extracts from both Bridget of Sweden and Mechtild of Hackeborn; see also Dublin Trinity MS 277; *Booke of Gostlye Grace*, 47–50.

79. Cambridge, Peterhouse MS 276, see Halligan, *Booke of Gostlye Grace*, 47–50.

80. See Manchester, John Rylands Library, MS 295.

81. See *Booke of Gostlye Grace*, 50; also *The Myroure of Oure Ladye*, ed. John Henry Blunt, EETS, o.s. 19 (London: Oxford University Press, 1973).

82. For other records of these works in manuscripts and wills, see Halligan, *Booke of Gostlye Grace*, 50–52.

83. See Hope Emily Allen's preface to *The Book of Margery Kempe*, lxvi; for the

dating of the *Revelations* and the *Orcherd*, see Hodgson and Liegey's preface to *Orcherd of Syon*, vii.

84. *Catalogue of the Library of Syon Monastery*, ed. Mary Bateson (Cambridge, 1898).

85. The Witham Charterhouse, for example, shows both works in its library, see E. Margaret Thompson, *The Carthusian Order in England* (London, 1930), 321. For holdings of English Carthusian libraries, see 313–24.

86. Halligan, *Booke of Gostlye Grace*, 53–54 and 51.

87. *Orcherd of Syon*, ed. Hodgson and Liegey, vii.

88. N. F. Blake, "Revelations of St. Matilda," *Notes and Queries* 20 (1973): 324n.

89. For the allegorical framework, see Hodgson, vii, and Sister Mary Denise, "*The Orcherd of Syon*: An Introduction," *Traditio* 14 (1958): 273–81; for the connection between Bridget's founding of the order and the title of the Middle English edition, see Phyllis Hodgson, "*The Orcherd of Syon* and the English Mystical Tradition," *Proceedings of the British Academy* (1964): 236.

90. See *The Book of Margery Kempe* for her visitation to Syon, 245; for references to Bridget, 47 and 95; for mention of Bridget's book, 39, 47, and 143; for Kempe's visit to an attendant of Bridget, 95.

91. See her preface to the Meech and Allen edition, lxvi. Allen planned a second volume to her edition in which she would print excerpts from these and other related mystical works, but she did not live to complete it.

92. See Vauchez, *Les laïcs*, 266, and Alexander Murray's discussion of Latin and literacy in the church, *Reason and Society in the Middle Ages* (Oxford: Clarendon Press, 1978), 293–98.

93. *Reason and Society*, 299–300.

94. Vauchez, *Les laïcs*, 266; for speculations on Catherine's learning, see Noffke, trans., *Catherine of Siena: the Dialogue*, 10–12.

95. See Mechtild, *Booke of Gostlye Grace*, ed. Halligan, 37. There is evidence to suggest that Mechtild of Hackeborn feared "exploitations" of her visions by her sisters and arousal of the suspicion of authorities, according to Bynum, *Jesus As Mother*, 223–24. I will return to this later in my discussion of the *Booke of Gostlye Grace*.

96. *Revelations of Saint Birgitta*, ed. Cummings, xxi, xxv. The original was destroyed except for a few surviving fragments of Birgitta's handwriting, xxvii.

97. See *Orcherd of Syon*, ed. Hodgson and Liegey, vi–vii and Noffke, *Catherine of Siena*, 11–12 and 19–20.

98. See Vauchez, *Les laïcs*, 267.

99. Rolle, *The Fire of Love*, trans. Richard Misyn, 3. I am not including the Monk of Farne among these instructional works because he addresses Christ, not his audience, in a prayerful meditation more akin to the mode of the women's texts. Rolle's lyrics and "Meditations on the Passion" are also excluded from this group, but the Latin and English works, the *Incendium Amoris* and *The Form of Living*, and others are not. As R. S. Allen argues, one could say that all of Rolle's works are instructive, but the mode of instruction differs (34).

100. See A. J. Minnis on this distinction in commentaries on the *Sentences* of Peter Lombard, *Medieval Theory of Authorship*, 97–99.

101. See *The Cloud of Unknowing*, ed. Hodgson, 128–30.

102. See Rolle's distinction between mystical knowledge and human knowledge in Misyn, *The Fire of Love*, 3.

103. For the different medieval uses of *speculum* to mean exemplary text, see Herbert Grabes, *The Mutable Glass: Mirror-Imagery in Titles and Texts of the Middle Ages and English Renaissance*, trans. Gordon Collier (Cambridge: Cambridge University Press, 1989), 38, 51–52.

104. The publicity is, of course, limited by the writer's intended audience. I am referring here to the text's primary engagement with a "reading public" which, as Walter J. Ong has pointed out, is fictional and absent from the writer, *Orality and Literacy: The Technologizing of the Word* (New York: Methuen, 1982), 101–3, 135.

105. *Booke of Gostlye Grace*, 69.

106. *Booke of Gostlye Grace*, 586–87.

107. *Booke of Gostlye Grace*, 67 and 600.

108. The institutionalization of secrecy is discussed by Frank Kermode, *The Genesis of Secrecy: On the Interpretation of Narrative* (Cambridge, MA: Harvard University Press, 1979). Jesse M. Gellrich examines the secrecy of Dante's allegory using the concept of *liber occultorum* from Rev. 20:12, *The Idea of the Book in the Middle Ages: Language Theory, Mythology, and Fiction* (Ithaca, NY: Cornell University Press, 1985), 162–66. He finds in Dante the same "concealing-revealing" gesture I have described, but he does not make the same distinction between public and private discourses that I do.

109. *Orcherd of Syon*, 68–69.

110. *Orcherd of Syon*, 163, 166.

111. See *Booke of Gostlye Grace*, 321–22, 326.

112. *Booke of Gostlye Grace*, 339, 417.

113. *Orcherd of Syon*, 281.

114. The Middle English text of Bridget's *Revelations* does not locate this place in the wounds of Christ. Instead, she finds this location in her vision of the speaking book on the pulpit, which is able to speak itself, see 68 and 86–87.

115. For examples of Mechtild's despair, see *Booke of Gostlye Grace*, 351 and 502–3; for God's reassurance, 224–25.

116. *Orcherd of Syon*, 237–39. Gladness and desire for virtue are the two traces of divine speech in the soul.

117. *Revelations of Saint Birgitta*, 3–4; Christ assures her in a later vision that she may speak without fear because he speaks through her and "there is none that schall preuayle ayenst me," 105.

118. *Revelations of Saint Birgitta*, 104.

119. *Sermon on the Song of Songs*, 31, 4; quoted in Kristeva, who discusses this aspect of Bernard's mystical theology in *Tales of Love*, 159–62.

120. *Orcherd of Syon*, 24.

121. *Orcherd of Syon*, 178–79 and 58–59.

122. *Orcherd of Syon*, 376.

123. See *Orcherd of Syon*, 317; Mechtild refers to these affective states, too, 235–36, 247–48, and 335. Bridget's *Revelations* include less of this affective dimension, except for her claims to hunger and satiety already quoted.

124. See the *Orcherd of Syon*, 59; *Booke of Gostlye Grace*, 248; a similar description appears in a later vision, 452; Mechtild experiences a liquefaction of the body, too, 78.

125. I am borrowing the term *sensorium* from Walter J. Ong, who defines it as "the entire sensory apparatus as an operational complex." He sees cultures as organizing and organized by this *sensorium*, in *The Presence of the Word*, 20.

126. *Booke of Gostlye Grace*, 459, 590–91.

127. *Revelations of Saint Birgitta*, 59, 15.

128. See Vauchez, *Les laïcs*, 242. As Vauchez points out, Bridget was more critical of church culture than was Catherine of Siena, whose ties to the Dominicans made her more respectful of Church doctors, 266–67.

129. See *Orcherd of Syon*, 273–305; *Revelations*, 5–6.

130. Halligan makes this argument in her introduction to her edition of the *Booke of Gostlye Grace*, 55.

131. Steven Ozment argues for the sixteenth century that mysticism is potentially anti-institutional, that it is a place for dissent from institutions, *Mysticism and Dissent: Religious Ideology and Social Protest in the Sixteenth Century* (New Haven, CT: Yale University Press, 1973), 4–6.

132. For a discussion of this election of feminine witnesses due to the corruption of the church, see Vauchez, *Les laïcs*, 241–43.

133. *Booke of Gostlye Grace*, 388. The *Ancrene Wisse* condemns the mouth as one of the windows of the senses; see Salu, *Ancrene Riwle*, 28–46.

134. For an argument that Kempe's struggles must be seen within the context of her class and community, see David Aers, *Community, Gender, and Individual Identity: English Writing 1360–1430* (London: Routledge, 1988), 73–116.

135. David Wallace warns against trying to fit Kempe into our critical categories of religious and secular, illustrious and popular. Using Bakhtin, he proposes instead that Kempe be considered a carnivalesque figure struggling to occupy official space, "Mystics and Followers in Siena and East Anglia: A Study in Taxonomy, Class, and Cultural Mediation," in *The Medieval Mystical Tradition in England: Papers Read at Dartington Hall, July 1984*, Proceedings of the Third International Exeter Symposium, ed. Marion Glasscoe (Cambridge: D. S. Brewer, 1984), 169–91.

136. Among the critical condemnations of Kempe are: David Knowles, who credits her only with having been a better wife than the Wife of Bath, *The English Mystical Tradition*, 139–48; Riehle, who deplores Kempe's excesses and distortions of perfectly respectable traditions in late medieval spirituality, *The Middle English Mystics*, 11, 38–40, 118 and elsewhere; Ute Stargardt, who finds Kempe exasperatingly simple-minded, "The Beguines of Belguim, the Dominican Nuns of Germany, and Margery Kempe," in *The Popular Literature of Medieval England*, ed. Thomas J. Heffernan (Knoxville: University of Tennessee Press, 1985), 301–8; and the editors of the modern English edition of Julian of Norwich's *Showings*, Colledge and Walsh, who simply refer to Kempe as "the egregious Margery Kempe," 18.

3. From Utterance to Text: Authorizing the Mystical Word

> This book is not written in order, everything after the other just as it was done, but as the matter came to this creature's mind when it was written down, for it was so long before it was written that she had forgotten the time and the order in which things befell.
>
> *The Book of Margery Kempe*

> And with the same traversing, dispersing gesture . . . , she breaks with explanation, interpretation, and all the authorities pinpointing localization. She forgets. She proceeds by lapses and bounds. She flies/steals.
>
> Hélène Cixous, *The Newly Born Woman*

The search for authority is a common practice among medieval texts, although the authorizing procedures of medieval texts vary across genres. Fourteenth-century literary texts, for example, often imitated the Aristotelian prologues of scriptural commentary by ascribing the authority of their works to the primary author, God, and to human *auctores*.[1] Nevertheless, their reference to authority differed from the authorizing idioms of exegetical texts in that their self-conscious manipulation of *auctores* drew attention to their own creativity. The art of preaching, by contrast, drew its authority not from any personal creativity or from ancient authors, but from the office of preacher itself. *Artes praedicandi*, in fact, disavowed personal responsibility for *auctoritas*, using instead the model of scriptural authors and deferring to divine authority.[2]

The difference in authorizing procedures among medieval texts calls attention to the importance of authorization itself to medieval discourse. No matter what method is used, the validity of the medieval text depends on its inscribed authorizing gesture, even if that gesture is purely rhetorical. Medieval literary practice, like medieval exegetical practice, consists in this authorizing gesture which founds the text as well as establishes the author as an *auctor* for the authorizing of future texts. A medieval text thus practices intertextuality to authorize itself at the same time that it sets itself up as "intertext" to some future work.

Medieval mystic texts, as we saw in chapter 2, depart from this tradition of authorization. The chief difference is that, while literary and theological texts appeal to a written tradition in order to authorize their own writing, mystic texts seek to authorize the oral text within their written texts. Utterance is central to mystical discourse. It is the sign of God's grace and the signal of His authorization. The mystic is required to verify the source of this utterance—that it comes from God rather than the devil. More importantly, she must verify that the place from which God speaks in her text is separate from that of the magisterium language. Her locus of utterance already threatens the Church's role as author of God's utterance. The mystic must authorize this utterance as the same as, and yet distinct from, the utterance proclaimed by the Church and her ministers.

Such authorization can be tricky, since the position of utterance is *ex cathedra*. The mystic text does not vie with the magisterium language of the Church for its position; rather, it defines and asserts an alternative location for divine speech altogether: the mystic's desire. The oral text is neither accurately rendered nor explicitly authorized by the written text. It lies beyond the capacity of the written text to apprehend except through various *signa* of the mystic's desire. The goal of mystical desire, as the Monk of Farne laments, is to imprint itself upon the hearts of readers even as written characters are presented to their eyes. Because this desire remains hidden in the mystic utterance, the mystic text must find other means of authorizing itself than the written text or the archive of authors available to other kinds of texts.

The task of authorizing the oral text is particularly problematic in the *The Book of Margery Kempe*. Kempe's illiteracy raises the question of the relationship of author to book and of author to the mystical tradition. Modern scholarship tends to privilege the written text, often ignoring the oral text of Kempe's *Book*. Furthermore, her very authorship is often called into question where evidence of familiarity with Latin or English mystical works may be found in her narrative. Scholars prefer to attribute the scriptural and mystical subtexts of Kempe's *Book* not to herself but to her scribe.[3]

Those scholars who do ascribe the book to Kempe's authorship often do so by way of criticism. Its lack of order, narrative repetitions, digressions, and general lack of spiritual depth are faults that some readers might attribute to Kempe's illiteracy and the oral production of her book.[4] Yet the problem of Kempe's illiteracy has never been directly addressed in connection with her writing and the authorization of her book. While scholars are aware of Kempe's quest for authority in her own life—through her visits to Julian of Norwich in 1413 and to various respected religious men—few have examined how that search works at the level of the text itself.[5]

Before looking at how Kempe's illiteracy functions in her narrative, we can observe an authorizing strategy in the story of how her book came to be written in the first place. Ironically, this story calls attention to her notoriety at the same time that it comments upon the relationship of oral to written text and her own role as author. In the proem to her *Book*, Kempe recounts in brief the story of her conversion and her subsequent efforts to substantiate her visions by "showing" them to clerics, including archbishops, bishops, doctors, bachelors of divinity, anchorites, and anchoresses. In spite of their urging her to write her revelations down, she waited more than twenty years until she was commanded by God to have her visions recorded. Her attempt to carry out His command turns into an ordeal lasting more than four years. She is at first unable to find anyone willing to transcribe or even "give credence" to her revelations. Finally, an Englishman who has been living in Germany agrees to move back to England to write her treatise.

When this scribe dies suddenly, Kempe takes her book to a friend, a priest, who offers to finish the book for her. To the surprise of both, he finds the writing incomprehensible:

> Þe booke was so euel wretyn þat he cowd lytyl skyll þeron, for it was neiþyr good Englysch ne Dewch, ne þe lettyr was not schapyn ne formyd as oþer letters ben. Þerfor þe prest leued fully þer schuld neuyr man redyn it, but it wer special grace.[6]

> (The book was so evilly written that he could make little sense of it, for it was neither good English nor German, nor were the letters shaped or formed as other letters are. Therefore the priest believed fully that man should never be able to read it, unless it was by means of a special grace.)

This muddled text of Kempe's revelations has raised much speculation about whether the first scribe knew English at all.[7] Whatever the first scribe's language problems might have been, Kempe's text blames the second scribe's inability to read the strange text rather than the "evil writing" itself: he simply fails to achieve the "special grace" needed to read it. In the meantime he also becomes intimidated by the "evil speaking" about Kempe and abandons the project out of cowardice. He does not wish, he tells Kempe, to put himself in peril.

Four years later, the priest finally agrees to try to read the strange book again because he has become "vexyd in his consciens" for not having fulfilled his promise to write it. This time, he has less difficulty in deciphering the words. Instead, he is afflicted by another problem: his eyesight is troubled whenever he tries to write, even though he can see everything else well enough. After trying spectacles without success, he complains to Kempe of his "dysese." She explains that the devil is afflicting his eyesight to prevent him from writing, but that he should persevere to the extent that God will give him grace to do so. The results are miraculous: "When he came again to his book, he might see as well, it seemed to him, as ever he did before by daylight and by candlelight both" (5). He is cured of his reading malady, and can finally read the text without any interference from the idiosyncratic script of the first text.

This ordeal is both wondrous and humorous at the same time—a feat which Kempe accomplishes throughout her narrative, as we shall see in chapter 4. Beyond this, however, the story serves a a parable of the relation between the oral and written texts. The first written text was a disaster. Not only did it suffer from a mutilated syntax and grammar, but it was incomprehensible at the level of the letters. The "evilly" written letters with their queer shapes must have wreaked havoc with the most basic level of language, that is, the literal meaning.[8] While scholars question the first scribe's grasp of English, Kempe does not blame or doubt the first scribe's literacy. The distortion of the letters is not, in fact, a writing problem at all, but the fault of reading.

The second scribe's dyslexia becomes apparent after he agrees to try to read the text for a second time and finds that "hys eyes missed so that he might not see to make his letters nor could he see to mend his pen." His vexation is caused by his own doubts about Kempe, which prevented him from reading in the first place and which invite the devil's interference. It is only through Kempe's intercession and his reliance on God's grace that his eyesight is repaired. More importantly, his ability to read, and hence to write, has been brought about through Kempe's interdiction, that is, her insertion of her own voice between text and reader.[9] This interdiction becomes her authorizing practice, which not only inaugurates the book but resurfaces in the text whenever the scribe (or reader) loses faith in her authority. Our own ability as readers to read, like the scribe's, is thus contingent both on belief and on Kempe's interdiction.

The radical contingency of the mystic text is exposed in the introduction to her treatise. She claims to offer this treatise as a comfort to sinners and as a witness to Christ's mercy. The reader should profit from the stories of Christ's works, but only if "lack of charity be not our hindrance" (1). Charity enables the profitable reading of mystical texts, just as lack of charity leads to misreading, perhaps even incomprehension, such as the scribe's. Doubt, fear, and cowardice all condition the priest's inability to read as much as any physical disability does. In view of this notion of the act of reading, interdiction serves the very important function of guiding the charitable reader. It does not, however, insure the text against misreading by uncharitable readers.

There is an analogy to be made between this authorizing practice of interdiction and the origins of mystic speech itself. Mystical desire creates the place for mystic speech, enabling God's interdiction in the mystic's soul. In Kempe's own conversion, this speech interrupts first her madness and then her sleep in the form of melody. Christ's interdiction is the source of the mystic text and continues to engender it in a series of locutions with Kempe. Thus, Kempe's own interdiction in the writing process imitates the practice of mystic speech. It interjects itself into the writing and reading processes to authorize itself at the same time that it instructs the reader's desire. In contrast to the Monk of Farne, who seeks a way to analogize mystic speech to writing, Kempe defers the written text to her speech.

This practice of interdiction in the written text needs to be considered in the context of Kempe's illiteracy. Specifically, we need to consider Kempe's illiteracy in the context of medieval notions of literacy and its consequences for the writing of her book. Her knowledge of other mystical texts and her role in the production of her narrative are at stake in our assessment of her literacy.

As we have known for some time, illiteracy in the Middle Ages is not the same as illiteracy today. The chief difference is that medieval literacy described the ability to read, but not necessarily to write, Latin. Although the term *litteratus* had been used before 1300 to include the abilities to read, understand, compose, and express oneself in Latin, after 1300, it meant simply "a person with a minimal ability to read" Latin.[10] By the fifteenth century a London tradesman with this minimum ability could be included among the ranks of the churchmen and scholars, according to M. T. Clanchy.[11] Whether or not one achieved the status of clerk, many among the laity dealt in Latin documents or, at the very least, were able to recite some Latin, such as the *Pater Noster* and the *Credo*.[12]

Thus literacy was not a fixed or homogeneous category in the Middle Ages. "The literacy and latinity of an individual are in part elusive because the definition of both is necessarily a matter of degree," according to Franz H. Bäuml. Neither are these categories of literate and illiterate necessarily allied with particular classes. Rather, a new category somewhere in between these two arises for the exercising of social functions, that is, a quasi-literacy defined by its *access* to the written word, including Latin.[13] The increase of written documentation in England in the twelfth and thirteenth centuries required that different classes of people learn as much Latin as necessary to conduct business and legal transactions. This meant that those among these classes who had access to the written word were minimally literate.

However, it is also important to remember that although documents might have been written, the medieval recipient of the document often received it orally. A public document, a financial report, and even a legal charter would be read aloud for their "readers."[14] Not only were business and political documents read aloud, but spiritual works were commonly read during meals in late medieval households.[15] Thus reading and speaking were not mutually exclusive language practices. Reading was more often linked with hearing or listening than it was with seeing. The written word was viewed as an extension of the spoken word. John of Salisbury's comment on the relationship between voice and written text interestingly conveys this notion of reading:

> Littere autem, id est figure, primo vocum indices sunt; deinde rerum, quas anime per oculorum fenestras opponunt, et frequenter absentium dicta sine voce loquuntur.
>
> (Fundamentally, letters are shapes indicating voices. Hence they represent things which they bring to mind through the windows of the eyes. Frequently they speak voicelessly the utterances of the absent.)[16]

The power of letters to speak the utterances of those who are absent suggests the fundamentally vocal experience of the written text. For the mystical text this notion of the written word is especially appropriate, since it is precisely absent speech that the written text seeks to capture.

At the same time, medieval culture reserved for the written text the power of letters to conceal the sacred. As Margaret Aston reminds us in *Lollards and Reformers*, in spite of the increasingly "everydayness" of reading and writing, "we must not forget the ability of letters to be arcane: that is to conceal rather than to reveal: to be symbols that enclosed a mystery rather than transmitting a message."[17] While this very reverence for the written word was viewed as idolatrous by the Lollards, it continued to persist in the culture alongside Lollard attempts to demystify it by making it more accessible.

So far, this discussion of reading and Latinity has been focused on the laity, but it has not distinguished between lay men and lay women. Were lay women, such as Margery Kempe, also able to participate in literate culture through business transactions and religious instruction? Clanchy makes no distinction between *laica* and *laicus*. Among the nobility laywomen were often schooled in Latin so that they might teach their children. However, among other social classes, the mother's capacity for such instruction was doubtful. As Susan Groag Bell has pointed out, "Medieval laywomen's knowledge of Latin was even rarer than that of laymen."[18] Medieval lay-women's access to the written documents, such as those available to the reeve, the bailiff, or the juror, would have been rare. Although they partici-pated in some of the business and commercial ventures that men did, they were excluded from positions of social, political, and legal power.[19] Mar-gery Kempe's brief ventures into brewing and milling, even had they been successful, would probably not have provided her access to written docu-ments or to positions of social or economic significance.[20] Furthermore, religious instruction probably did not provide the access they needed to be considered minimally literate. The Latin "Instructions" for an English layman, for example, advise him, "Expound something in the vernacular which may edify your wife and others."[21] Thus women did not have the same access to written culture that men did except through Church ser-mons.

Kempe's dictation of her *Book* may thus be viewed in the context of this general exclusion of women from the written culture of commerce and public transactions. It is true that women were increasingly literate in the vernacular, as the numerous commissions for vernacular translations of Latin texts and wills of books to daughters attest.[22] Yet this does not necessarily mean that women could write. While our modern notion of literacy tends to pair the ability to write with the ability to read, the same is not true in the Middle Ages, for men or for women.

As Clanchy has pointed out, reading was more often associated with dictating than with writing in the Middle Ages. This was because writing was viewed as a separate skill in itself and one which required a good deal of sheer physical labor.[23] The act of composition was equated not with the physical act of writing, as it is today, but with dictation.[24] The branch of rhetoric which included the writing of letters was called *ars dictaminis*, "the art of dictation." This prevalence of dictating as a means of composition further links the oral word (and reading aloud) to the written text. At the same time, neither the reader nor the author needs to be intimately familiar with the written text itself.[25] Except in the case of monks, then, an author and a reader might both maintain a primarily oral/auditory relationship to the written text.

A vivid representation of the relationship of *dictator* to written text appears in the prologue to Peter of Poitiers's *Compendium*. In a roundel on the upper left corner of the page, Peter holds open a blank, ruled book with his right hand and points to the roundel on the opposite side of the page with his left. In the roundel on the right, a scribe with his back to Peter twists around to hear him, a knife poised in his left hand over a blank parchment while his right hand dips his quill in his inkhorn behind him. In between the two are the words of the prologue presumably being dictated.[26] The written text is created in the midst of the act of dictation. The blank parchments are associated with the oral texts themselves, both the oral text dictated by Peter and the aural text received by the scribe. John of Salisbury's notion of writing as speech which voicelessly proclaims the utterances of the absent is rendered quite literally in this illustration of the dictation of Peter of Poitiers's book.

It is not only for Margery Kempe, then, that the written text was both the creation and the expression of an oral text; it is true for manuscript culture as a whole. While the book in a print culture is dissociated from oral production and identified by its appearance, the book of manuscript culture is more an utterance, or a "proclamation." As Walter J. Ong reminds us, "What gave a work its identity consisted very little in what it looked like. The work was what it *said* when someone was reading it, converting it into sound in the imagination or, more likely, aloud."[27] For those who cannot read, such a conversionary understanding of the written text was not only fundamental: it constituted the very basis for differentiating the contents of books. Bridget of Sweden's vision of the book speaking from the pulpit provides a useful *trope* for the orality of written texts. As she tells it in her *Revelations*, the book in the pulpit shone as brightly as gold:

> Which boke, and the scriptur þer-of, was not write with ynke, bot ych worde in the boke was qwhik and spak it-self, as yf a man shuld say, doo thys or that, and anone it wer do with spekyng of the word. No man redde the scriptur of that boke, bot what euer that scriptur contened, all was see in the pulpyte, . . .[28]

(This book, and the scripture thereof, was not written with ink, but each word in the book was alive and spoke itself, as if a man were to say, do this or that, and immediately it were done with the speaking of the word. No man read the writing of that book, but whatever was contained in the writing, all of it was seen in the pulpit, . . .)

The written word here proclaims and bodies forth before the gaze of the reader/listener. Each word is alive and "speaks itself," thereby producing action in the world. Reading is akin to attending to speech-acts.

In the context of this notion of the speaking text and the medieval equation of dictation and composition, Margery Kempe's authorship is hardly anomalous. Why, then, her opening defense of her own interdictive powers over the written text? Apparently, Kempe feels it necessary to justify her own dictation of the book as much as modern scholars insist upon questioning her authorship. One of the reasons for Kempe's insecurity has already been suggested: that is, her own exclusion from written culture demanded that she justify her intrusion. A second reason is that, in spite of the fundamentally oral modes of composing and reading the written text, modes of authorizing a text draw upon a written tradition. While the methods of inscribing *auctores* into a text differ among literary, theological, and exegetical works, the sources (even if they are fictional) are written. The written tradition of *auctoritas* was conceived of as both continuous and hierarchically arranged, with the Scripture at the top and the works of pagan philosophers and poets at the bottom.[29]

Kempe's anxiety about the oral text of her treatise is rooted in the subtext of the medieval written text, the *auctoritas*. This subtext gives cause for further anxiety because it is a patently male one. Any medieval woman author would have had to contend with this gendered, authorizing tradition from which she was excluded. This subtext, in turn, practices what Robert Hanning has termed "textual harassment" in the sense that the woman author is by definition excluded from the very operation of textual authority.[30] This subtextual authorization is not only unavailable to Kempe: it is positively hostile to women. The medieval antifeminist tradition, consisting of scriptural, exegetical, and literary works, explicitly forbids women from teaching or preaching, as we shall see. Kempe is forced to seek an alternative authorization for her mystical treatise at the same time that she must justify her own voice. Because woman's voice is censured from public discourse, particularly the discourses of preaching and instruction, Kempe needs to create a place for her own voice in the text and in the world.

As we saw in chapter 2, the mystic always endeavors to verify the speech-acts in her soul, seeking signs that they come from God and that they produce acts of contrition, devotion, and compassion. Kempe's *Book* places marked emphasis on these speech-acts and hearing through what she calls "dalliance" and "colloquies" with Christ.[31] Her preface cites the "wonderful speeches and dalliance which our Lord spake and dallied to her soul" which should cause such wonder and doubt among her fellow townspeople (2–3). These same holy speeches constitute her *secretys* which she *shows* to clerics. Her self-authorization proceeds from divine locution in the soul to showing her *secretys* to clerics and holy men, and ultimately, to her readers. Her method of authorizing her own voice, then, might be construed as a series of showings of the speech-acts in her soul. These showings, in turn, occur in the form of further locutions, even dalliances, with clerics.[32]

Christ instructs Kempe to "speak boldly in my name in the name of Jesus, for they [his speeches] are no lies" (26). His authorization of Kempe's speech, however, is continually contested by the clerks and doctors of divinity who oppose her. Her ability to speak boldly and well about holy subjects nevertheless astounds some of the holy men she encounters. When Kempe visits Richard of Caister, the Vicar of St. Stephens in Norwich, in order to speak with him, he responds with skepticism:

> Benedicite. What cowd a woman ocupyn on owyr er tweyn owyrs in þe lofe of owyr Lord? I xal neuyr ete mete tyl I wete what ʒe kan sey of owyr Lord God þe tyme of an owyr (38).

> (Bless us. How could a woman occupy an hour or two in the love of our Lord? I shall never eat meat until I know what you can say of our Lord God during the space of one hour.)

Kempe then "showed him all the words which God had revealed to her in her soul." Not only does Kempe occupy an hour or two with her speech, but she convinces the vicar that she is learned in the law of God and visited by the grace of the Holy Ghost(40).

Even more impressed with Kempe's speech is Thomas Marchale who invited Kempe to meals "to hear her dalliance." He is so drawn to her "good words" that he becomes a new man, weeping with tears of contrition and compunction (108). Earlier in the book, Kempe visits William Southfield, a White Friar of Norwich, to "show him the grace that God wrought in her" and to determine whether visions were illusions or not (41). Her showing elicits the friar's assurance that her mystical experience is the working of the

Holy Ghost in her soul. In both cases dalliance serves as Kempe's way of converting bold speech into action at the same time that it converts divine speech into showing. In this sense, her showing functions as oral proof of the veracity of divine speech in her soul.

The most significant endorsement of Kempe's visions comes from Julian of Norwich. Kempe shows Julian "very many holy speeches and dalliance that our Lord spoke to her soul" to determine whether there is any deceit in these spiritual locutions. Julian instructs Kempe to measure these experiences according to the worship they accrue to God and the profit to her fellow Christians. She also justifies Kempe's tears as tokens of the Holy Spirit in her soul. Finally, Julian encourages Kempe, "Set all your trust in God and fear not the language of the world" (43). Kempe's "holy dalyawns" and "comownyng" in the love of God with Julian last several days, providing a kind of oral testimony to the dalliance of God in Kempe's soul. Julian's advice that Kempe not fear the language of the world is a significant one, for it advocates the divine locutions in the soul—dalliance—over and against all those speeches and writings which threaten to silence her.

Kempe's assertion of her own right to speak and teach directly challenges the "language of the world," including the writing of the Church Fathers and the clerical prerogative of speech. This challenge is complicated by the fact that it runs dangerously close to the boundaries of the Lollard heresy in fifteenth-century England. The prescriptions against woman's speech in scriptural and patristic writing are invoked to protect the clerical prerogative to preach.

The most famous scriptural text used to support women's silence is that of St. Paul: "But I suffer not a woman to teach, nor to use authority over the man: but to be in silence. For Adam was first formed; then Eve. And Adam was not seduced, but woman being seduced, was in the transgression" (I Tim. 2:12–14). Various treatises on preaching further reinforce Paul's prohibition of women's assuming the pulpit, signifying as it does, a reversal in the natural hierarchy which leads to the downfall of humanity. In a later elaboration of St. Paul's doctrine by the Dominican Humbert de Romans (d. 1277), Eve herself becomes a sort of false priest who, being corrupted in her own soul, provokes immorality in the souls of others. "'She spoke but once,'" he quotes Bernard, "'and threw the whole world into disorder.'"[33]

Lollard activity in England during the fourteenth and fifteenth centuries circulated the antifeminist fears of woman's speech. One English preacher in Kempe's time, outraged over the growing number of laymen and -women who were usurping the clerical prerogative to read, interpret, and spread the Gospel, exclaimed: "Behold now we see so great a scattering of the Gospel, that simple men & women and those accounted ignorant laymen [*laici ydiote*] in the reputation of men, write and study the Gospel, as far as they can & know how, teach and scatter the Word of God."[34] Not only were these laywomen and men reading and scattering the gospel, but they were being so presumptuous as to dispute clerks in public.[35]

Records from the diocese of Norwich indicate that women Lollards were in fact "scattering the Gospel" in English translation.[36] While Lollards did not explicitly advocate that women should become preachers, they believed that any lay person could preach and teach the gospel and that all good people, even the *laici ydiote*, were priests.[37] In the words of one woman Lollard, Hawisia Moone, "every man and every woman beyng in good lyf oute of synne is as good prest and hath [as] muche poar of God in al thynges as ony prest ordred, be he pope or bisshop." The publicity of the Lollard belief in lay preaching can be inferred from Archbishop Courtenay's alarm at the Leicester Lollards, who argued that "any layman can preach and teach the gospel anywhere."[38] While Lollards were being tried and sometimes burnt at the stake at Smithfield, Parliament tried to curb the activities of unlicensed preachers by issuing the statute, *De heretico comburendo*, which called for their punishment.[39]

Kempe's own preaching and teaching raise the specter of Lollardy, causing townspeople to curse her and clerics to accuse her of Lollard beliefs.[40] After Kempe criticizes some clerics at Lambeth for swearing, she is confronted with an angry townswoman who says, "I wish you were in Smithfield, and I would carry a fagot to burn you with; it is a pity that you live" (36). In another encounter with a group of Canterbury monks, she is followed out of the monastery by the same monks who taunt her, "You shall be burned, false Lollard. Here is a cartful of thorns to burn you with" (28). They are prepared to make good their threat to the encouragement of the Canterbury townspeople until she is rescued by two young men. Her own trembling, quaking, and standing stock still indicate that she, at least, believes their threats and is very much afraid of them.

Kempe's efforts to authorize her own voice are thus very politicized and dangerous. She must assert her own orthodoxy as a Christian at the same time that she argues for her right to speak. Obviously, this is a contradiction which continually threatens to brand her as a Lollard. She has few *auctores* whose writings she can bring to her own defense. If she tries to quote Scriptures, she again incriminates herself, for Lollards were said to have been able to read English translations of the Bible.[41] In fact, when Kempe does quote Luke to justify her speech to the Archbishop of York and his ministers, the clerics respond in unison: "Ah, sir, . . . we know well that she has a devil within her, for she speaks of the Gospel" (126). Access to vernacular translations of the gospels was tantamount to possession by the devil. Clearly, Kempe's access to the written word, like her bold speech, is both controversial and dangerous.

At issue in Kempe's first arraignment before Henry Bowet, Archbishop of York, is her publicity and her speech. The clerics declare their fears quite openly:

> We knowyn wel þat sche can þe Articles of þe Feith, but we wil not suffyr hir to dwellyn a-mong vs, for þe pepil hath gret feyth in hir dalyawnce, and perauentur sche myth peruertyn summe of hem (125).

> (We know well that she knows the Articles of Faith, but we will not suffer her to dwell among us, for the people have great faith in her dalliance, and she might by chance pervert some of them.)

Her knowledge and belief in the Articles of Faith seem to be a ruse for her "dalyawnce" by which she perverts her listeners. The choice of words here—"dalyawnce"—is crucial, since dalliance is the source of her mystical and authorial credibility, as we have seen. The charges of the clerics echo the fears of Humbert de Romans and St. Bernard for the consequences of woman's speech. The archbishop attempts to assuage their fears by demanding that Kempe swear she will neither teach nor challenge the people of his diocese.

Kempe not only refuses to swear: she makes a case for her right to speak which is key to her authorization of herself as a mystic and her book as a whole. She defends her speech by citing a passage from Luke 9:27–28:

> And also þe Gospel makyth mencyon þat, whan þe woman had herd owr Lord prechyd, sche cam be-forn hym wyth a lowde voys & seyd, 'Blyssed be þe wombe þat þe bar & þe tetys þat ӡaf þe sowkyn.' Þan owr Lord seyd a-ӡen to hir, 'Forsoþe so ar þei blissed þat heryn þe word of God and kepyn it.' And þerfor, sir, me thynkyth þat þe Gospel ӡeuyth me leue to spekyn of God (126).

> (And also the Gospel makes mention that, when the woman had heard our Lord preach, she came before him with a loud voice and said, 'Blessed be the womb which bore you and the teats which gave you suck.' Then our Lord responded to her, 'In truth so are they blessed who hear the word of God and keep it.' And therefore, sir, it seems to me that the Gospel gives me leave to speak of God.)

What is curious is that the Gospel passage does not explicitly endorse woman's speech, but rather her "hearing and keeping" of the word of God. Kempe's gloss of Luke seems rather forced and self-serving. However, there is an interesting precedent for Kempe's interpretation of Luke from a contemporary of hers. The self-confessed Lollard William Brute cites precisely the same passage in his argument for women's right to preach. His extensive gloss of the passage provides us with evidence of the Lollard argument for women preachers, and perhaps, of the subtext of Kempe's gloss. While acknowledging Paul's virtual command that women be silent listeners rather than teachers of the Word, Brute nevertheless makes a clever argument for women preachers:

> Docere et predicare verbum Dei competit sacerdotibus et ad hoc tam a Cristo quam ab apostolis sunt in ecclesia ordinati, et Paulus docet mulieres in silencio discere cum omni subieccione et docere mulieri non permittit neque dominari in virum. Quod tamen non possunt docere neque in virum dominari non dicit Paulus, nec ego audeo affirmare, cum mulieres, sancte virgines, constanter predicarunt verbum Dei et multos ad fidem converterunt sacerdotibus tunc non audentibus loqui verbum, et an predicare verbum Dei sit maius vel minus vel equale cum ministracione corporis Cristi Deus novit qui respondit mulieri dicenti: 'Beatus venter qui te portavit et ubera que suxisti dicendo quin ymmo beati qui audiunt verbum Dei et custodiunt illud,' si beati qui audiunt et custodiunt, magis beati qui predicant et custodiunt verbum Dei, quoniam beacius est magis dare quam accipere.[42]

> (Teaching and preaching the Word of God belongs to the priests and moreover, they are ordained in the Church as much by Christ as by his apostles. Paul teaches that women learn in silence with all subjection and that it is not permitted to woman to teach nor to have mastery over a man. Because, nevertheless, Paul does not say they are not able to teach nor to dominate a man, neither do I venture to affirm it, since women, holy virgins, have constantly preached the word of God and converted many to the faith at times when priests were too faint-hearted to speak the word. God considered the question of whether preaching the word is superior, inferior, or equal to the administration of the body of Christ, when he responded to the woman who said, 'Blessed be the womb that bore you and the breasts which gave you suck,' saying, 'Rather, blessed are they who hear the word of God and keep it.' If they are blessed who hear and keep the word of God, they are even more blessed who preach and keep it, because it is more blessed to give than to receive.)

A two-fold strategy emerges from Brute's defense of women's preaching. Brute negotiates the Pauline prohibition of women's speech by distinguishing between what women are capable of and what they are permitted, between what Paul explicitly forbids and what he fails to affirm. The example of teaching virgins contradicts Paul's prohibition, allowing Brute to insert exceptions to Paul's rule. His second strategy is to conflate the teaching that "it is more blessed to give than to receive" with the Christ's answer to the woman, rendering preaching the word more blessed than hearing and keeping it. In this way, Brute circumvents Paul's prohibition of women preachers.

Brute's defense helps to elucidate Kempe's own argument for her right to speak. Her "reading" of Luke and her assertion of her own teachings could be labeled Lollard. They are, in fact, Lollard arguments. She further threatens to speak of God "until the Pope and Holy Church ordain that no man shall be so bold as to speak of God." However, she does make a distinction between teaching and preaching which Lollards do not make. When a cleric produces the inevitable passage from St. Paul that "no woman should preach," she answers, "I preach not, sir, I come into no pulpit. I use but communication and good words, and that will I do while I live" (126). Kempe may seem to be quibbling here between preaching—coming into the pulpit—and teaching in order to rescue herself from the damning Pauline edict. Her distinction is not entirely original, though. In the beginning of the popular fifteenth-century treatise, *Speculum Christiani*, the author marks similar boundaries between preaching and teaching:

> A Grete differens es be-twene prechynge and techynge. Prechynge es in a place where es clepynge to-gedyr or foluynge of pepyl in holy dayes in churches or othe[r] certeyn places and tymes ordened ther-to. And it longeth to hem that been ordeynede ther-to, the whych haue iurediccion and auctorite, and to noon othyr. Techynge is that eche body may enforme and teche hys brothyr in euery place and in conable tyme, os he seeth that it be spedful. For this es a gostly almesdede, to whych euery man es bounde that hath cunnynge.[43]

> (There is a great difference between preaching and teaching. Preaching occurs in a place where there is a summoning together or following of people on holy days in churches or other special places and times ordained thereto. And it belongs to them who are thereto ordained, who have jurisdiction and authority, and to no one else. Teaching means that each body may inform and teach his brother in every place and at a suitable time, as he sees it necessary. For this is a spiritual almsdeed, to which every man who possesses cunning is bound.)

Whether or not the author meant to include women among those bound to the spiritual almsdeed of teaching, his argument is very similar to Kempe's. The basic difference between teaching and preaching is the institutionalization of the words by means of specified places, times, and circumstances.

The authority and jurisdiction of preaching belongs, the *Speculum Christiani* author is quick to remark, only to ordained priests. Teaching confers no such authority or jurisdiction on its speaker, yet it occupies the dangerously vast position of any place which is outside the pulpit. Kempe's appeal to this argument allows her to claim that crucial positionality of the mystic voice as separate from the magisterium one, and as legitimate in the eyes of God. It is also, then, a marginal, straying position which threatens to blur the boundaries between authorized and heretical speech.

Obviously, such a distinction does not diminish the threat which her speech poses for the clerics who oppose her and the archbishop, who merely wishes his diocese to be left in peace. In fact, it renders her speech immune from their authority and jurisdiction. We can observe clerical frustration when one monk curses her, saying that he wished she were closed up in a house of stone so that no man could speak with her (27), or when some men of Beverley gently suggest that she return to spinning and carding (129). Attempts to silence Kempe, however, are not always so innocuous. The Steward of Leicester tries to intimidate Kempe by speaking to her in Latin, and when that fails, by threatening to rape her (112–13).

Kempe's argument for woman's speech makes use of a popular debate of her time. But she is not the last to use the Lucan passage to authorize her own speech. In her *Book of the City of Ladies*, Christine de Pizan in the fifteenth century searches likewise for an argument for woman's speech which would refute the cultural idioms identifying it as "blameworthy and of such small authority." The allegorical figure of Reason, who appears to the despairing Christine, points to Christ's favoring of woman's speech by having his resurrection announced by a woman, Mary Magdalene, as well as to other examples from the Gospels. She concludes her testimony to woman's blessed speech with the same passage from Luke cited by Kempe. Interestingly, Christine does not include Christ's response, which is so crucial to Brute's exegesis of the passage. Instead she considers the woman's speech itself as a model of wisdom, boldness, and "great force of will." From this and her other examples she infers, "Thus you can understand, fair sweet friend, God has demonstrated that He has truly placed language in women's mouths so that He might be thereby served."[44]

This, too, is the lesson of Kempe's disputation with the clerics of York. Christ confers authority on women's speech when he blesses those "who hear the word and keep it." This authority, in turn, privileges the spoken word over the written word. Her defense of her own "bold speech" provides Kempe a means of interdicting the written tradition of *auctoritas* which prohibits that speech. Both in her exchanges with Church authorities and in her mystical locutions, Kempe's voice "speaks between" the written antifeminist tradition and the written text of her own life, locating divine locution, and hence, true authority, in the place where she—and not the written text—is. True authority is always displaced elsewhere than the written text or textual tradition. Dalliance replaces *auctoritas* as the foundation of authorship and textual authority.

Dalliance also intercedes in the written traditions in Kempe's *Book*, as is the case with Kempe's vision of St. Paul, the primary scriptural *auctoritas* against woman's speech. In one of Christ's colloquies of reassurance, He thanks Kempe for her suffering and particularly for her weeping. As consolation for the hostility she endures, Christ reminds her, he once sent St. Paul to her:

> Dowtyr, I sent onys Seynt Powyl vn-to þe for to strengthyn þe & comfortyn þe þat þu schuldist boldly spekyn in my name fro þat day forward. And Seynt Powle seyd vn-to þe þat þu haddyst suffyrd mech tribulacyon for cawse of hys wrytyng, & he behyte þe þat þu xuldist han as meche grace þer-a-ȝens for hys lofe as euyr þu haddist schame er reprefe for hys lofe (160).

> (Daughter, I once sent Saint Paul to you to strengthen you and comfort you in order that you should boldly speak in my name from that day forward. And Saint Paul said to you that you had suffered much tribulation because of his writing, and he promised you that you should have as much grace in return for his love as ever you had shame or reproof for his love.)

We do not learn which writings of St. Paul's have caused Kempe so much tribulation, but his encouragement of Kempe to "boldly speak in my name from that day forward" points to the passage from 1 Timothy quoted earlier. Paul's endorsement of Kempe's bold speech undermines those very writings which have caused her suffering. In effect, he interdicts his own writings in order to authorize Kempe's speech. Ironically, the same Pauline texts so often cited as authorities against woman's speech become for Kempe the source of her grace. She places the textual harassment experienced by all women writers at her own disposal as evidence of her grace, and hence her authority. While Julian had urged her not to fear the language of this world, Paul assures her that she need not heed the writings of this world that would silence her bold speech.

Interdiction is the practice by which Kempe establishes and justifies her own voice within the text. Her locutions with St. Paul and Christ occur in between the written texts of her life and the experience, just as her own dictation intercedes between the acts of reading and writing. Interdiction performs that "dispersing gesture" which Cixous attributes to women's writing—one which "breaks with explanation, interpretation, and all the authorities pinpointing localization." Kempe dislocates herself as author by breaking with written authority. In the place of textual authority she substitutes the *volo* of mystical desire which gives habitation to her speech.

This does not mean, however, that Kempe makes no reference to textual authorities; in fact, her *Book* does draw upon spiritual texts, and, oddly enough, she clearly views it in the context of a Latin tradition. On two separate occasions in her *Book*, a collection of texts is cited in connection with Kempe's own spiritual practices, including the *Scala Perfectionis* by Walter Hilton, the *Liber Revelationum Celestium S. Birgitta* of St. Bridget, Rolle's *Incendium Amoris* and the Pseudo-Bonaventure text, *Stimulus Amoris*.[45] As we have seen, some scholars would simply attribute these Latin sources to Kempe's scribe.[46] Meech and Allen note that Kempe could have known these Latin works only through "extemporaneous translations" by the priest who read to her over a period of seven or eight years or through actual English translations.[47]

These references are further complicated by Kempe's own testimonies. She asks the Steward of Leicester to direct his questions to her in English instead of Latin because she cannot understand it (113). Yet when another clerk asks her what the biblical command, "Crescite & multiplicamini," means in order to see whether she advocates the heretical interpretation of this passage to justify free love, she responds without difficulty (121). In Book II, when she is chided for her weeping, she quotes the Latin Psalm 126:5 and 6: " 'Qui seminant in lacrimis' & *cetera* 'euntes ibant & flebant' & *cetera*, and swech oþer" (235). She clearly understands some Latin phrases and scriptural texts even if she cannot speak or hear in Latin. Nevertheless, it is remarkable in her book that Latin seems to comprehend her whether she comprehends it or not. A German priest who becomes Kempe's confessor in Rome understands no English, yet he is able to translate Kempe's stories into Latin to the astonishment of a group of her fellow pilgrims (97).

Though we cannot know how much Latin Kempe knew, neither can we ignore the Latinity of her book. We need to be aware of the fact that the priest who read to her probably read from Latin texts of Hilton, Rolle, and Bridget even if he then translated or paraphrased his readings. Kempe's own spirituality seems to be most markedly influenced by the writings of Richard Rolle, particularly the *Incendium Amoris*. This is one of the works which Kempe had read to her before the Latin text was translated into Middle English by Richard Misyn in 1434–35.[48] In fact, traces of Rolle's

Latin work survive in Kempe's book, not only in her images and mystical concepts but in her mystical idioms.

Kempe's text frequently makes reference to the "fire of love," a very common mystical idea attributed to Rolle in the *Incendium Amoris*.[49] Early in her book, she describes how her heart was consumed by the "ardowr of lofe." Since most other references are made to the fire, rather than the ardor, of love, Hope Emily Allen speculates that maybe Kempe is making a distinction between two types of fires (271n). Yet a reading of the Latin text of Rolle's treatise reveals that the Latin *ardor* was often used as a synonym for *ignis* (fire) and *amor* (love). Rolle explains in his prologue that he uses *ignis* metaphorically to describe *ardor*, the flame or heat of love.[50] It is interesting to note that Misyn translates the *ardor* of the Latin text as "hete," "lufe," and "flaume," but not the English derivative, "ardor." Clearly, more than one translation of the Latin text is possible in Middle English. Kempe's use of the word "ardowr" follows the Latin more closely than Misyn's does, even though the word in Middle English does not have the same meaning as the Latin word. This could be the result of a literal translation of the Latin, either the priest's or her own. Whichever is the case, this is just one example of the Latin residues in Kempe's text.

Other borrowings from Rolle likewise recall the Latin text of the *Incendium Amoris*. Kempe's description of the first visitation of the fire of love, for example, is very close to Rolle's description of the same in his prologue. Kempe experiences the fire she feels in her breast and heart as truly "as a man would feel the material fire if he put his hand or his finger in it" (88). This material analogy is provided by Rolle as well in his prologue and in his English work, *The Form of Living*.[51] In this case, Kempe's use of Rolle could have come from either his Latin or his English writings.

She also renders the Rollean experience of the fire of love in her use of the verb "languryn." Rolle's fullest explication of the mystical lover's languor appears again in the *Incendium Amoris*. His explication of languishing comes from the declaration from the Song of Songs 5:8: "I adjure you, O daughters of Jerusalem, if you find my beloved, that you tell him that I languish for love." Rolle attributes this languishing to the lover's abundant love, which lacks the object of his love. More importantly, this languishing accompanies the fire of love, according to Rolle:

Amoris ergo diuini incendii est mentem quam capit uulnerare: ut dicat, 'Uulnerata sum ego caritate,' et eciam languidam facere pro amore, (unde dicitur *Amore langueo*,) et inebriare: ut sic tendat ad dilectum, quod sui ipsius et omnium rerum obliuiscatur preter Christum.[52]

(Therefore it is the mind which is wounded by the fire of divine love that is meant by, "I am wounded with love." Also when one is made languid and intoxicated for love, it is said, "I languish for love." For this is how one strives towards the beloved to the extent that he forgets himself and all things apart from Christ.)

Elsewhere in his Latin works, Rolle likewise attributes this "languor" to the wounding of the heart and the unsatisfied longing of the lover for his beloved.[53] Kempe's understanding of mystical languor closely approaches Rolle's, for she reserves the English verb *languren* only for her experience of the terrible lack of the object of her love. When she desires to be rid of the world, Christ instructs her that she must remain and "languren in lofe" (20). Her "languor" is often triggered by the "gret sowndys & gret melodijs" reminding her of Heaven and her own impatience for it (185). She needs only to hear the words uttered in a sermon, "Owr Lord Ihesu langurith for lofe" to be reduced to boisterous weeping (185). Her choice of words again invokes the Latin works of Rolle to her text. It is interesting to note that Kempe uses the verb "languryn" where the Middle English translation of the *Incendium Amoris* consistently translates *langueo* into "longyn."[54] Her choice of the English cognate for the Latin words *languor* and *ardor* echoes Rolle more directly than does the Middle English translation by Misyn.

Kempe's clearest echoes of Rolle occur in her metaphorical renderings of mystical union in terms of song or melody and smell. Rolle's three-fold distinction among the stages of mystical ascent—*calor*, *dulcor*, and *canor*, fire, sweetness, and song—is made in his *Incendium Amoris*, although it appears in his Middle English works as well.[55] Kempe experiences the heavenly melody described by Rolle in his Latin work when she awakens in the middle of the night to "a sound of melody so sweet and delectable, she thought, as though she were in Paradise" (11). She later speaks of the "sowndys & melodijs" which she heard over a period of twenty-five years and which were so loud as to interfere with her conversations with people (87–88). These mystical references compare with Rolle's account of his own experience while he is reading the Psalms of a "suavitatem inuisibilis melodie" (sweet invisible melody) which overwhelms him. Not only does the divine voice become transformed into this invisible music, but the human response is also converted into song.[56]

More significant is Kempe's reference to the heavenly smells, because she could have been familiar with this mystical sensation in Rolle only through his Latin works.[57] The mystical comfort Kempe receives comes in the form of "sweet smells" which exceed all earthly odors and the power of speech to describe (87). Christ also offers Kempe the comfort of knowing that at her death he will remove body from soul "with great mirth and melody, with sweet smells and good odors" (51). The mysterious odors of divine visitation infuse Rolle's *Melos Amoris* as they do few of his other Latin or English works.[58] While these heavenly scents may be found in continental mysticism, in England they are almost exclusively characteristic of Rolle and Kempe.

This brief overview suggests that Kempe draws upon the Latin writings of Richard Rolle to characterize her mystical experiences. Her references to divine fragrances, heavenly melodies, and the "ardor" and "languor" of love are only a few examples of the Latinity of her *Book*. Other examples from Hilton, Pseudo-Bonaventure, Bridget's *Liber Revelationum Celestium*, and the *Stimulus Amoris* need to be explored more seriously in Kempe's text than they have been previously. Although the *Book*'s Latinity rarely surfaces, we can observe the process in the scribe's own authorization of Kempe's tears. After suffering from doubt about Kempe's tears because of a friar's preaching against her, the scribe reads several works which restore his faith in her, including the biography of Marie d'Oignies and the *Stimulus Amoris*. The scribe refers to the Pseudo-Bonaventure text, *Stimulus Amoris*, by its English title, "Þe Prykke of Lofe." Walter Hilton translated this Latin work into English using the same title, but the scribe's quotation in Middle English actually corresponds more closely to the Latin than it does to the English text. Compare the Middle English version with the Latin:

> A, Lord, what xal I mor noysen er cryen? Þu lettyst & þu comyst not, & I, wery & ouyrcome thorw desyr, begynne for to maddyn, for lofe gouernyth me & not reson. I renne wyth hasty cowrs wher-þat-euyr þu wylte. I bowe, Lord, þei þat se me irkyn and rewyn, not knowyng me drunkyn wyth þi lofe. Lord, þei seyn 'Lo, ȝen wood man cryeth in þe stretys,' but how meche is þe desyr of myn hert þei parceyue not (154).

> (Sed quid vociferabor amplius? Tardas, et non venis, et jam lassatus desiderio incipio insanire. Amor regit, et non ratio, et curro cum impetu, quocumque me volueris inclinare. Nam qui me vident, derident, et quod tuo amore sim ebrius, non cognoscunt. Dicunt enim: Quid iste insanus vociferatur in plateis? Et quantum sit desiderium non advertunt.)[59]

The scribe seems to be translating from the Latin rather than quoting from Hilton's Middle English translation, for there are some distinct differences in Hilton. Instead of the clause, "I run with a hasty course wherever you wish," Hilton's text has "I run with great noise witherso my love inclines." Further, Hilton inserts a phrase found in none of the Latin texts, substituting for "desire" "desire of Jesus burneth in my heart."[60] Although the Latin text cannot be established conclusively as a source for the scribe's quotation, it can be seriously considered. It is possible that he translates from a text at hand as he writes this portion of the narrative. Since Kempe mentions the Latin title elsewhere, there is a good chance she was familiar with both.[61]

We have evidence that the scribe's memory of another Latin text fails him even though there is a clear resemblance between the Middle English and its source. The story of Marie d'Oignies, like the Pseudo-Bonaventure text, restores the scribe's faith in Kempe's tears. He quotes the *incipit* of chapter 18 and paraphrases the contents of chapter 19 of Jacques de Vitry's *Vita Maria Oigniacensis*. A comparison of the Latin source and the scribe's recollection again reveals a correlation:

> Of þe plentyuows grace of hir teerys he tretyth specyaly . . . in þe xix capitulo wher he tellyth how sche, at þe request of a preyste þat he xulde not be turbelyd ne distrawt in hys Messe wyth hir wepyng & hir sobbyng, went owt at þe chirche-dor, wyth lowde voyse crying þat sche myth not restreyn hir þerfro. & owr Lord also visityd þe preyste beyng at Messe wyth swech grace & wyth sweche deuocyon whan he xulde redyn þe Holy Gospel þat he wept wondirly so þat he wett hys vestiment & ornamentys of þe awter & myth not mesuryn hys wepyng ne hys sobbyng, it was so habundawnt, ne he myth not restreyn it ne wel stande þerwyth at þe awter (153).

> (Quadam autem die ante Parasceven, cum jam imminente Christi Passione majori lacrymarum imbre, cum suspiriis et singultibus, se cum Domino mactare inchoasset; quidam de Sacerdotibus ecclesiae eam ut oraret cum silentio, et lacrymas cohiberet, quasi blande increpando hortabatur. Illa . . . impossibilitatis [*sic*] suae conscia, egressa clam ab ecclesia in loco secreto et ab omnibus remoto se abscondit, impetravitque a Domino cum lacrymis, ut praedicto Sacerdoti ostenderet, quia non est in homine lacrymarum impetum retinere, quando flante spiritu vehementi fluunt aquae.)[62]

The basic elements of de Vitry's story survive in Kempe's version, including the priest's prohibition against Marie's weeping, her inability to restrain her tears which forces her to leave the church, and, finally, the priest's own experience of uncontrollable tears. Yet the Middle English here does not follow the Latin syntax and wording the way the previous passage did. Is this an example of the scribe's faulty memory, or is he reading from a different text of Marie's life?

Kempe offers a parenthetical explanation which, because it is so uncharacteristic, should alert us to an important distinction between texts alluded to by memory, which need justification, and texts more directly available, which need no justification:

> Than þe preste whech wrot þis tretys . . . had seyn & red þe mater beforn-wretyn [the story of Marie d'Oignies] meche mor seryowslech & expres-siowslech þan it is wretyn in þis tretys (for her is but a lityl of þe effect þerof, for he had not ryth cler mende of þe sayd mater whan he wrot þis tretys, & þerfor he wrote þe lesse þerof) (153).

> (Then the priest who wrote this treatise . . . had seen and read the matter before written [the story of Marie d'Oignies] much more seriously and in more detail than is written in this treatise [for here is but a little of the story's meaning, because he did not have a very clear memory of the said matter when he wrote this treatise, and therefore he wrote less about it.])

Kempe points out two important things in this passage, both of which are instructive as exceptions to the rule of her dictation. First, the story of Marie d'Oignies is the scribe's and not her own; and second, the written account is but a trace of the Latin story because the scribe's recollection was "not ryth cler." The clear attribution of the Latin texts to the scribe's reading (and not Kempe's), along with her apology for his faulty memory, suggests by way of exception her own relationship as author to her text and to her Latin sources. The Latin traces of Rolle's works are not the result of scribal mediation, nor do they reflect the efforts of Kempe to authorize her own discourse. Rather, they represent Kempe's own inscription of the Latin culture which excludes her into her text by way of translation. At the same time that her own text echoes Rolle, it rejects Latinity and authoriza-tion of written discourse altogether.

The story of Marie d'Oignies and the translation from the *Stimulus Amoris* are used specifically to authorize Kempe for the scribe's sake. He has doubts about her weeping and her credibility, and therefore it is he who needs the comfort of these Latin texts to restore his faith in her. In a curious way these authorities serve not as signs of textual or authorial validity but as guides for reading Kempe's text. Kempe's own scribe is both her *scriptor* and her reader. In order to carry out his function as *scriptor*, he must learn to be a good reader. When he loses faith in Kempe, he also loses his ability to read, and hence to write, as we saw in the dictation scenario described in the *Book*'s prologue. In this case, his faith and his ability to read are restored through the application of Latin texts—Marie's *Vita* and the *Stimulus Amoris*—as glosses to Kempe's life. Jacques de Vitry's life of Marie allows the scribe to accept Kempe's tears by means of comparison:

Þan he leuyd wel þat þe good woman, whech he had be-forn lityl affeccyon to, myth not restreyn hir wepyng, hir sobbyng, ne hir cryyng, whech felt meche mor plente of grace þan euyr dede he wyth-owtyn any comparison" (153).

(Then he believed well that the good woman, whom he had had little affection for earlier, was not able to restrain her weeping, her sobbing, nor her crying, that she felt much more fullness of grace than he ever had, without comparison.)

Likewise, the passage quoted from the *Stimulus Amoris* moved him to believe in Kempe (154). These Latin references are aimed at resolving the reader's doubt and restoring his/her credence in the author.

The Latinity of Kempe's text functions to direct her readers by resolving their doubts as she did the scribe's. While she never privileges this Latinity, she nevertheless inscribes it in her text in order to guide and direct readers, to jar their lapsed faith and renew their reading. Even where these Latin texts are not explicitly translated by the scribe, as they are in the passages described above, they "speak" to a readership that is literate in Latin and that relies on Latinity as a hermeneutic.

Interlinear and marginal annotations in Kempe's *Book* suggest that it was read (as well as dictated) in the context of a Latin archive of mystical texts. Four different sets of late medieval notations appear in the text of *The Book of Margery Kempe*. Three of these in brown ink are thought to be earlier than the fourth set, which appear in red ink in the manuscript. The three sets of brown annotations are chiefly emendatory, with a few merely calling attention to passages with the symbol *n* for *nota*.[63] The red annotations, by contrast, consist of commentary, summary, and emphasis of specific passages of the text. Written in a late fifteenth- or early sixteenth-century hand probably at the Carthusian monastery of Mount Grace where this manuscript was housed, these annotations may be construed as one late medieval reading of the text.

Among the marginal annotations are several Latin references to the fire of love and to Richard Rolle specifically. Textual allusions to the "flawme of fyer" and the "fyer of loue brennyng in her brest" are attributed by the reader to "R. hampall" and labeled *ignis divini amoris*. The reader's identification of Kempe's mystical experience with the experiences of the Latin works and concepts of Rolle is significant, since he does not always use Latin labels or commentary.[64]

Next to another passage where Kempe describes herself as weeping uncontrollably and turning as blue as lead, the reader has written *langor amoris*. This concept, as we saw earlier, comes from Rolle and entails the lover's longing for his or her beloved, who is absent. Both the Latin marginalia construct a sixteenth-century reading of Kempe in terms of the Latin works of Richard Rolle. Here the marginal comment does not bear an obvious relationship to Kempe's text. What does weeping have to do with Rolle's concept of *langor amoris*? The answer may lie in Kempe's cries, which accompany her weeping, "I die, I die," for Rolle often juxtaposes his languishing love with the mystic's desire for death.[65] In this case the reader's invocation to Rolle helps to place Kempe's roaring exclamations into a context we might not otherwise have considered.

Another marginal comment is more puzzling, although it appears two times in similar contexts. *Amor impaciens* appears in conjunction with two separate incidents of Kempe's roaring. In the second case, the Latin seems to comment upon the fact that she is unable to restrain her tears. *Impaciens* seems to be used here in the sense of "ungovernable," because at issue in the passage is Kempe's controlling her tears during a Grey Friar's sermon. The reader's note is placed next to the Grey Friar's complaint that "she [Kempe] annoys the people," and his request that she be removed from the church. The reader's comment, from whatever source it derives, seems to contradict the Grey Friar's assumption that Kempe can and should govern her boisterous cries. The reader is clearly familiar with a tradition of ungovernable love which he finds expressed in Kempe's clamor.

One of the fifteenth-century annotations in brown ink likewise "reads" Kempe's more extraordinary behavior in terms of Rolle, producing what Allen considers to be a "misunderstanding" of Rolle. Where the scribe mentions that Richard Rolle's *Incendium Amoris* helped him to regain faith in Kempe's loud cries, this reader adds the word *clamor* out to the side. While the scribe does not cite any specific aspect of Rolle's work, the reader interprets one, giving us a glimpse of late medieval receptions of both Rolle and Kempe. As Allen notes, the reader is probably linking Kempe's loud cries with Rolle's description of mystical song as a kind of cry: "clamor iste canor est" (the shout is the song).[66] Even though we might understand Rolle to mean something quite different from Kempe's boisterous cries, the late medieval reader clearly did not. This reading, in turn, raises the question of whether Kempe regards her own cries as the mystical *clamores* of which Rolle speaks.

Finally, at least four marginal comments appear to be quotations from Latin texts that the reader thinks Kempe's own English text invokes. In other words, he seems to be supplying the Latin source for Kempe's text.

The closeness of the Latin annotation with Kempe's own words causes one to speculate whether even more of her text is Latin-based than I have been discussing thus far. After a period of temptation in which Kempe apologizes to Christ for doubting him, she vows to become "buxom" to his will, and she adds: "I pray thee, Lord, speak in me whatever is most pleasant to thee" (146). The reader interjects the following: "Loquere, Domine, quia audit seruus tuus. Audiam quid loquatur in me, Dominus Deus" (146) ("Speak, Lord, because your servant hears. I will hear that which is spoken in me, Lord God"). This annotation could hardly be mistaken for a simple translation of Kempe's text into Latin. Instead, it clearly invokes another text entirely, possibly the biblical text of 1 Sam. 3:9 and 10.

Similarly, next to the passage described above in which Kempe is reprimanded for not controlling her tears, the reader remarks: "Non est in hominis potestate prohibere spiritum s[anctum]" (It is not in the power of men to prohibit the holy spirit) (149). This comment differs from the previous one in that it does not attempt to draw a connection between Kempe's text and another one; rather, it comments upon the words and actions of the Grey Friar. Instead of reinforcing the Latinity of Kempe's text, it suggests a sympathetic reading of Kempe's controversial behavior— a reading that situates Kempe's text within a Latin medieval mystical tradition, not on the fringes. In chapter 6, this reading will be explored further to see how her text was read in terms of the late fifteenth-century contemporary, Richard Methley, as well as of Kempe's precursors.

The Latinity of Kempe's text, like that of the sixteenth-century reader's reading of it, serves to authorize it in contradiction to her claims not to know Latin. Her authorization is underhanded, perhaps even sleight-of-handed, since she everywhere insists on her own ignorance and Christ's coaching. She allows only that her scribe resorted to Latin works in order to restore his own faith in her. Kempe thus links Latin mystical texts and saints' *vitae* with the scribe's need for authority rather than her own. She does not acknowledge the debt of her own text to the Latin tradition so reassuring to her scribe. In fact, her text endeavors to deny its own Latinity. It has been largely successful, if contemporary scholarship's neglect of it is any indication.

What is the relationship of this authorizing Latinity to her privileging of the mystic utterance, of voice? In chapter 2, we saw how the mystic text is always unstable because it situates itself both within the authorized institution of the Church and outside it. Instead of drawing upon that "objective organization of statements" which are the foundation of theological, doctrinal, devotional, and homiletic texts, the mystic text affirms the place from which the other speaks. That is, it insists upon the "dialogic spaces" created by the mystic's desire and consequent voiding of self.[67] It is important to recognize that Kempe does not create this space *within* the Latinity of her text. The Latinity serves to restore the scribe's faith, but it is not the source of her own utterance. Instead, her locutions with Christ take place at the site of her interdiction in the written text.

Such interdiction is what Kempe seems to be describing in the passage quoted at the beginning of this chapter. This book, she tells us, is not written according to any order but according to her recollection of the events recounted: "And therefore she had nothing written until she knew it for the very truth" (5). Kempe is careful to situate the truth of her text not in the written testimony but in the oral one, which relies upon memory and pays little heed to the linear demands of written narrative. It is the utterance itself that intercedes on behalf of the written text, rather than the written inscription of Latin authorities authorizing the mystic text. Interestingly, Kempe's apologia is itself an interdiction, interrupting her account of the second scribe's difficulties in reading the first scribe's text.

It remains to be seen how this interdiction is established in the written text. The opening scenario of the scribe's ordeal in reading the first version of the book provides us with one example of how the written text, reader, and scribe rely upon Kempe's dictation for comprehension. Interdiction, too, plays an important role in Kempe's own conversion. Following the birth of her first child, Kempe despairs for her life and wishes to confess a sin she had previously kept hidden. She is interrupted on the point of revealing her sin by her confessor's sharp rebukes, and she goes mad, fearing at the same time her confessor's disapproval and damnation. The confessor's interdiction in the process of confession silences Kempe and ultimately forces her to go mad. It is repaired only by Christ's interdiction in her madness after more than six months to restore her to her mind. This sequence of events constitutes the violent process by which the mystic's soul is made the site of divine utterance. Kempe's wits are restored when she is able to listen to Christ. Divine locution, then, occurs at the rupture of the mystic's will and speech.

The temptations which are visited on Kempe also serve to condition her receptivity to divine interdiction. The first occurs soon after Kempe's conversion. She falls victim to the sin of vainglory when she desires Christ to come down from the cross to embrace her. As the text makes clear, Kempe's presumption lies in relying too much on herself and her desires

(16). Three years of temptation prepare her, as Christ tells her, to "think such thoughts as I will put in your mind." He concludes, "Then you shall lie still and speak to me in thought, and I shall give to you high meditation and true contemplation" (17). In fact, Christ here gives her permission to abandon her vocal prayers for this divine dialogue in her soul. This is a crucial step in the establishment of interdiction as a principle of the mystic text and utterance.

In a second incidence of Kempe's willfulness, she doubts God's interdiction, attributing a painful vision of the damned to the devil's deceit rather than to God's revelation. After a twelve-day period of suffering in which her holy thoughts and sweet meditations are withdrawn from her, she is restored to that proper desire which awaits divine utterance in the soul. She prays Christ to "speak what is most pleasant to him" in her soul, signifying her own submission to his will. The presence of divine speech in the mystic's soul depends on the mystic's desiring and creating an empty place for it—empty of will, speech, and human affections.

The self-abandonment which precedes mystic locution in the soul may be observed in other places in the text. Kempe seeks out divine interdiction to guide and direct her meditation, for example, when she begins her meditation on the life of Christ by asking, "Ihesu, what schal I thynke?" (18) This does not mean that Kempe acts as a passive vessel for divine utterance, because this request for interdiction already begins in the mystic's desire.

From the interdiction of divine speech in the soul, the mystic proceeds to interdiction in the discourses of the world and the text. Kempe does this explicitly by disregarding a discursive order in her book in favor of what she calls the "very trewth schewyd in experiens" (220). Her apology that her book "is not wryten in ordyr" is no humble pose, for indeed her book does proceed by "lapses and bounds," as Cixous puts it, repeating, backtracking, rearranging, and qualifying itself.[68]

"To fly/steal is woman's gesture, to steal into language to make it fly," claims Cixous, explaining the passage quoted at the beginning of this chapter. She plays upon the two meanings of the French verb *voler* meaning "to fly" and "to steal." To these may be added the mystic's *volo*, that contractual statement of desire that permits the flying and stealing. It is this desire which enables utterance and which produces that *corpus verborum*—the text—out of abundance. Kempe's flying will be explored more fully in chapters 4 and 5, where we shall see how Kempe finds entry into the mystical text through laughter and tears. The "woman's gesture" of stealing offers us a way of understanding the relationship of the Latinity of Kempe's

Book to the privileging of voice. As we saw in chapter 2, women are excluded from culture in the Middle Ages because they are denied access to Latin and the institutions it circumscribes. In spite of the fact that many people might have been quasi-literate in the language as their business transactions required, women still remained largely excluded from the magisterium language. Kempe somehow steals into the charmed circle, robbing the Latin works of Richard Rolle, and the *Stimulus Amoris*. This stealing is partly what makes the writing of her book possible at all, since her scribe shores up his own belief in her through these texts. It is also what enables his reading. Her scribe needs the authorization of the Latin texts of Marie d'Oignies and the *Stimulus Amoris* in order to read Kempe's. The text's sixteenth-century reader likewise read Kempe's book in the context of a Latin tradition of devotional writings.

Yet, though Kempe steals into culture by means of inscribing Latin works and concepts into her text, she never remains there. She always crosses the boundaries through her interdiction and by privileging the voice in the text over the written text. Dalliance, colloquy, and bold speech fissure the Latin text of her *Book* in order to provide passage to that "elsewhere" where mystical experience takes place.[69] Her speech begins in what the sixteenth-century reader called *amor impatiens*, "impatient, ungovernable love" and passes beyond the clamor of her cries and her text. This is her "dispersing gesture."

Mystical utterance which attempts the impossible—to utter God—is always blasphemous. Kempe is aware of her own failure to utter (much less to dictate) "the unspeakable love that burned so fervently in the soul" (69–70). Although she views herself as God's secretary, she always acknowledges the insufficiency of her speech:

> Ne hyr-self cowd neuyr telle þe grace þat sche felt, it was so heuenly, so hy a-bouen hyr reson & hyr bodyly wyttys, and hyr body so febyl in tym of þe presens of grace þat sche myth neuyr expressyn it wyth her word lych as sche felt it in hyr sowle. (3)

> (Nor could she herself express the grace that she felt, it was so heavenly, so high above her reason and her bodily wits, and her body so feeble during the presence of grace that she might never convey it with her words as she felt it in her soul.)

Her speech is already undermined by the inadequacy of language; it blasphemes in its presumption and in the tainted nature of all human utterance.

Yet her voice is not silenced or intimidated by its own presumption or failure. The failed human utterance is, in fact, what mystic texts practice as a rule. However, the location of this failure is what is important to the politics of mystical utterance.[70] In fact, her own speech points to the breakdown of the Latin discourse. Kempe situates her own failed speech in a Latin mystical tradition, at the same time drawing upon it and leaving it behind. Hers is not an enterprise of instruction, but one of desire. This desire, in turn, seeks out the hearts of her readers where it longs to make an impression like that of written characters upon the sight. Her voice charges the boundaries of uncharitable hearts and textual traditions. Like her *clamor*, which disrupts all human activity, her utterance tears at the fabric of the written text, instilling disorder, impatience, lapses, and verbal insurgency at its core. These are the effects of mystical desire.

This privileging of voice is not without its sleight-of-hand. Kempe plays the innocent with the Latinity of her text. She claims to be ignorant of Latin and clerical wit. Considering the evidence of her own use of Rolle and the sixteenth-century reader's reading, we must finally wonder whether she is as ignorant as she claims. We might explain *The Book of Margery Kempe* as the work of her more learned scribe. Or we might speculate that his simultaneous translations of these Latin works might have introduced Kempe to the words and concepts. Or perhaps it is time we read Kempe a bit more closely and seriously to consider her own acquaintance with Latin texts. If we do, we will find a curious and surprising comment by Christ made in passing. Near the end of Book 1, Christ assures Kempe that he is pleased with her meditations and holy thoughts, her prayers and her suffering. In the course of his assurance, Christ makes a startling revelation:

> . . . I haue often seyd on-to þe þat wheþyr þu preyist wyth þi mowth er thynkist wyth thyn hert, wheþyr þu redist er herist redyng, I wil be plesyd wyth þe. (218).

> (. . . I have often said unto you that whether you pray with your mouth or think with your heart, whether you read or hear reading, I will be pleased with you.)

Christ here recognizes both her reading and her hearing works read. The distinction itself points to her ability to read, although neither her editors nor modern scholars have commented on this puzzling evidence. It is interesting that her scribe does not dispute it either. Perhaps this is the ultimate sleight-of-hand: the literate author has slipped through her own text. If so, we are left with a gap which is as much a creation of modern scholarship as it is of Kempe herself. She pretended to be ignorant, perhaps, to steal; we have no such excuse. We have the precedent of Christina the Astonishing (1150–1224), who claimed also to be illiterate, yet she knew Latin and the Holy Scriptures.[71] If Kempe could read after all, it is time her late twentieth-century readers realized it. Yet Kempe's reading must not be forgotten or subsumed by her "loud voice," for it represents the very means by which she steals and finally enables her own voice.

Notes

1. See the discussion of literary theory and practice by A. J. Minnis, *Medieval Theory of Authorship: Scholastic Literary Attitudes in the Later Middle Ages* (London: Scolar Press, 1984; 2nd ed. Philadelphia: University of Pennsylvania Press, 1988), 160–217.

2. See Minnis on *artes praedicandi*, *Medieval Theory of Authorship*, particularly 136–38 and 174–77.

3. See for example, Anthony E. Goodman, "The Piety of John Brunham's Daughter, of Lynn," in *Medieval Women*, ed. Derek Baker (Oxford: Basil Blackwell, 1978), who argues that the scribe was responsible for the argument of the *Book*, 348–49; John C. Hirsh attributes all that is worthwhile in the *Book* to the second scribe's authorship, "Author and Scribe in *The Book of Margery Kempe*," *Medium Aevum* 44 (1975): 145–50.

4. For a summary of the criticism, see Maureen Fries, "Margery Kempe," in *An Introduction to the Medieval Mystics of Europe*, ed. Paul E. Szarmach (Albany: State University of New York Press, 1984), 227–29.

5. One exception is an excellent paper presented at the 1988 MLA Convention in New Orleans, David Lawton, "The Voice of Margery Kempe's Book." Lawton makes the only case I know of for Kempe's privileging of voice and the clear signs of Latinity in that voice. Some of my own ideas presented here are indebted to Lawton's paper.

6. *The Book of Margery Kempe*, ed. Sanford B. Meech and Hope Emily Allen, EETS, o.s. 212 (London: Oxford University Press, 1940), 4. All quotations from this text will hereafter be cited in the text. Translations are my own unless otherwise noted. For a modern English translation, see Barry A. Windeatt, *The Book of Margery Kempe* (New York: Penguin, 1985).

7. Ute Stargardt has suggested that the anonymous scribe was Kempe's daughter-in-law, her son's Prussian wife, since she was likely to have been inexperienced in writing, "The Influence of Dorothea von Montau on the Mysticism of Margery Kempe" (Dissertation, University of Tennessee, 1981), 8n.

8. Walter J. Ong reveals the illusory connection in written language between the segmented letters and words on the page and a fixed and neatly separable literal meaning. He cautions that "a complex and polysemous utterance is no clearer when it is written down, nor is its meaning any simpler. We are surer that we can recover it

word for word. That is all. But word for word, it may convey only a very obscure sense." *The Presence of the Word*, 47–48.

9. I am using the term "interdiction" here to describe the interference of the dictating author in the written text, as well as in the writing process. My use differs from Lawton's notion of the "writing interdiction," in which the written text refers its authority to the spoken one, "The Voice of Margery Kempe's Book," 7. Lawton borrows the notion of "writing interdiction" from Domna C. Stanton, "Autogynography: Is the Subject Different?" in *The Female Autograph*, ed. Domna Stanton (Chicago: University of Chicago Press, 1987), 13.

10. M. T. Clanchy, *From Memory to Written Record: England, 1066–1307* (Cambridge, MA: Harvard University Press, 1979), 181–87. Clanchy points out that the terms for laity (*laicus*) and illiterate (*illiteratus*) were synonymous and analogous to another synonymous pair, *clericus* and *literatus*. According to these pairs of synonyms, lay and clerical were equivalent to illiterate and literate. Thus, a knight who possessed a knowledge of Latin might be called a cleric for his learning, while presumably, a monk or priest who was not "lettered" could be called a *laicus*, 175–81.

11. *From Memory to Written Record*, 185.

12. *From Memory to Written Record*, 189. Clanchy notes that knowledge of Latin extended from the central government to the manors and villages, where stewards, bailiffs, beadles, and reeves possessed a "pragmatic literacy" by 1200 (187).

13. Franz H. Bäuml, "Varieties and Consequences of Medieval Literacy and Illiteracy," *Speculum* 55 (1980): 239. Bäuml makes a case for quasi-literacy in terms of access to the written language, 246–49. Clanchy confirms the existence of a "pragmatic literacy" among the English after 1200, including peasants, *From Memory to Written Record*, 187.

14. See Clanchy, *From Memory to Written Record*, 202–26.

15. Of course, the *lectio* of monastic tradition also called for reading aloud: Clanchy, *From Memory to Written Record*, 216–17. This practice was also encouraged along with edifying conversation among the laity in the late Middle Ages, William Abel Pantin, "Instructions for a Devout and Literate Layman," in *Medieval Learning and Literature: Essays presented to Richard William Hunt*, ed. J. J. G. Alexander and M. T. Gibson (Oxford: Clarendon Press, 1976), 408–9.

16. *Metalogicon*, I, 13. Quoted and translated in Clanchy, *From Memory to Written Record*, 202. For the relationship between speaking and reading, see 218–19.

17. Aston attributes this everydayness to the Lollard practice of posting bills to air their complaints, *Lollards and Reformers: Images and Literacy in Late Medieval Religion* (London: Hambledon Press, 1984), 108. I will be discussing some connections between Lollardy and literacy later in this chapter. Lollardy was an heretical religious movement associated with the teachings of John Wyclif. It lasted through the late fourteenth and early fifteenth centuries, and it represented a variety of heretical beliefs, such as that lay people could read and interpret scriptures and preach and administer the sacraments, that images and pilgrimages fostered idolatry, and that the sacrament of the altar remained bread after being consecrated. See Claire Cross, "'Great Reasoners in Scripture': Women Lollards, 1380–1530," in *Medieval Women*, 359–80.

18. Clanchy mentions that noblewomen took an active role in the education of

their children. How far this extended to the other social classes is not clear from his assertion that "by 1300 conscientious or ambitious parents of all social classes had strong motives for seeing that their children were *clerici* and *litterati* in the new minimal sense of being capable of reading a verse from the Bible" (196). Susan Groag Bell reminds us that women were excluded from Latin culture, and that this was a factor in their instigation of vernacular translations for the purposes of education, "Medieval Women Book Owners: Arbiters of Lay Piety and Ambassadors of Culture," in *Women and Power in the Middle Ages*, ed. Mary Erler and Maryanne Kowaleski (Athens: University of Georgia Press, 1988), 165. Joan M. Ferrante argues that we know little about women's education, but she notes that after the thirteenth century the education of women suffered a decline because of their exclusion from the universities, "The Education of Women in the Middle Ages in Theory, Fact, and Fantasy," in *Beyond Their Sex: Learned Women of the European Past*, ed. Patricia H. Labalme (New York and London: New York University Press, 1980), 9, 17.

19. See Judith M. Bennett, "Public Power and Authority in the Medieval English Countryside," in *Women and Power in the Middle Ages*, 18–36.

20. Women were excluded from all "basic political, legal, and economic rights," according to Judith M. Bennett, "The Village Ale-Wife: Women and Brewing in Fourteenth-Century England," in *Women and Work in Preindustrial Europe*, ed. Barbara A. Hanawalt (Bloomington: Indiana University Press, 1986), 28. Even though they might be commercially successful as ale-wives, they were still viewed by the manorial courts as wives. In fact, it is often difficult to determine how many ale-wives there were because local court records list ale fines under the names of the heads of household, i.e., the husbands. See Maryanne Kowaleski, "Women's Work in a Market Town: Exeter in the Late Fourteenth Century," in *Women and Work in Preindustrial Europe*, 151.

21. Pantin, "Instructions for a Devout and Literate Layman," 400. It is interesting that the text also instructs him at dinner to "let there be reading, now by one, now by another, and by your children as soon as they can read " (399). Whether the wife was one of the readers here is not clear; however, the writer seems to be making a distinction between the Latin readings and the vernacular speeches of edification, as well as between their recipients. If the wife is one of the readers, the devotional guide seems to be advocating some additional vernacular instruction.

22. See Bell, "Medieval Women Book Owners," 135–61.

23. Clanchy, *From Memory to Written Record*, 97; for the perception of writing as labor, see 41 and 90.

24. Suzanne Fleischman has recently investigated how an understanding of the orality of medieval culture enhances our knowledge of "medieval textual language," "Philology, Linguistics, and the Discourse of the Medieval Text," *Speculum* 65 (1990): 19–37.

25. Clanchy makes this point, particularly as it is important to the illiterate person's access to written documents, *From Memory to Written Record*, 219. Only when reading and writing become silent activities do illiterate people become fully excluded from written texts.

26. See Plate XII of Clanchy, *From Memory to Written Record*.

27. Ong, "Orality, Literacy, and Medieval Textualization," *New Literary History* 16 (1984): 2.

28. Bridget, *The Revelations of Saint Birgitta*, ed. William Patterson Cumming, EETS, o.s. 178 (London, 1929; rpts. 1971), 68.

29. See Minnis, *Medieval Theory of Authorship*, 10–12, 158–59.

30. Robert W. Hanning uses this term to describe the late fourteenth-century view of the medieval practice of glossing as a kind of violence done to a text for the purpose of self-aggrandizement. He further links this to the situation of women in Chaucer's texts—Criseyde in particular—who are "harassed" in effect by the anti-feminist texts, "'I Shal Finde It in a Maner Glose': Versions of Textual Harassment in Medieval Literature," in *Medieval Texts and Contemporary Readers*, ed. Laurie A. Finke and Martin B. Shichtman (Ithaca, NY: Cornell University Press, 1987), 27–50.

31. Lawton notes the numerous verbs for speech to be found in Kempe's book, including *spak, dalyid*, and others, "The Voice of Margery Kempe's Book," 8.

32. References to speech and speaking run throughout *The Book of Margery Kempe*, making them difficult to list in their entirety. A partial list of these instances includes 11, 26, 28, 29, 36, 38–39, 42, 47, 90, 93, and 230.

33. Humbert of Romans, *Treatise on Preaching*, ed. Walter M. Conlon, trans. The Dominican Students, Province of St. Joseph (Westminster, MD: Newman Press, 1951), 48. G. R. Owst discusses Humbert's remark in the context of the medieval sermon, *Preaching in Medieval England* (New York: Russell and Russell, 1965), 5.

34. Quoted in Owst, *Preaching in Medieval England*, 136. He notes that Robert Rypon, sub-prior of the monastery of Durham and prior of Finchale, also comments on the activities of Lollard lay preachers, 135n. Claire Cross documents the participation of women in the Lollard movement, "'Great Reasoners in Scripture': The Activities of Women Lollards 1380–1530," in *Medieval Women*, ed. Derek Baker (Oxford: Basil Blackwell, 1978), 359–80.

35. Aston, *Lollards and Reformers*, 130. Reginald Pecock, bishop of Chicester, complained especially of the arrogance of women Lollards who "make themselves so wise by the Bible, that they "are most haughty of speech regarding clerks" (quoted in Aston, *Lollards and Reformers*, 51).

36. See Norman C. Tanner, ed., *Heresy Trials in the Diocese of Norwich, 1428–31* (London, 1977).

37. See Archbishop Courtney's examination of the Lollards of Leicester, including women, in Cross, "'Great Reasoners in Scripture,'" 362. As Cross points out, Lollard activity in East Anglia where Kempe lived has been especially well documented.

38. For the testimony of Hawisia Moone, see Tanner, *Heresy Trials in the Diocese of Norwich*, 142. For Archbishop Courtenay's comment, see Margaret Aston, "Lollardy and Sedition, 1381–1431," *Past and Present* 17 (1960): 12.

39. Aston, "Lollardy and Sedition," 31.

40. For more on Kempe in the context of the Lollard movement, see Clarissa W. Atkinson, *Mystic and Pilgrim: The Book and World of Margery Kempe* (Ithaca, NY: Cornell University Press, 1983), 103–12; 151–54. David Aers also sees Kempe's re-

sistance to authority as identifying her with the Lollard movement; see *Community, Gender, and Individual Identity: English Writing 1360–1430* (London: Routledge, 1988), 84.

41. Women Lollards often knew Scriptures from having them read to them. In addition, however, they seem to have taught others including their own children passages from the Bible. See Cross, "'Great Reasoners in Scripture,'" 370. Some of these Lollard women boasted of their learning. Margery Baxter claimed to have deceived a Carmelite, while another woman Lollard publicly declared that "she was as well learned as was the parish priest, in all things, except only in saying mass." See Meech and Allen's commentary in *The Book of Margery Kempe*, 315n, and Cross, 371.

42. William W. Capes, *The Register of John Trefnant, Bishop of Hereford* (Hereford, 1914), 345. The translation is my own. Meech and Allen cite Brute's feminism in connection with Lollard advocacy of women preachers, but they do not mention the parallel between Kempe's argument and Brute's, 315n. Margaret Aston summarizes Brute's defense of women's preaching, *Lollards and Reformers*, 52.

43. G. Holmstedt, ed., *Speculum Christiani*, EETS, o.s. 182 (London: Oxford University Press, 1933; rpt. 1971), 2.

44. Christine de Pizan, *The Book of the City of Ladies*, trans. Earl Jeffrey Richards (New York: Persea Books, 1982), 30. I have discussed this passage in connection with Kempe's search for authority elsewhere, "*The Book of Margery Kempe*: A Marginal Woman's Quest for Literary Authority," *Journal of Medieval and Renaissance Studies* 16 (1986): 33–56.

45. Hilton's text is not mentioned by title in either place, but the *Incendium Amoris* is twice referred to by its Latin title, as is the *Stimulo Amoris*, 39 and 154. As I will show, Kempe's use of these references differs in these two passages in important ways.

46. Lawton is the only one to point to the "signs of Latinity" in Kempe's text, particularly to her use of the *Meditationes Vitae Christi*. Lawton argues that this Latinity needs to be explored in more detail and that it signifies "a certain far from naive intertextuality in the work of Margery Kempe," "The Voice of Margery Kempe's *Book*," 4.

47. Meech and Allen, 276n. H. E. Allen also speculates that local copies of English translations might have existed at one time and have since vanished.

48. She mentions having this book read to her after she returns from her visit to the Holy Land, which was at least fifteen years before Misyn's translation (153).

49. While this work is the main source for the "fire of love," other Latin and English writings by Rolle elaborate on this mystical experience, including the *Melos Amoris, Emendatio Vitae, The Form of Living, The Commandment*, and the lyrics.

50. *The Incendium Amoris of Richard Rolle of Hampole*, ed. Margaret Deanesly, Publications of the University of Manchester, Historical Series, 26 (London, 1915): "Necessitas quoque corporalis atque affecciones humanitus impresse, erumpuosique exilii anguscie ardorem ipsum interpolant, et flammam quam sub metaphora ignem appellaui, eo quod urit et lucet, mitigant et molestant" (146). Rolle also calls this warmth or love a "spiritual ardor" (147).

51. *English Writings of Richard Rolle, Hermit of Hampole*, ed. Hope Emily Allen (Oxford: Clarendon Press, 1931), 105.

52. *Incendium Amoris*, 195. The subject of languishing also comes up in the English work, *The Form of Living*, but it is more fully elaborated in the Latin works, see *English Writings*, ed. H. E. Allen, 103–4.

53. See Rolle, *Emendatio Vitae* in *The Fire of Love and the Mending of Life*, trans. M. L. Del Mastro (Garden City, NY: Image Books, 1981); and *Melos Amoris*, ch. 55, in *The Melos Amoris of Richard Rolle of Hampole*, ed. E. J. F. Arnould (Oxford: Basil Blackwell, 1957).

54. For a comparison with the Latin passage quoted, see ch. 18, 40, where even *Amore langueo* is translated "for lufe I longe." For another example, compare Deanesly's edition of *Incendium Amoris*, 216–19, with Richard Misyn's Middle English translation, *The Fire of Love and the Mending of Life, or the Rule of Living*, ed. Ralph Harvey, EETS, o.s. 106 (London, 1896; rpt. 1973), 56–58.

55. See Rolle, *Incendium Amoris*, 182–91; also *The Form of Living* in *Richard Rolle*, trans. R. S. Allen, 170–180.

56. See Wolfgang Riehle's discussion of Rolle's musical imagery, *The Middle English Mystics*, trans. Bernard Standring (London: Routledge and Kegan Paul, 1981), 119–22. The *Melos Amoris* as well as the *Incendium Amoris* uses the related notions of song and melody to convey mystical dalliance; see Arnould, *Melos Amoris*, 20, 138–40.

57. In fact, Riehle claims that this particular mystical sensation is limited in English mysticism to the Latin works of Rolle, except for the negative experience of the devil's stench in Julian of Norwich's *Showings*: *Middle English Mystics*, 115–16.

58. *Melos Amoris*, ed. Arnould, 49, 83, 99, 119. Riehle also finds reference to smells in conjunction with the fire of love in *Emendatio Vitae*: *Middle English Mystics*, 116. The Misyn translation of this work describes the mystic's love as "swete smelland" and a "plesand odur," *The Mending of Life*, 125, 126.

59. The Middle English reads: "Ah, Lord, what shall I more make noise or cry out? You delay and you come not, and I, weary and overcome through desire, begin to go mad, for love governs me and not reason. I run with hasty course wherever you wish. I bow, Lord, and they who see me are irked and pity me, not knowing that I am drunk with your love. Lord, they say, 'Lo, yonder crazy man cries in the streets,' but how great my heart's desire is, they perceive not." The Latin text appears in Meech and Allen, 323n. Although Hilton's text has not been edited, it has been translated by Clare Kirchberger, *The Goad of Love* (London, 1952): "But whereto shall I cry more thus? Thou tarriest and comest not and I as man weary in yearning begin for to fonne. For love stirreth me and no reason and I run with great noise whitherso my love holdeth. And they see me, scorn me, for they know not that I am made as I were drunken, for longing in love. They say thus: 'Why crieth this wood man thus in the streets?' but they take no heed how that "desire of Jesus burneth in my heart" (59).

60. The additions to the Middle English versions seem to be present in all of the ten surviving manuscripts, according to Kirchberger, *The Goad of Love*, 20. This makes the added phrase in this modern English translation particularly important for distinguishing between the scribe's Latin and English sources.

61. As Kirchberger points out, the Latin and Middle English texts are quite

different, for Hilton tempered much of the excessive affectivity of the Latin texts, *The Goad of Love*, 28–44. Clearly, Kempe would have found more affinities with her own spirituality in the Latin texts than she would have in Hilton's.

62. The Middle English passage reads: "Of the plenteous grace of her tears he treats especially . . . in the 19th chapter where he tells how she, at the request of a priest so that he would not be troubled nor distraught in his Mass with her weeping and her sobbing, went out at the church door, with loud voice crying because she could not restrain herself. And our Lord also visited the priest at Mass with such grace and with such devotion when he would read the Holy Gospel that he wept wondrously so that he wet his vestment and the ornaments of the altar and he could not measure his weeping nor his sobbing, it was so abundant, nor might he restrain it nor well stand therewith at the altar." The Latin is quoted in H. E. Allen's notes to *The Book of Margery Kempe*, 323n. The corresponding passage in the Middle English version of Marie's life may be found in C. Horstmann, *Prosalegenden: Die Legenden des MS Douce 114. Anglia* 8 (1885): 135–36.

63. See Meech's summary of these emendations and annotations in Meech and Allen, xxxvii and xliii–xliv.

64. Examples of English labels and commentary include: "nota A sotel & a sore temptacion. In siche a case we shold be more strange & bold a-ga[n]ste our gostly enmy," 177/n.2; "manheyd of cryst," 183/n.4; "trew it is blyssyd lord," 191/n.1; and others. I should note here that the reader sometimes alternates English translations of the Latin, such as "langyng loue" for *langor amoris*, 176/n.3, 197/n.2, and 140/n.1. The reader does not seem to be making any distinction when he uses the English instead of the Latin in this case.

65. See Rosamund Allen's discussion of the desire for death in Rolle, including passages from *Emendatio Vitae* and *Melos Amoris*, *Richard Rolle*, 31–32.

66. *Incendium Amoris*, ed. Deanesly, 243.

67. Michel de Certeau, *Heterologies: Discourse on the Other*, trans. Brian Massumi (Minneapolis: University of Minnesota Press, 1986), 92 and 91; see also chapter 2 above.

68. Robert Karl Stone considers the repetition in Kempe's narrative monotonous, *Middle English Prose Style: Margery Kempe and Julian of Norwich* (The Hague: Mouton, 1970), 111. One example of the rearrangement occurs at the end of chapter 16, where the reader is instructed to read chapter 21 before reading any further (38). An example of qualification occurs where the scribe's story of Marie d'Oignies is said to be only a rough approximation of the real story, which he couldn't quite recall, as I have discussed above.

69. See my discussion of this fissuring of the mystical text, chapter 2.

70. I agree with de Certeau: "Mystics are engaged in a politics of utterance." The essence of the politics lies in the mystic's reconstruction of a language which has broken down. In de Certeau's words, "This kind of 'politics,' like contemporary rhetoric, sets forth operational rules determining the relational usage of a language that has become uncertain of the real. It *reconstructs*, where the *ontological* relation between words and things has come undone, *loci* of *social* communication," *Heterologies*, 91.

71. See the Middle English translation of her life in C. Horstmann, *Pros-alegenden*: "She vndirstood sooþly alle latyn and knewe plenirly alle the menynge in scripture, þof sche neuer knewe lettir syþen she was born; and whan she was asked moost dyuyne questyons of holy wrytte, she wolde declare hem moost openly to summe of hir spritual freendes" (129).

4. Fissuring the Text: Laughter in the Midst of Writing and Speech

> In the midst of writing, there is merriment.
>
> Gertrude Stein, *Lifting Belly*

Margery Kempe's desire for acceptance and tolerance from the English clergy, her confessors, her fellow townspeople, and her readers is urgent both in her visionary conversations with Christ and in her disputes with the Church. Considering the unpopularity of her mystical practices, her desire is understandable. Yet, in spite of her insistence on authorizing the mystical discourse of her *Book* and the "truth shown in experience," she seems continually to undermine her own efforts. By reporting her ordeals of writing the book and of finding only grudging acceptance from many, including the Archbishop of York and her second scribe, Kempe appears determined to call her own authority as writer and mystic into question even as she attempts to authorize it. This double gesture of authorizing and undermining her own discourse often goes unrecognized by those who consider Kempe's whole enterprise to be a rather outlandish accomplishment of naiveté.

The fierce criticism, vituperation, and even mockery that she experiences are usually attributed to her desire for suffering and sympathy. By that account, her own failure to consider how her narrative of rejection might prejudice her reader testifies to her lack of self-consciousness. Yet the possibility that her undermining of authority works in conjunction with her search for the same authority needs to be considered, particularly in light of the evidence in the preceding chapter of her skillful authorization of her own voice.

In a sometimes shocking counterpoint to her search for authority, Margery Kempe exhibits an obvious irreverence for the very authority she seeks. This irreverence is usually overlooked by critics who focus on Kempe's

excessive weeping and emotional identifications with Christ.[1] In the midst
of the weeping, suffering, accusations, and interrogations of Kempe's mystical practices is the locus of her own irreverence: her laughter. This laughter
belies Kempe's naiveté and suggests, instead, something more "monstrous," according to Catherine Clément's analysis of the sorceress's laughter:

> All laughter is allied with the monstrous. . . . Laughter breaks up, breaks out,
> splashes over . . . . It is the moment at which the woman crosses a dangerous
> line, the cultural demarcation beyond which she will find herself excluded.[2]

Kempe uses laughter and what she calls "good game" to mock, disperse,
and subvert the culture which excludes her. The evidence of this irreverent
laughter in Kempe's narrative, in turn, raises questions about the role
laughter plays in her discourse. To put it another way, the laughter in the
text just might be *of* the text as well, a discursive practice aimed at readers of
her book. If her laughter is neither innocent nor naive—if it verges on the
monstrous, as Clément suggests—we need to observe how it functions in
Kempe's text to authorize her own discourse at the same time that it
establishes that separateness from the magisterium language of the medieval Church. If her laughter is subversive, we also need to examine how our
critical assumption of her naiveté has repressed this feature in Kempe's text.

Before looking at how laughter functions in Kempe's book, it is
important to consider how it functions in culture, particularly in relationship to that culture which relies on the integrity of bodily, moral, and social
boundaries. The monstrosity of laughter suggested by Clément is derived
from its ability to degrade—an ability which is made possible by the
culture's taboos against defilement at all levels. Bakhtin claims that laughter
degrades because it materializes, that is, it brings language, society, and
culture down to the level of the grotesque body.[3] In medieval culture, the
female body represented the grotesque body as Bakhtin defines it, excessive, corporeal, and accessible. The power of laughter lies in its ability to
invoke this grotesque body which is gendered in the Middle Ages.

I do not want to adopt a Bakhtinian model for Kempe's use of laughter
here, though, because his fails to account for gender and because it tends to
celebrate the grotesque in the form of carnival. I do not wish to celebrate
the kind of carnival Bakhtin outlines. Rather, I want to suggest that
laughter invokes the bodily, and that in doing so, it threatens the very
boundaries of social and institutional bodies which, in the Middle Ages,
rely on the repression of the grotesque female body. We saw in chapter 1

how the construction of the female body is based in part on fear of pollution, or abjection. At the level of society, this fear manifests itself in oppression, hatred, and persecution of social and religious groups. R. I. Moore has argued that the persecution of heretical groups and religious sects in medieval society is based on this fear of pollution.[4] Kempe's own persecution in England and Europe can be viewed in the context of her laughter, by which she not only recalls that medieval grotesque—the feminine flesh, with all its heaving powers and permeability—but she also transgresses the other cultural boundaries dependent on this grotesque, including the prerogatives of the Church. Laughter allows Kempe to trespass on sacred territories—of interpreting Scripture, teaching, speaking, and claiming divine authority. In effect, she adopts the position of the monstrous, a position which would not even exist without the medieval notions of the flesh, the female body, and social, moral, and spiritual *integritas*. In a culture which attempts to place the flesh (and woman) in parentheses, Kempe uses laughter to disperse the parentheses and contaminate the boundaries which preserve the power of the medieval Church and society.

Medieval scholars rarely comment on laughter or humor in Margery Kempe's book. Only one scholar that I know of, Martin Thornton, has even mentioned Kempe's humor in the context of her claims in the book as a whole: "I think it is a very important work; it is also very amusing, in places hilariously funny, which is all to the good so long as we are not too much distracted from its solid worth."[5] Thornton's suggestion that the humor of Kempe's book should be considered in conjunction with its serious claims to mystical revelation might give some readers trouble. Students in my graduate and undergraduate classes have themselves thought some of Kempe's book humorous, but they could not even consider the possibility that Kempe is conscious of the humor. I would like to look first at the evidence for Kempe's own laughter in her narrative and then at the humor she creates in the context of a larger serious purpose.

Traces of Kempe's laughter appear in the context of two separate incidents in her narrative. The first incident occurs after her second arraignment before the archbishop of York on a variety of charges, including disparaging the clergy, displaying her tears of contrition at will, and bearing secret Lollard missives about England. The archbishop protests that he has already examined Kempe and, finding no fault in her, even paid one of his own men to escort her out of his diocese so that she would no longer be a disturbance to him. The suffragan to the archbishop levels a further charge against her that she counseled Lady Greystoke to leave her husband. Kempe denies the charge, but recounts a tale instead which she told Lady Greystoke about a woman who was damned for not loving her enemies and a man who was saved for loving his. In exasperation the archbishop asks Kempe what he should do with her. She requests and is granted a letter excusing her of the charges of heresy.

Kempe receives a blessing from the archbishop and leaves him marveling over her enterprising ability to raise money from supporters for her travel. On her way out of the archbishop's hall, she is stopped by one of his stewards, who is annoyed that "she laughed and made good cheer." He rebukes her, "Holy folk should not laugh." Kempe's response reveals the essential connection between her laughter and the mystical project of her life and book: "Sir, I have great cause for laughing, for the more shame and spite I suffer, the merrier I may be in our Lord Jesus Christ" (135). Far from indulging in self-pity or appeals for sympathy at this point in her ordeals, Kempe finds "cause for merriment" in her troubles. Her narrative does not record her laughter elsewhere in the text, but if the sheer volume of shame and "despite" she suffers is any indication, we can suppose that she laughed even where her text is silent. Learning to read these silences amidst which there is Kempe's laughter, then, becomes the key to the reader's own transaction with the text and his or her "profit." For, as Kempe reminds us in her introduction, we can profit from the examples and instruction of others only if "lack of charity does not hinder us." The reader must bring her charity to the text, and this charity produces laughter; the mirthless reader, like the remonstrating steward, remains resistant to the mystical project of Kempe's life and book.

Kempe's text, then, is one in which "there is merriment," to borrow Gertrude Stein's vision of the transformative powers of language. The merriment which lurks in Kempe's text, however, is not always articulated. It is a private, secret laughter which celebrates the worldly complicity in her mystical desire for union with Christ. Her laughter has the power to mock the culture in which she travels, to enrage those representatives of the Church who, like the steward, fail to restrict her activities or speech, and to disable the very Church authority which interrogates and threatens her. As a social practice, her laughter provides her a way of slipping through the criticism and abuse she endures. Yet it is a mystical practice as well, for, as she claims, her merriment resides in Christ. What exactly does she mean by this?

Many readers mark the beginning of Kempe's conversions with her postpartum depression after giving birth to her first child. She provides a rather frightening account of how, fearing that she is about to die, she tries to confess some unshriven sin too terrible to mention even to her readers. Her confessor's sharp rebuke prevents her from telling the whole sin, leaving Kempe distraught and assured of her own damnation. Her subsequent madness clearly frightens even her husband, who has her restrained in order to protect her from herself. Only Christ's visitation to her in one of her mad fits stabilizes her. Her resolve to give up her old life and devote her life to Christ is soon abandoned. Her first conversion is thus a failed one.

The second conversion is quite different in nature, yet it is more significant for Kempe's mysticism and narrative than is the first. In this second conversion, Kempe takes up the cause of merriment as a mystical practice. In the middle of the night, Kempe tells us, she was awakened by "a sound of melody so sweet and delectable" that she thought she was in paradise. She starts right out of her bed and exclaims, "Alas, that ever I did sin, it is full merry in heaven" (11). What Kempe means by "merry" in this context is not clear, but she obviously does not mean simply "full of joy." She often uses the words *joye, joyen*, and *joyis* elsewhere in her *Book* to refer to the "joys of this world." Our modern notion of merriment and mirth is closer to this sense of worldly joy than it is to Kempe's experience of spiritual communion. We cannot detect Kempe's meaning from the context alone, nor can we simply rely on a modern understanding of mirth and merriment.

In fact, medieval attitudes toward mirth and laughter were often disparaging. John Chrysostom, for example, inveighed against laughter and frivolity as dangerously allied with excess, gluttony, and lechery. Chrysostom is careful not to condemn all laughter by distinguishing between that which is excessive and that which contributes to the soul's rest. However, he is quick to condemn all laughter which accompanies the more pernicious types of entertainment, such as dance. In one of his *Homilies on the Epistle to the Hebrews*, he asks the one who laughs, "Tell me, dost thou laugh? Where dost thou hear of Christ doing this? Nowhere; but that He was sad indeed oftentimes."[6] Clearly, Christ's example is behind the steward's offense at Kempe's laughter as well. Her own conception of mirth departs from the prevailing view of laughter exemplified by Chrysostom.

One clue to Kempe's meaning comes from Richard Rolle's *Incendium Amoris*. His equivalent term for mirth is *iocunditas* in a chapter devoted to the necessity for praising God in adversity and to the proper behavior of pious human beings. Although *iocunditas* can be translated as "delight," "enjoyment," or "pleasantness," Rolle suggests a meaning closer to "laughter" or "merriment." In particular, Rolle counsels that God's lover be neither too sad nor too lighthearted; instead, lovers aspiring to God should adopt a "mature merriment." He then considers the difference between spiritual merriment and frivolity:

> Porro risum quidam reprobant, quidam laudant. Risus igitur qui est ex leuitate et uanitate mentis, reprobabilis est: qui uero est ex hilaritate consciencie et leticia spirituali, laudabilis est, qui solum in iustis est, et dicitur iocunditas in dileccione Dei.[7]

> (Furthermore there are those who disapprove of laughter and those who praise it. Laughter which comes from levity and a vain mind is reprehensible; surely that which derives from a cheerful conscience and spiritual buoyancy deserves to be praised. This kind of laughter exists only in the righteous and it is called mirth in the love of God.)

Rolle's comment on people like the steward who reproaches Kempe for her laughter is a telling one. Such reproach derives from vanity and presumptuousness, as Rolle explains in the passage following this one. In fact, Rolle casts laughter as an expression of *iocunditas* or *hilaritas*, both of which mean "mirth." Rolle's laughter bespeaks not only a spiritual bouyancy but humility. One of the ironic consequences of this laughter is that it arouses the indignation of others whose vanity makes them obsessed with the appearance of holiness: holy folk, after all, should not laugh.[8] Richard Misyn's Middle English translation of Rolle's work, *The Fire of Love*, expressly renders *iocunditas* as "myrth." This version of Rolle's distinction between kinds of laughter praises "gostely myrth," and it advocates the same expression of this mirth in laughter. Elsewhere Misyn associates mirth with the fire of love in the soul by which "all þe inar forpartis of my saule with swetnes of heuenly myrth ar fulfild" (all the inner parts of my soul are filled with the sweetness of heavenly mirth). God also has the power to invest this sweetness in souls, "making (them) merry" ("myrthand") through his burning love. Under the heat of this intense burning, the mind is "myrthyd" or "made merry" with the gifts of His love.[9] All this merriment participates in mystical love of and union with God. The laughter of which Rolle approves takes this mirth into the world, where it is rarely appreciated.

One further link between Kempe's use of mirth and Rolle's can be found in heavenly song, a characteristic feature of Rolle's threefold system of spiritual ascent. After the heat and sweetness of love, the mystic experiences the heavenly song and, along with it in Misyn's translation, mirth. Kempe's introduction to heavenly mirth along with heavenly song replicates Rolle's own understanding of the relationship between the two in the progress toward mystical union. Kempe takes her mirth as far as Rolle has suggested a holy person may go, that is, into the world where it proclaims her "spiritual buoyancy" and her humility. Yet, too, her laughter exceeds the mirthful enjoyment of her conversion: it becomes a practice for upsetting the calculated attempts to discredit her, discomfiting the authorities who examine her, and making a place for her bold speech and her text beyond the circuit of her exclusion from medieval culture.

Most of Kempe's merriment occurs in the midst of her interrogations by English Church authorities. Her laughter serves not only as an affront to the likes of the mirthless steward but as a way of displacing the culture which excludes her with her own parables. Storytelling is Kempe's main strategy for unsettling the accusations against her with their implicit intentions of silencing her speech. She uses parables to make sport of her detractors' abuse—to have "good game" at their expense, as she puts it. The parables she tells, in turn, teach lessons in spiritual buoyancy. They also undermine the accusations of her detractors by confounding them.

In an especially nasty confrontation with some monks in Canterbury, Kempe is chided for her claim to be able to speak about God and to quote stories from Scripture. One monk in particular wishes she were an anchoress "shut in a house of stone so that no man could speak with you." Another younger monk attributes her scriptural knowledge either to the gifts of the Holy Ghost or to the promptings of the devil, for "what you say here to us is Holy Scripture, and that you do not have of yourself" (27–28). At this point, Kempe begs leave to tell a tale rather than take their advice and hold her tongue. The tale she tells bears quoting in full because it is too clever to be summarized adequately:

> Þer was onys a man þat had synned gretly a-ȝens God, &, whan he was schrevyn, hys confessowr jnyoined hym in party of penawnce þat he schuld o ȝer hyer men to chyde hym & repreuyn hym for hys synnes & he xuld ȝeuen hem syluer for her labowr. & on a day he cam a-mong many gret men as now ben her, God saue ȝow alle, and stod a-mong hem as I do now a-mong ȝow, despysyng hym as ȝe do me, þe man lawhyng er smylyng & hauyng good game at here wordys. Þe grettest maystyr of hem seyd to þe man, 'Why lawhyst þu, broþel, & art þow gretly despysed?' 'A, ser, I haue a gret cause to lawh, for I haue many days put syluer owt of my purse & hyred men to chyde me for remyssyon of my synne, & þis day I may kepe my syluer in my purs, I thank ȝow alle.' Rygth so I sey to ȝow, worshepful serys, whyl I was at hom in myn

owyn contre day be day wyth gret wepyng & mornyng, I sorwyd for I had no
schame, skorne, & despyte as I was worthy. I thank ȝow alle, serys, heyly what
fore-noon & aftyr-noon I haue had resonably þis day, blyssed be God þerof
(28).

(There was once a man who had sinned greatly against God, and, when he was
shriven, his confessor enjoined him as a part of his penance that he should for
one year hire men to chide him and reprove him for his sins and he should give
them silver for their labor. And on a day he came among many great men as
now are here, God save you all, and stood among them as I do now among
you, despising him as you do me, the man laughing or smiling and having
good game at their words. The greatest master of them said to the man, "Why
do you laugh, scoundrel, since you are greatly despised?" "Ah, sir, I have a
great cause to laugh, for I have many days put silver out of my purse and hired
men to chide me for the remission of my sin, and this day I may keep my silver
in my purse, I thank you all." Right so I say to you, worshipful sirs, while I was
at home in my own country day by day with great weeping and mourning, I
sorrowed for I had no shame, scorn, and spite as I deserved. I thank you all
highly, sirs, for what I have had in reasonable measure this day, before noon
and afternoon, blessed be God.)

Using a mock reverence for the "gret men" and "maystyrs" among her
accusors, Kempe turns their serious charges into her sport. The parable
allows her to move from object of their ridicule into subject of her own
story. Given the strict comparisons she draws between the abusive crowd in
the story and the Canterbury monks, between the penitent man who hires
others to abuse him and herself, we must assume that she is smiling,
laughing, and having good game at their words, just as the man in the tale
is. The fact that they threaten to burn her as a "false Lollard" and pursue her
with a cartful of thorns in order to carry out their threats is further evidence
of the power her laughter has to discompose the mastery—including the
magisterium language—which tries to objectify her. She accomplishes this
through a kind of exhibitionism which situates revelation in the place of
laughter. It is through laughter that the secret of the story and of Kempe's
own spiritual practice is revealed. Without laughter, there would be no
revelation, no disclosure of truth, no exposure of the emptiness of the
monks' moral authority, no confounding of the power of their speech.

Even more importantly, with this tale Kempe defines her own economy of laughter as a code indecipherable to the great masters. It has the
power to break the circuit of exchange upon which their power and authority rest. The man in the story enacts his own penance by seeking out abuse
and even paying for it. Thus he sets up a system of exchange very similar to

that which the Church uses through its own commerce in pardons and indulgences. In return for a sound scolding for his sins, the man pays his accusers—pieces of silver in exchange for revilement. The difference between his actions and those of the medieval Church is that he seeks to be reminded of rather than forgiven for his sins. The monetary transaction is not made in exchange for penance but in addition to physical (or verbal) penance. By keeping the silver, the man in Kempe's story reverses the usual transaction of money in return for and in place of actual penance for his sins.

For Kempe the story has more to do with laughter than with money, but her transaction is linked to the same system of exchange. In return for abuse, she offers laughter rather than money. This laughter explodes the economy underlying the man's payment and the Church's commerce in sins. because it returns something without value in exchange for something which seems to be without value but in fact is not. Her laughter is something which accrues to no one's profit, yet it is exchanged by the man in the tale instead of money and by Kempe herself. It confounds the Canterbury monks, but, more importantly, it undermines their authority. In the story the great men and masters are the ones left out of the exchange as the man offers only smiles in return for their abuse. In short, they unwittingly give something in exchange for nothing. The weight of their authority is thus denied, just as it is in Kempe's telling of the story, because it fails to intimidate. It is not even worth paying for.

Kempe's parable about the good game constructs a larger game in her narrative around the economy of exchange. Her laughter is monstrous in the sense that it perverts this economy by reducing it to good game. Her failure to be intimidated by the threats and criticisms of the Canterbury monks in effect denies their authority over her and the force of their words. Her laughter becomes a sign of her resistance, a refusal to exchange words of guilt, contrition, shame, or fear in return for their judgments of her. At the same time, she proclaims through her laughter a spiritual mirth which exceeds institutional authority. Hence her dual gesture of resistance and celebration in her good game.

Kempe's laughter displaces their threats, making a place for her own stories. Laughter is not only the subject of the story: it is the hermeneutic of the story as well. That is, the story itself is good game—sport—and it requires laughter on the part of its readers and listeners for the decoding of its meaning. The enraged reaction of the monks to Kempe's tale is directly proportional to their inability to laugh, which, in turn, is due to their

slighted authority. Kempe's ability to laugh comes from her own irreverence for the economy of words which ultimately demands her silence. Her
laughter allows her a place from which to speak and a sign through which
she may be read and heard.

Kempe's treatise offers a theology and hermeneutic of mirth which
periodically erupts in her narrative, but which often runs like a silent
subtext within it. Her own expressed purpose in telling her story conspires
with the mirthful economy of her narrative. In the prologue to her *Book*, she
reveals its spiritual program: "Here begins a short and comforting treatise
for sinful wretches, wherein they may have great solace and comfort" (1).
This statement seems to be redundant: sinful wretches are to be comforted
with solace and comfort. The apparent circularity of this statement, however, becomes more meaningful once "solace and comfort" are viewed as
distinct, component parts of the "comfortabyl tretys." The two terms are
not, in fact, redundant. We may recall from the general prologue to Chaucer's *Canterbury Tales* that Harry Bailey promises the pilgrims a free dinner
at the Tabard Inn for the one who tells "tales of best sentence and moost
solaas." Here *solaas* and *sentence* strike the literary balance between pleasure
or "pley" and profit toward the larger end of "confort."[10] While "comfort"
and "solace" are nearly synonomous by their modern definitions, they are
not in medieval usage. Bailey uses "solace" to mean "entertainment,"
"amusement," "pleasure," and even "mirth." In this context, "solace" is
equivalent to the Latin term, *gaudium* "joy" or "cheerfulness," as it was
applied to the goal of literature.[11] A Middle English translation of the
popular Latin verse, *Disticha Catonis*, places solace in the company of game
and joyousness:

> Sumtyme among thi bysynesse
> Melle solace, gamen and ioyowsnesse,
> That thou may the lyghtlyker
> With mery thouht thi trauayll ber.[12]

> (Sometimes among your business
> Mix solace, games, and joyousness,
> That you may the lighter
> With merry thought your travail bear.)

According to Glending Olson, literature which contained the proper mix-
ture of solace and comfort was considered spiritually and psychologically

beneficial.[13] The one satisfied the external man by inducing a "temperate cheerfulness" which lead ultimately to mental repose; the other repaired the internal man by profiting his soul with spiritual instruction.[14] As opposed to dishonest game, honest literary game not only relieved travail of mind and body with "merry thought," but was thought to repair the vice of *acedia*, or sloth.

The *solaas* of medieval literature was thus not without its spiritual aspect, nor was comfort without its game. In a defense of her convent place, a sixteenth-century Florentine playwright, Giovan Maria Cecchi, makes a case for the profit of what she calls "spiritual fun" (*spasso spirituale*):

> [E]verything, in fine, needs to rest. For this reason, I believe, those who established the convents saw fit to allow the nuns to put on *sacre rappresentazioni* and comedies in this season, making sure they were always above reproach and apt to produce spiritual fun and learning.[15]

Learning occurs in conjunction with this spiritual fun, even though the purpose of such activity is rest.

Kempe's own notion of mirth clearly shares in the concepts of spiritual fun and literary merriment. We can see this particularly in her story of the laughing penitent who gets abuse for a bargain. However, both her mirth and her solace serve more disturbing ends than simple entertainment. Neither supplies the rest prescribed for nuns. Kempe associates the words "solas" and "cowmfort" elsewhere in her treatise with "dysese" which she suffers for the love of God (2). Not coincidentally, she also finds merriment in this same "disease." As she reports soon after her story of laughter and good game,

> thys creatur þowt it was ful mery to be reprevyd for Goddys lofe; it was to hir gret solas & cowmfort whan sche was chedyn & fletyn for þe lofe of Ihesu for repreuyng of synne, . . ." (29).

> (this creature thought it was full merry to be reproved for God's love; it was to her a great solace and comfort when she was chided and scolded for the love of Jesus for the reproof of sin, . . .)

Like the man of her story, she seeks out merriment, solace and comfort in her own dis-ease. Her laughter, too, comes at her own expense.

Returning to the opening lines of her prologue, we find that she offers her treatise for the solace and comfort of sinners, that is, her readers. In directing the same solace at her readers that she seeks for herself, she constructs a hermeneutic of laughter and dis-ease in her prologue. Readers who are unable to take solace in her narrative are like the peevish steward who shuns laughter or the Canterbury monks who have too much invested in their own authority to laugh at her story. Laughter itself, as we recall, was the gesture—the sign—of the man's spiritual profit. Kempe, too, responds to the recriminations against her with laughter and merriment. Spiritual profit is achieved through laughter, but at the cost of one's own comfort. Kempe's laughter unsettles her contemporaries and her twentieth-century readers, causing us both to wonder at her sheer capacity for rejection and abuse. More than this, her laughter asserts a language of its own, one that disrupts the interrogatory discourse of clerks and monks and that interferes in the social system, causing her fellow townspeople to protest. It is a language of gesture which refuses the customary habits of the dominant discourse, authorizing positions of power and constructing social communities. It represents an excess of spiritual buoyancy dispersing the controlling efforts of her culture. Finally, Kempe's laughter spreads dis-ease like a contagion among her fellow townspeople and her readers.

As a mystical practice, Kempe's laughter demands a certain humility, a willingness to be discomfited. Her laughter inverts, even mocks, her culture, just as her conversion produces an inversion in her own life by turning all things "vp-so-down." As a hermeneutic, Kempe's offer of solace and comfort is double-edged, for it is really dis-ease that she instigates. Such dis-ease can lead to our own merriment only if lack of charity does not hinder us. What Kempe calls for in her introduction is a radical practice of charity through laughter—a hermeneutic designed to upset our conventions of reading, our expectations of authority, and our models of piety. In the midst of Kempe's writing, there is merriment leading to spiritual solace and mystical union.

The role of laughter in women's mystical practice, including Kempe's, is usually overlooked. Yet the laughter of women mystics does peal in their texts if only temporarily. It functions in different ways not only as an expression of mystical desire, but also as the disruptive force we have observed in Kempe's encounters with her critics. The capacity of laughter to recall the body accounts, in part, for its power to transgress. The laughter of the woman writer and mystic derives from the excess described by Rolle, and it becomes a sign of her triumph—over the devil, society, and their culture's ideology. It may not be possible to discern a tradition of laughter in women's writings, but we can collect traces of it in their works.

Kempe reports that St. Bridget "had a lawhyng cher," according to the saint's own handmaiden whom Kempe visited in Rome (95). More than this cannot be determined from the Middle English life or book of Bridget's *Revelations*. The Middle English life of Elizabeth of Hungary in Bokenham's *Legendys of Hooly Wummen* gives one startling account of the saint's laughter. Elizabeth is granted a vision of heaven during which she gazes on the face of Christ. Her first response is to laugh since it seemed most appropriate: "I thought I could no better express it than with laughing." As with Kempe, Elizabeth's laughter occurs during mystical ecstasy, as Elizabeth explains, "in joy and mirth I was entirely, . . ."[16] When Christ later withdraws this vision, her laughter turns to sorrow and weeping.

While the Middle English text of Elizabeth's life does not detail her cause for laughter, Julian of Norwich's *Showings* provides some explanation for her laughter. In the fourth revelation, Julian witnesses the suffering of Christ on the cross. In the fifth revelation, she contemplates God's glory in overcoming the devil. The vision prompts her to laugh and to justify a kind of pious laughter:

> Also I saw oure lorde scornyng hys malys and nowghtyng hys vnmyght, and he wille that we do so. For this syght, I laght myghtely, ... But I saw not Cryst laghyng; but wele I wott that syght that he shewed me made me to laugh, for I vnderstode that we may laugh in comfortyng of oure selfe and joyeng in god for the feend is overcome.

> (Also I saw our Lord scorn his malice and despise him as nothing, and he wants us to do so. Because of this sight I laughed greatly, . . . ; but I did not see Christ laughing, but I know well that it was the vision he showed me which made me laugh, for I understood that we may laugh to comfort ourselves and rejoice in God, because the devil is overcome.)[17]

Julian sketches three aspects of the Crucifixion, one of which is "sport." This is the sport of overcoming the devil which caused her to laugh greatly. As Colledge and Walsh point out, Julian's laughter invokes the figure of the "valiant woman" from Proverbs 31:25 who "shall laugh at the latter day." Like the valiant woman who laughs at the Last Judgment, Julian celebrates the overthrow of the fiend in her vision. In both cases, spiritual strength enables the mirthful acknowledgment of evil overcome. Laughter is a token of the mystic's strength and of the irreverent expression of her mirth. Her laughter compares with that described by Rolle proceeding from a cheerful conscience and love of God.

The difference between these examples of mystical laughter and Kempe's is that her mirth and laughter are integral to her discourse and to her social practice of irritating people. Her laughter provides the passage-way—the fissure in the text—through a manner of self-voiding. Although she draws attention to herself through her laughter, she slips through it to displace it with her own parables, including her narrative. Laughter is that excess which destabilizes the mystic self and text, permitting a passageway through which mystic and reader may approach God. The game—the sport—of mystical discourse in Kempe's *Book* lies in this mirthful progress through language to the secret transactions with God. Kempe calls herself one of the "Lord's own secretaries," by which she means "one who is entrusted with His secrets" (71). The secrets are both revealed and concealed in her laughter and in the silent merriment in the midst of her written text.

This merriment which runs throughout the narrative can be found most often in those places where she is confronted with great men. Her good game sometimes functions as a riddle, confounding others in order to teach. After Kempe decides to visit the Holy Land as a pilgrim, she pro-ceeds to Bristol to wait for a ship. There she is arrested and brought before the bishop of Worcester to be interrogated on her faith. Upon entering his chambers, she is greeted by some of the "most worshipful men in the town," who are dressed in finely cut and dagged clothes. Instead of greeting them in the customary fashion, she blesses herself. The bishop's men are baffled by her gesture, since it is ordinarily used to ward off devils rather than to greet the "worshipfullest men in town." In their naiveté they ask what devil ails her, and she answers, "Whose men are you?" Instead of catching on to her game, they reply with the obvious answer, "the Bishop's men." Kempe shakes her head, saying, "Nay, in truth, you are more like the Devil's men" (109). Whether she says this with a straight face or a "smiling cheer," Kempe is clearly making sport of them. They react predictably enough with anger at the fact that they have unwittingly had a joke played on them. At the same time, her joke is instructive. Their very inability to understand her riddle demonstrates the depth of their pride. Because they are men of the world, they fail to read the world, including its gestures, language, and appearances, as a token of God's love. When they are con-fronted with Kempe's signs, they read them carnally, that is, literally. The same carnality of their dress can be found in their speech and their literal interpretation of Kempe's gestural riddle. They chide and rebuke her before they are finally silenced by her wisdom. They end up thanking her for her guidance.

Such riddling gestures constitute a kind of code to which her laughter performs revelation. Kempe's laughter is a sign of her own excess of desire, of love for God, which imbues even casual social interactions, such as the one with the bishop's men. It is both the language of her desire and the source of her pleasure, as she makes clear to the Canterbury monks in her parable about laughter. Similarly, in her exchange with the bishop's men, she uses laughter—or good game—to repair lapsed desire. But laughter also defiles when it crosses cultural boundaries, serving as a spectacle of grace before skeptical spectators, such as the monks of Canterbury. At the same time, laughter has the power to defile the one who laughs, since it mocks conventional notions of piety and holiness. She who laughs takes defilement on herself, making a spectacle of it, in order to disperse speech, authority, and models of holiness, where a culture's power is located. The monks are reduced to threats to have her burned at the stake made good with a cartful of thorns, while the bishop's men become instructed through their own embarrassment.

The relationship between laughter and defilement is dramatically enacted in one of Kempe's parables about a priest. During her first arraignment before the Archbishop of York, he begs her not to teach or bother the people in his diocese. She refuses to promise not to do so. One of her examiners, trying to find one charge that will stick, accuses her of telling "the worst tales about priests that I ever heard" (126). In her own defense, Kempe clarifies the story to which the Church doctor refers:

Sir, wyth ȝowr reuerens, I spak but of o preste be þe maner of exampyl, þe whech as I haue lernyd went wil in a wode thorw þe sufferawns of God for þe profite of hys sowle tyl þe nygth cam up-on hym. He, destytute of hys herborwe, fond a fayr erber in þe whech he restyd þat nyght, hauyng a fayr pertre in þe myddys al floreschyd wyth flowerys & belschyd, and blomys ful delectabil to hys syght, wher cam a bere, gret & boistows, hogely to beheldyn, schakyng þe pertre & fellyng down þe flowerys. Gredily þis greuows best ete & deuowryd þo fayr flowerys. &, whan he had etyn hem, turnyng hys tayl-ende in þe prestys presens, voydyd hem owt ageyn at þe hymyr party. (126–27)

(Sir, by your reverence, I spoke but of one priest by way of example, who as I have learned went astray in a wood through the sufferance of God for the profit of his soul until night came upon him. He, destitute of lodging, found a fair arbor in which he rested that night. It had a fair pear tree in the midst of it, all adorned and embellished with flowers and blossoms full delectable to his sight. There came a bear, great and rough, ugly to behold, who shook the pear tree and caused the flowers to fall. Greedily this grievous beast ate and devoured those fair flowers. And, when he had eaten them, turning his tail-end to the priest, he discharged them out again at his rear end.)

Kempe's story is about the defilement of a priest who has lost his way in a wood. The spectacle of the bear first spoiling the beautiful pear tree and then nearly defecating in the priest's face causes him great horror and "heaviness," as one could imagine. He is baffled and shamed by the experience, but he is unable to interpret its meaning. This inability itself is a sure sign of his guilt.

An old hermit finally interprets the loathsome experience to the priest. The priest is himself the pear tree, the old man begins, who flourishes by administering the sacraments and saying the divine service. However, the priest's recent habit of babbling his service without devotion, occupying himself with worldly pursuits, and indulging in sins of gluttony, swearing, lying, backbiting, and detraction makes him also the bear in the story:

> Thus by thy mysgouernawns, lych on-to þe lothly ber, þu deuowryst & destroist þe flowerys & blomys of vertuows leuyng to thyn endles dampnacyon & many mannys hyndryng lesse þan þu haue grace of repentawns & amendyng. (127)

> (Thus by your misgovernance, like the loathly bear, you devour and destroy the flowers and blossoms of virtuous living to your endless damnation and many a man's hindrance unless you have the grace of repentance and amending.)

The priest in the story has to be defiled in order to recognize his own self-defilement through his squandering of the "flowers and blossoms of virtuous living" entrusted to his care.[18]

The tale ends here, but the reactions to it are crucial to the larger purpose of Kempe's narrative. The archbishop likes it. The man who had accused Kempe of telling bad tales says that he himself is "smitten to the heart" by her story. The success of Kempe's tale is, in part, its scatalogical humor—the bear defecating before the horrified priest. Her story is like many others in medieval literature which expose through its scatology the hypocrisy of religious figures. One good example by Chaucer is the *Summoner's Tale* in which a false friar is requited with a fart for his greedy exploitation of penitent sinners.[19] Yet the success of Kempe's tale lies not only in its scatalogical subject but in its rhetoric of defilement. That is, the tale, too, is the bear in that it smites the hearts of false sinners by defiling them, by making a spectacle of their own abomination. The near pun of the bear's *tayl* and Kempe's *tale* renders the "voiding" of one equivalent to the telling of the other. The effects are the same. Both religious figures, the priest in the story and the cleric in Kempe's audience, are smitten by the "loathly sight" and the hermit's gloss. Defilement is thus both the subject of the tale and the medium of its message. Through defilement the tale offers passage to holiness.

Where is the laughter? Given the pervasiveness of scatalogical humor in the medieval fabliau and in religious tales, there is little doubt that Kempe's story was greeted with laughter by some. Only those who, like the priest in the story, are guilty of spiritual defilement are unable to laugh. Kempe clues us into this when she answers the cleric who was smitten to the heart by her story: "If any man is ill pleased with my preaching, let him note it well, for he is guilty" (128). Those who are pleased with the story must have laughed, even if the narrative does not record it. Those evilly pleased will, of course, neither laugh at it nor much like it.

Laughter requires a reverence for spiritual and religious ideals and an irreverence for their institutionalization. As Mikhail Bakhtin writes, laughter accompanies "unbridled game with all that is most sacred and important from the point of view of official ideology."[20] Yet laughter is not as universal or endemic to medieval culture as Bakhtin argues. Kempe's laughter partakes of fabliau and dramatic parody with their capacity for scatalogy of evil and sin, but she also uses her humorous stories to establish a position for her own voice in the text and in the world separate from Church dominion.

This is comically illustrated by the fact that the archbishop of York, in spite of his approval of her story, offers payment to the man who will escort her out of his diocese. When one offers to lead her away for a noble instead of five schillings, the archbishop quibbles, saying he does not wish to "spend so much on her body." He offers five schillings and instructions to "lead her fast out of this country." Although he asks for Kempe's blessing, he is anxious to be rid of her because her "bold speech" is incompatible with his authority. One can imagine his frustration when Kempe is brought before him again by the Duke of Bedford's representatives. He makes it explicit: "What, woman, are you come again? I would willingly be delivered of you" (131). Her stories, like her speech, produce as much dis-ease as they do her own mirth.

Humor in her stories, then, is meant to instruct by defiling the guilty with laughter. Merriment is possible only at someone's expense. In the tale about the bear and the pear tree, that someone is the guilty priest. Most of the time, however, Kempe's merriment is achieved at her own expense. Laughter at her own ordeals not only brings her dis-ease: it is her chief mystical strategy for travelling what she calls "the way of high perfection." Mirthless readers are likely to miss the opportunity for spiritual buoyancy as well as Kempe's secret source of communication with God. Within the text of Kempe's suffering and visionary experiences, there is merriment tracking the way to high perfection.

In the first part of the book, Kempe struggles with her husband to regain control of her body. She desires to become celibate for Christ. John's resistance comes to a climax during one hot midsummer's eve as he and Margery bear cakes and ale homeward from York. He hits upon what he imagines to be the perfect riddle. It will force Kempe to become reconciled to her marital obligation by reminding her of her wifely devotion to him:

> Margery, yf her come a man wyth a swerd & wold smyte of myn hed les þan I schulde comown kendly wyth ȝow as I haue do be-for, seyth me trewth of ȝowr consciens—for ȝe sey ȝe wyl not lye—wheþyr wold ȝe suffyr myn hed to be smet of er ellys suffyr me to medele wyth ȝow a-ȝen as I dede sum-tyme? (23)

> (Margery, if a man came here with a sword and would smite off my head unless I made love to you as I did before, tell me the truth of your conscience—for you say you will not lie—whether you would suffer my head to be cut off or else suffer me to sleep with you again as I did at one time?)

Recognizing the threat to their agreement that they will live chastely together, Kempe begs him not to ask such questions. He insists, and she finally replies, "In truth, I would rather see you be slain than that we should turn again to our uncleanness." John's reaction is understandable: "You are no good wife." Scholars agree with John, but Kempe might have explained herself in the words of Mae West in a decidedly different context: "goodness has nothing to do with it." The way of high perfection, Kempe might have answered John, is not peopled with good wives. The humor of this encounter is partly at John's expense as well as her own, but it does not trivialize Kempe's struggle to reclaim her own body. Kempe's argument with John is as serious as are the threats to her chastity and the accusations of her heresy. The humor merely enables her to negotiate the boundaries of her culture, allowing her to inhabit the paradoxical position of being a worldly mystic, a chaste wife, and a woman worth listening to and reading.

Kempe even creates merriment out of the temptations through which she is punished for her pride. The first occurs soon after her conversion when Kempe presumptuously decides that she loves Christ more than he does her. Knowing her vulnerabilites, Christ visits her with the "snare of lechery." A man she knew well propositions her in her parish church of St. Margaret shortly before evensong services. Kempe is vexed by his proposal all through the service and finally agrees to it. In fact, she shamelessly propositions him only to be rebuffed by his remark that he would rather be hewn as small as meat in a pot than sleep with her (15). Her humiliation causes her great distress, but his unexpected rebuff and put-down has a different effect upon the reader. It is comical even if Kempe suffers as a result of it.

Her second temptation is brought about by her refusal to recognize God's vision of the damned as His. She mistakes it for the devil's, and He vows to teach her to know the difference. Again, she is tested by lecherous suggestions. This time, the devil presents her with religious men "showing their bare members to her." The devil then instructs her to choose which one she likes best, for she shall have them all: "And he said she liked one of them better than all the others. She thought that he spoke the truth; . . ." (145). While the temptation is vexing to her, only the most phlegmatic medieval reader would need to search for cause to laugh at her ordeal. Failed lechery, like lechery itself, is often occasion for laughter in medieval literature. Again, Chaucer provides some pertinent examples. One need only think of the Wife of Bath's Prologue, the *Miller's Tale*, or the *Merchant's Tale* to recover the spirit of mirth by which medieval narratives turned *sentence* into laughter. Pride, as Kempe and Chaucer know, finds its most comical expression in lechery.

In spite of the suffering this particular vision causes her, it has significant consequences for her ongoing disturbance of priestly authority. Clearly, this vision mocks the exposed members of the priests as much as it brings Kempe shame and fear. The ideological implications of this vision have been described by Sarah Beckwith:

> here she might be seen as lifting the veil, the priestly skirts that hid the Phallus which reproduces priestly law as God. She shows it to be merely a penis, or in her own words an "abhominabyal [sic] membre."[21]

What appears to Kempe as an evil vision contrived by the devil conveniently suits two purposes: her own penance through dis-ease, and her ongoing dismantling of the language and authority of the magisterium. This vision is a revelation in the sense that it reveals what was hidden, but it is a revelation which reduces the symbolic to the literal and physical, rather than offering the possibility of mystical ascent from the literal to the symbolic. It embarrasses the discourse and authority of priests by reducing them to this spectacle of "abhominacyons." Kempe is made to endure this horrifying vision for twelve days so that, as an angel tells her, "you will know thereby whether it is better that God speaks to you or the Devil" (146). At stake in this lesson is ecclesiastical authority to proclaim law, doctrine, and learning. Kempe's own persecution by this vision disguises its real force, which is to dismantle priestly authority, to subvert it, and finally, to establish her own right to speak. Her vision de-mystifies priestly authority by reducing it to an "abominable member."

Considering how important it is that the mystical text authorize its own separate discourse alongside the magisterium discursive site, Kempe's vision helps accomplish this positioning in a radical way. At the same time that she clearly seeks out clerical approval of her mystical visions and practices, she undermines the discourse which excludes her as a woman and a member of the *indocti* who presumably could not read or write. Her own embarrassment at this vision does not diminish its power to embarrass the priestly caste and to call their authority into serious question.

It is important to remember that, although Kempe falls into despair over both temptations, her narrative maintains a twenty-year distance over these events. She refers to herself as "this creature," thereby creating a tale of her own life in which she is merely a representative figure. Furthermore, one should never forget the conditions under which her narrative was produced: she dictates these events to a scribe who belongs to the same group of religious men as those who are exposing themselves in her vision. One is certainly permitted to speculate about their interaction at these points in the narrative. Embarrassment might cause Kempe to stumble through these parts, but it is hard to imagine that the woman who believed that holy folk who had suffered for Christ's love had cause to laugh dictated these sections soberly. In any case, readers need not attribute these temptations to Kempe's neurosis; instead, they should remember Kempe's caution that he who is evilly pleased beware, for he is guilty.

Kempe's visions, as we have seen in these examples, are not exempt from her mirth. It is the humor of her visions, rather than of her life, which is the most troubling of all. When we feel inclined to laugh at some of her visions, we may consider this laughter inappropriate to mystical contemplation or meditation. Yet before we blame Kempe for naiveté, we need to remember Elizabeth of Hungary, Bridget of Sweden, and Julian of Norwich, all of whom are reported to have laughed during highly serious mystical revelations. Kempe's visions do not always induce her own laughter so much as they do ours. Her own merriment exists not in the visions themselves but in the text, in the writing/telling of them. Although this type of merriment is the most threatening to her authority as a mystic and author, she insists upon it.

The best example of visionary merriment is her vision of the Virgin's death. The apostles kneel before the body of the Virgin praying for grace. As Kempe witnesses this, she bursts out into her customary loud crying and weeping. Curiously, the apostles turn and command her to "cease and be still." Even they, apparently, could not brook her disruptive weeping. Kempe refuses to be intimidated, however, and ends up reprimanding *them*:

> Wolde ʒe I xulde see þe Modyr of God deyin & I xulde not wepyn? It may not be, for I am so ful of sorwe þat I may not wythstonde it. I must nedys crying & wepyn. (175)

> (Do you desire that I see the Mother of God die and that I should not weep? It cannot be so, for I am so full of sorrow that I cannot withstand it. I simply must cry and weep.)

Her presumptuousness at instructing the apostles is only part of the outrageousness of this vision. The humor of it lies in the gap between the world of the vision and the world of Kempe's response to it. In the rest of her book we can observe the type of vision in which Kempe converses with Christ or with the Virgin. These visions are quite different from those narrative visions in which Kempe observes and participates in the life of Christ. The latter type are encouraged by such spiritual treatises as the *Meditations on the Life of Christ*. Although participation in the events of Christ's life is consistently enjoined, nowhere does the mystical narrative "break" in the way it does here in Kempe's vision.[22] The apostles cease to be objects of Kempe's meditation as they speak across the boundaries of the mystical spectacle. It is as if her own vision turns on her in the ultimate reprimand. Modern readers might be familiar with this kind of occurrence in contemporary literature, drama, and film where characters break the fictional conventions by directly addressing author, audience, or reader. In medieval mystical discourse, such an occurrence is highly unusual as well as humorous.

This breaking vision allows Kempe to travel between the worlds of her visions and those of her ordeals. In addition, she tampers with the world of the text and the world of the vision. As in other kinds of mystical discourse that we examined in chapter 2, Kempe's visions and colloquies with Christ constitute a secret oral text which exists apart from the written text we read. However, Kempe breaks down the barriers between the two, allowing the visionary text to seep into the physical text. She creates the gap through her own weeping, but her readers can do the same with their laughter. Laughter here opens up the text to the other place from which the divine speaks. It is significant that Kempe's exchange with the apostles is immediately followed by the Virgin's speech in her soul. She creates that place for divine speech through her deconstruction of the boundaries between mystical and worldly experience. For her readers the same place is created by laughter.

Kempe's mirth resides in the midst of her written text, whether it is proclaimed by her own laughter or not. Laughter itself constitutes her own version of the mystical *volo*, that desirous utterance which makes possible the visitation of divine speech. At the same time, her merriment undermines the discourse which excludes her through an act of defilement. Finally, her merriment and mirth, together with her laughter, enact a dis-ease in her listeners and readers—a displacement through which they discover the true discourse within the text. Mirth is created by and creates the excess of desire which fissures language and permits extravagant speech.[23]

Ultimately, Kempe's mirth and laughter engender a crisis of reading, for they undermine the authority of her own speech and text. As readers we may conclude that the merriment throughout her text is unintentional, that it is the result of the disjunction between her own self-image and our reading of her. Yet the incidences of her laughter discussed above suggest that she deliberately creates and participates in the humor. Her understanding of mirth and solace also sets up a mystical discourse in the midst of which there is merriment. Finally, the narrative distance between Kempe as author and Kempe as "creatur" of her tale allows for a retrospection which knows more than the experience. She herself distinguishes at the end of Book 1 between what she calls the "trewe sentens" of her book and the "experiens" (220). Such a distinction allows for merriment in the narrative.

As we have seen, the spirit of Kempe's conversion and of her mission in the world depends on heavenly mirth and worldly good game. She uses good game to restore the wayward and spiritually negligent to God's grace. Perhaps Kempe's own parable of her laughter has more to tell us about the way in which she views her function as a mystic. By making herself the object of derision, she follows the way to high perfection of the holy fool of God. Like the fool of St. Paul who suffers the revilement of the world, (1 Cor. 4:10–13), Kempe endures the scorn of her contemporaries as well as our laughter to earn her own salvation. Kempe's holy folly also serves God's purpose as it is formulated in 1 Cor. 1:19–20:

> I will destroy the wisdom of the wise, and the prudence of the prudent I will reject. . . . Hath not God made foolish the wisdom of this world? For seeing that in the wisdom of God the world, by wisdom, knew not God, it pleased God, by the foolishness of our preaching, to save them that believe.

In this passage Paul is arguing that salvation lies not in human wisdom or eloquence but in foolishness. A world blinded by its own excessive reverence for learning and eloquence must be turned upside down in order to be set aright; it must be made sane by being confounded; and it must learn divine wisdom in the fool's folly.

Kempe tells us that God turned everything *vp-so-down*, including her health, prosperity, and the respect she commanded in society (1). Later, Christ calls her a "mirror amongst men" in that she reminds them of their own unregeneracy, their foolishness, and their pride. She is thus an inverted mirror—a holy fool—whose mystical project is the world's salvation through dis-ease, even laughter. She endeavors to do to others what Christ did to her own life, to de-stabilize them so that they may find the way to high perfection in their own dis-ease. She clearly sees herself as living in a topsy-turvy world where the wisdom of clerics is foolishness and her own laughter proclaims wisdom. Her powers come from Christ himself who continually promises to give her "grace enough to answer every cleric in the love of God" (17). The way of high perfection for Kempe as a holy fool is the *via paradoxica*, or as she might have called it, the "up-so-down" way, and it is fraught with suffering, along with laughter and good game.

The fool's folly comes from excess of love which does violence to the mystic and her speech. It is excessive in that it transgresses the safe boundaries of human reason, leading to that paradoxical new wisdom which is holy folly and spiritual buoyancy. To the world, this kind of love has always seemed sheer madness.[24] For the holy fool, such love requires excess which spills over from mystical contemplation to action in the world.

Holy folly brings the violent charity of mystical contemplation into the world. This kind of charity was described by Richard of St.-Victor as the third stage of contemplation. He called this love alternately *excessus mentis* and *alienatio mentis*, because it produces a self-alienation and an excess which makes union with God possible. Various Middle English mystical treatises, including the *Cloud of Unknowing* and the *Book of Privy Counselling*, explicitly link this "excess of mind" to an excess of love. Thus, "excess of loue" in *Privy Counselling* causes one to become "ravished out of mind."[25] Richard of St.-Victor gives a dramatic account of this alienation of mind:

> In hoc itaque statu plene compescitur profundeque sopitur carnalium desideriorum turba, et *fit in celo silentium quasi hora dimidia*. Et quicquid molestis inest absorbetur a gloria. In hoc statu dum mens a seipsa alienatur, dum in illud divini arcani secretarium rapitur, dum ab illo divini amoris incendio undique circumdatur, intime penetratur, usquequaque inflammatur, seipsam

penitus exult, divinum quemdam affectum induit et inspecte purchritudini configurata tota in aliam gloriam transit.[26]

(In this state the turbulence of carnal desires is entirely subdued and profoundly quieted, and *there was in the heavens a silence for about half an hour.* (Apoc. 8:1) And any remaining vexation is absorbed into glory. In this state when the mind is alienated from itself, it is carried away by the secret of divine mystery. Then it is embraced by the fire of divine love which, having penetrated it inwardly, inflames it utterly, until divested completely of itself, the soul assumes a certain divine affection and, having become like the beauty it contemplates, it passes over into a new glory.)

For the holy fool, this fire of love produces an alteration of mind through alienation. While the turbulence of carnal love is quieted in the holy fool's madness, it is superseded by the tumult of his or her violent charity. Kempe calls it alternately the "ardor of love" and "grace" which passes "above her reason and bodily wits" (29, 3). The Middle English equivalent of this excess of love is "ravyshing," another term Kempe often uses to describe the ineffable sundering of the self from the surrounding world.[27] Both Richard of St.-Victor and Richard Rolle identify *excessus mentis* with the final grade of love, *singularis*.[28] The "singular love" to which Kempe aspires demands an infiltration of the secular world with this mystical state. There, it promises public contempt, rather than mystical union. Christ warns her, "You shall be eaten and gnawed by the people of the world as the cod is gnawed by rats (17). Holy folly clearly carries none of the protection or allowances made for the court fool.

The fool of God is required to "proclaim and live, through his word and daily life, the gospel of the beatitudes, to participate in Christ's *kenosis*, passion and divine folly through infinite love."[29] The tradition of the holy fool in Western culture is usually identified with St. Francis. Two main features of his life provide a model for holy folly: a rejection of worldly things and institutions and a spiritual vocation which combines the contemplative life with the active life.[30] In addition, the fourteenth-century account of St. Francis' life, the *Speculum Perfectionis*, reports that St. Francis even encouraged his followers to become holy fools:

Brothers, brothers! The Lord has called me by the way of humility, and he has shown me the way of simplicity; and I do not want you to mention to me any other rule, neither that of S. Augustine, or of S. Benedict, nor of S. Bernard. And the Lord told me that he wished me to be a new fool in the world, and that he did not want to lead us by any other way than by that wisdom; for by your learning and your wisdom God will confound you.[31]

Whether apocryphal or not, this story points to the main justification for holy folly, the imitation of Christ through the way of simplicity.

There is evidence in Kempe's *Book* that she envisions herself as a holy fool and that others do as well. Kempe is mistreated by the group of pilgrims with whom she is to visit the Holy Land. Among the abuses she endures at their hands is one which occurs in the English town of Constance:

> They cuttyd hir gown so schort þat it come but lytil be-nethyn hir kne & dedyn hir don on a whyte canwas in maner of a sekkyn gelle, for sche xuld ben holdyn a fool & þe pepyl xuld not makyn of hir ne han hir in reputacyon.[32]

> (They cut her gown so short that it came just barely below her knee and made her wear a white canvas in the manner of a sackcloth apron, in order that she should be considered a fool and the people should not make much of her nor hold her in high repute.)

The attempt by the Constance pilgrims to undermine her reputation is merely one of many indignities she suffers, yet it is a significant one. The passage suggests that they are deliberately trying to dress her up to be a fool and to discredit her among her contemporaries. It is an action which marvelously recapitulates Herod's mocking of Christ according to the account in the *Meditations on the Life of Christ*:

> Herod, longing in truth to see miracles performed by Him, rejoiced, but was unable to obtain a miracle or even a word. Therefore, thinking Him a fool, in derision he had Him dressed in white, and sent Him back to Pilate. Thus you can see how He was regarded by everyone not only as a criminal but as a fool; but He bore everything most patiently.[33]

Kempe, of course, also bears her treatment patiently. My point here is not that the painful incident that Kempe suffers is the result of her own self-fashioning. Nor, of course, would her detractors wish anyone to see a connection between the two events. It is possible, though, that Kempe's narrative alludes to the treatment of Christ as a fool—that here, too, she imitates Christ. The typology of holy folly outlined above receives a new twist in *The Book of Margery Kempe*. The habit of her folly—the white sackcloth—is a curious parody of the wedding habit Christ instructs her to wear. Early in her *Book* after her conversion, Christ instructs her to wear white and a wedding ring as tokens of her espousal to Him. Since she is the mother of fourteen children, Christ's request promises to expose her to ridicule and charges of hypocrisy. She is often interrogated about her white habit. "Are you a maiden?" the archbishop of York asks her. "Nay, sir, I am no maiden; I am a wife" (124). Kempe's response is itself a kind of riddle, since the white clothing signifies her betrothal to Christ. In effect, Christ makes her his fool by demanding that she dress in white. The one action by the angry Constance townspeople merely recapitulates the other. It is as Christ's bride that Kempe accepts the vocation of holy fool.

Kempe's holy folly is "singular," to use her own word. A female fool of Christ is defined differently than is a male fool. Because she is outside the dominant culture, a female fool is already anomalous. Her proclamation of this fact in the person of a holy fool renders her anomalousness dangerous. From the position of holy fool, she makes public assaults on her culture and the institutions which authorize it. Even though the male fool rejects the world, he does not risk his own culture as the female fool does. His holy folly finds institutional acceptance, as St. Francis's did, and it benefits from the patriarchal prerogatives of his culture. For example, St. Francis was able to travel freely around Italy, while the feminine representatives of his order, the Clares, were not. The domain of holy folly is the world; because men have always inhabited their societies and cultures, their holy folly is merely a change in lifestyle within that world. By contrast, holy folly demands of women that they assault the world which excludes them, not in order to become a part of it but to give it considerable discomfort.

Kempe's shame and dis-ease are consistently induced by her pre-sumptuous insistence on proclaiming the mirth of heaven—of being, in effect, a new fool, a female fool, *in the world*. This is why monks wish her behind a wall of stone, why archbishops pray her to leave their dioceses, why she is advised to return to spinning and carding like other wives, and why she is despised by men and women. Her holy folly violates the medi-eval ideal of chastity which, as we have seen in chapter 1, depends as much on the sealed body as it does on the privatized woman's sphere. That is, the chaste female body exempts itself from any kind of publicity, from the world of transactions, including discursive ones. As Peter Brown has ar-gued, female chastity differed from male chastity because the female body was already defined as private, untouched by the corruption of the public.[34] Chastity further interred the female body safely within the private sphere, while the chaste male body was viewed as already corrupted by learning and public responsibilities. Kempe's insistence on remaining in the world, therefore, threatens the very boundaries of holiness and medieval culture.

The desire of her contemporaries to have her shut up in an anchorage or returned to her husband reflects the investment medieval culture had in the sealed female body. Holy women were not supposed to roam or to laugh even during the late Middle Ages, when new forms of religious life became available to women.[35] While women in the mendicant orders might have been allowed to devote themselves to works of charity in the world, the female mystic who attempted to do the same was subjected to ridicule and the Church's stringent controls. As Weinstein and Bell have pointed out about the female saint,

> in religion as in other walks of life women were discouraged from aspiring to autonomous, much less public, roles. A reading of hundreds of accounts of male saints' lives renders again and again a picture of the faithful beating a path to the door of the hermit's cell, swarming to touch the bishop's robe, flocking to hear a holy preacher. For saintly women an equally vivid but sharply contrasting picture emerges: they gave unasked advice; they sought out the poor and the sick; if they preached at all, it was only to a very few who would listen. A woman claiming divine inspiration was immediately subject to special supervision, a male confessor assigned to review her every manifestation; and a woman whose religious impulses led her into the streets became fair game for every form of ridicule and even violence.[36]

These restrictions were operative even among the Beguines, who resisted strict enclosure and fashioned religious lives in the world. They ultimately earned church approval by staying within their communities.[37]

We can observe the violence to which Kempe is subjected for her publicity. Rape is a very real and recurrent threat to her travels in England and abroad. Her fears of rape prove to be justified when she is taken aside by the Steward of Leicester after one of her arrests. After attempting to intimidate her with Latin, he resorts to "lewd suggestions," translating his discursive threats into sexual ones. She explicitly says that he nearly carried out his plan to "for-lyn" ("violate") her. She is forced to travel with a male companion and even young women to protect herself from other such assaults. Yet some scholars dismiss her fears, attributing them to her "sick, neurotic psyche" or even making fun of them.[38] Rape is merely one of the many ways in which Kempe's contemporaries try to avenge her refusal to play the holy woman: silent, sequestered, her body erased from public discourse.

Margery Kempe has no model for the holy folly she practices. She does have Richard Rolle's defense of holy mirth to guide her, but her laughter has no source of legitimacy. It is always disruptive. If "all laughter is allied with the monstrous," as Clément has argued, Kempe's laughter and her holy mirth proclaim this alliance by placing her culture at risk. She crosses the boundaries of the "masculine integrity of the body" which underlies the repression of women's bodies, their interaction with their world, and their speech. Kempe's laughter breaks up the discourse of power circumscribed by learning and the repressed female body. She breaks out of the circle of interrogators who attempt to objectify her with their learning and abuse. It is because her laughter does not belong to models for holy living that it is monstrous.

An early Christian story about Mary, the sister of Martha provides an interesting comment on the monstrosity of women's laughter. In the second century A.D., gnostic Christians maintained "whoever the Spirit inspires is divinely ordained to speak, whether man or woman." Orthodox Christians responded with a rationale for the exclusion of women from the priesthood. They cited a discussion between Christ's disciples and Mary and Martha over this same topic. In the course of this discussion, John reminded Mary and Martha that at the Last Supper Christ blessed the bread and cup and offered them to the men, not the women. The reason for this, as Martha interjects, is that Mary laughed while Christ blessed the bread and wine. Over Mary's protests that she no longer laughs, the disciples agree that her laughter is the reason women should not become priests.[39] Mary's laughter is monstrous because it seems to undermine the highly serious ritual of the Sacrament. Clearly, holy folk should not laugh during the partaking of Christ's body and blood. Laughter disperses and disrupts such ritual and the institutional power it celebrates.

Like Mary of the early Christian story, Kundry the witch in Wagner's opera *Parsifal* was cursed for laughing at Christ's passage.[40] In both cases, women's laughter is a sign of their irreverence and weakness and an excuse for excluding them from high religious ritual and society. Women's laughter instills fear in the society which excludes them. Kempe recasts her own laughter as a sign of her own wisdom and spiritual strength, while exploiting the fear it creates in others. Her laughter exposes corruption, hypocrisy, and pride; at the same time, it redeems those who are able to share in her merriment. This is the central paradox of her text: that laughter is both monstrous and redemptive, that it redeems by defying and defiling what society holds sacred.

Kempe's laughter is especially important because it makes room for her speech and her mystical narrative. Her laughter not only provides a place within the dominant discursive system for her narrative and parables, it is the parable itself, the sign which must be decoded even in the midst of silence and of writing. Kempe's narrative as a whole can be seen to imitate the little parable about the man who laughed when he was reviled by others. The great men and masters are unable to solve the riddle of the man's laughter. They are also incapable of laughing. Both incapacities are expressions of their own lack of charity. Those unable to laugh are likewise unable to read mirth and good game in the midst of writing. Kempe knows that lack of charity is the main hindrance to the reading of her own text, as her prologue suggests. Yet that is the fate of parables, especially those in which there is merriment. Whether Kempe's readers discover the merriment in Kempe's narrative or not, it is crucial to her speech. It is the sign of her excess of love and the place from which she speaks. Yet though her laughter explodes into the narrative in a few places, she still regarded mirth as her secret. She viewed herself as a guardian and proclaimer of that secret, as one of the Lord's 'secretaries' in the medieval sense of the word, and as the site of his speech. Her good game and merriment constitute the secret through which she and her readers may discover high perfection by way of the monstrous.

Kempe's laughter, however, is not her only strategy for defying the language of the world and inscribing mystical desire in her text. Her tears provide a second method for disrupting the clerical discourse of power and inserting her own body and speech in the world and the text. The next chapter will show how Kempe returns reading and writing to the body in order to privilege her own meditations over the textual culture from which she is excluded.

Notes

1. While Kempe's naiveté is almost universally assumed, it continues to be a subject for discussion and criticism. Louise Collis characterizes Kempe's visionary colloquies with God as "naive and tedious," *Memoirs of a Medieval Woman: The Life and Times of Margery Kempe* (New York: Crowell, 1964), 256. David Knowles finds much of Kempe's treatise the work of "a sincere and devout, but very hysterical woman," *The English Mystical Tradition* (London: Burns and Oates, 1961), 147. Wolfgang Riehle considers her naive sincerity to be the product of a morbidly exaggerated sensibility," *The Middle English Mystics*, trans. Bernard Standring (London: Routledge and Kegan Paul, 1981), 118. Anthony Goodman's probing beyond the *Book*'s "plausible naivetés of expression" discovers autobiographical material which "has been shaped in a sophisticated and highly selective way," "The Piety of John Brunham's Daughter, of Lynn," in *Medieval Women*, ed. Derek Baker (Oxford: Basil Blackwell, 1978), 349. For Ute Stargardt, Kempe's sincerity reveals an exasperating simple-mindedness, "The Beguines of Belgium, the Dominican Nuns of Germany, and Margery Kempe," in *The Popular Literature of Medieval England*,

ed. Thomas J. Heffernan, Tennessee Studies in Literature, vol. 28 (Knoxville: University of Tennessee Press, 1985), 301–8.

2. Hélène Cixous and Catherine Clément, *The Newly Born Woman*, trans. Betsy Wing (Minneapolis: University of Minnesota Press, 1986), 33.

3. See his analysis of laughter in *Rabelais and His World*, trans. Helene Iswolsky (Bloomington: Indiana University Press, 1984), 20–58. Stallybrass and White also discuss the power of laughter to invoke the grotesque body, *The Politics and Poetics of Transgression* (Ithaca, NY: Cornell University Press, 1986), 8–20.

4. See Moore, *The Formation of a Persecuting Society: Power and Deviance in Western Europe, 950–1250* (Oxford: Basil Blackwell, 1987), 100–23. As the basis for his analysis, Moore uses Mary Douglas's ideas about pollution in *Purity and Danger: An Analysis of the Concepts of Pollution and Taboo* (London: Routledge and Kegan Paul, 1966).

5. Thornton, *Margery Kempe: An Example in the English Pastoral Tradition* (London: SPCK, 1960), 2.

6. John Chrysostom, *Homilies on the Epistle to the Hebrews*, ed. F. Gardner, *A Select Library of Nicene and Post-Nicene Fathers*, vol. 14 (Grand Rapids, MI: Eerdmans, 1978), Homily 25.

7. *Incendium Amoris of Richard Rolle of Hampole*, ed. Margaret Deanesly, Publications of the University of Manchester, Historical Series, 26 (London, 1915), 170.

8. See Rolle's discussion of this problem, *Incendium Amoris*, 171–72.

9. Rolle, *The Fire of Love* in *The Fire of Love, and the Mending of Life, or the Rule of Living*, trans. Richard Misyn, ed. Ralph Harvey, EETS, o.s. 106 (London, 1896; rpt. 1973), 38, 10, 87, and 82.

10. Glending Olson discusses the Host's game in terms of medieval ideas of play and recreation, *Literature as Recreation in the Later Middle Ages* (Ithaca, NY: Cornell University Press, 1982), 156–63.

11. For the medieval theory of literature as a source of cheerfulness, see Olson, *Literature as Recreation*, 55–89.

12. III, 6. Quoted in Olson, *Literature as Recreation*, 94.

13. For both the "hygenic" and "literary" justifications for the use of solace in literature, see Olson, *Literature as Recreation*, 39–127.

14. The idea of "temperate cheerfulness" leading to repose is a physician's explanation for the therapeutic effects of literature; see Olson, *Literature as Recreation*, 39–89.

15. *L'Acquisto di Giacobbe*, Prologo, ll. 69–77. Quoted in Elissa Weaver, "Spiritual Fun: A Study of Sixteenth-Century Tuscan Convent Theater," in *Women in the Middle Ages and the Renaissance: Literary and Historical Perspectives*, ed. Mary Beth Rose (Syracuse, NY: Syracuse University Press, 1986), 176.

16. Osbern Bokenham, *Legendys of Hooly Wummen*, ed. Mary S. Serjeantson, EETS, o.s. 206 (London: Oxford University Press, 1938; rpt. 1971), 284.

17. *A Book of Showings to the Anchoress Julian of Norwich*, Part 2, ed. Edmund Colledge and James Walsh (Toronto: Pontifical Institute of Mediaeval Studies, 1978), 348–49. Translated by Edmund Colledge and James Walsh *Julian of Norwich, Showings* (New York: Paulist Press, 1978), 202.

18. The only analogue I have found for this tale comes from medieval sermons

against backbiters who "deflower" the "tree of good doctrine" with their nasty speech. See G. R. Owst, *Literature and the Pulpit in Medieval England* (Oxford: Basil Blackwell, 1961), 454.

19. Larry D. Benson, ed., *The Riverside Chaucer* (New York: Riverside, 1987), 3.1709–2294.

20. *Rabelais and His World*, 84.

21. Sarah Beckwith, "A Very Material Mysticism: The Medieval Mysticism of Margery Kempe," in *Medieval Literature: Criticism, Ideology and History*, ed. David Aers (Brighton: Harvester Press, 1986), 53. Beckwith goes on to argue that the vision fails to embarrass the myth of God's transcendence and the law's power because it is sent as a punishment. In the context of Kempe's laughter, however, the one does not rule out the other.

22. Pseudo-Bonaventure, *Meditations on the Life of Christ*, trans. Isa Ragusa, ed. Isa Ragusa and Rosalie Green (Princeton, NJ: Princeton University Press, 1961), 15–21, in particular.

23. See ch. 2 above.

24. See Roland Maisonneuve's discussion of the holy fool in eastern and western religious traditions, "Margery Kempe and the Eastern and Western Tradition of the 'perfect fool,'" in *The Medieval Mystical Tradition in England: Papers Read at the Second Exeter Symposium, July 1982*, ed. Marion Glasscoe (Exeter: University of Exeter, 1982), 1–17.

25. For Richard's discussion of *excessus mentis*, see Richard of St.-Victor, *Richard de Saint-Victor: les quatre degrés de la violente charité*, ed. and trans. Gervais Dumeige (Paris, 1955), 155. Riehle explains how this idea of excessive love becomes translated in English mysticism, *The Middle English Mystics*, 92–94. *Alienatio mentis* has been linked to holy folly particularly in the poetry of Jacopone da Todi, see George T. Peck, *The Fool of God: Jacopone da Todi* (University: University of Alabama Press, 1980), 170–71. A more general history of *alienatio mentis* in the Middle Ages is provided by Gerhart B. Ladner, "*Homo Viator*: Medieval Ideas of Alienation and Order," *Speculum* 42 (1967): 239–46.

26. *Richard de Saint-Victor*, 167. Examples of the violence of this excessive love may be found in the *laude* of Jacopone da Todi, particularly numbers 82 and 90 in *Jacopone da Todi: The Lauds*, ed. Serge and Elizabeth Hughes (New York: Paulist Press, 1982).

27. Riehle, *Middle English Mystics*, 92. Riehle claims that Kempe confused the erotic and mystical meanings of the verb *ravishen* in her work, 96.

28. For a thorough study of Rolle's indebtedness to Richard, see Rosamund Allen, "'Singuler Lufe': Richard Rolle and the Grammar of Spiritual Ascent," in *The Medieval Mystical Tradition: Papers Read at Dartington Hall, July 1984*, ed. Marion Glasscoe, Proceedings of the Third International Exeter Symposium (Cambridge: D. S. Brewer, 1984), 28–54. It is interesting that Richard's concept of *excessus mentis*, according to R. Allen, derives from his Vulgate mistranslation of Psalm 67:28: "Ibi Beniamin adulescentulus, in mentis excess," 49n.

29. Maisonneuve, "Tradition of the 'perfect fool,'" 1.

30. John V. Fleming, *An Introduction to the Franciscan Literature of the Middle Ages* (Chicago: Franciscan Herald Press, 1977), 8–11.

31. Quoted in John Moorman, *The History of the Franciscan Order* (Oxford: Clarendon Press, 1968), 55. Moorman explains that a later version of the *Speculum Perfectionis* uses *novellum pactum* "a new way or pact," rather than *novellus pazzus* "a new fool." However, the earlier version is the correct one, according to Moorman, 55n. See Fleming's account of the controversy surrounding the *Speculum*'s authenticity, *Introduction to the Franciscan Literature of the Middle Ages*, 54–59.

32. *The Book of Margery Kempe*, 62. Meech and Allen suggest that the word *gelle* might have alluded to *gill*, "a familiar or contemptuous term applied to women," 286n.

33. Ragusa and Green, *Meditations on the Life of Christ*, 328.

34. *The Body and Society*, 227.

35. Carolyn Walker Bynum discusses the new forms of religious life available to women, *Holy Feast and Holy Fast: The Religious Significance of Food to Medieval Women* (Berkeley: University of California Press, 1987), 14–21.

36. Donald Weinstein and Rudolph M. Bell, *Saints and Society: The Two Worlds of Western Christendom, 1000–1700* (Chicago: University of Chicago Press, 1982), 232.

37. For an account of the Beguines, see Ernest W. McDonnell, *The Beguines and Beghards in Medieval Culture* (New Brunswick, NJ: Rutgers University Press, 1954); see also Elizabeth Alvilda Petroff, *Medieval Women's Visionary Literature* (New York: Oxford University Press, 1986), 171–78; Susan Dickman contrasts Kempe and other mystics like her who inhabit the world with the beguines who remain sequestered from it, "Margery Kempe and the Continental Tradition of the Pious Woman," in *The Medieval Mystical Tradition*, 156.

38. Meech and Allen's commentary, 112; see also 236 for another example. Ute Stargardt follows T. W. Coleman in calling Kempe's fear of rape "inordinate," *English Mystics of the Fourteenth Century* (Westport, CT: Greenwood Press, 1971), 158. Stargardt goes further to claim that Kempe's fears of rape are ludicrous when Kempe reaches the age of 60 and demands protection from younger women during a pilgrimage in Germany: "Thus Margery's abnormal fears resulted in the ludicrous situation of an old crone's virtue being guarded by young women instead of their honor being protected by an old woman past her prime and sexual allure," "The Beguines and Margery Kempe," in *The Popular Literature of Medieval England*, ed. Thomas J. Heffernan, Tennessee Studies in Literature, vol. 28 (Knoxville: University of Tennessee Press, 1985), 299. The underlying implication here that rape has anything to do with sexual allure is inexcusable and irresponsible, considering the many studies available which show rape to be a crime of violence rather than of sexual desire. In addition, Kempe experienced enough threats of rape to make Stargardt's criticism an insensitive one. Maureen Fries makes this same point about Stargardt's argument in "Margery Kempe," in *An Introduction to the Medieval Mystics of Europe*, ed. Paul E. Szarmach (Albany: State University of New York Press, 1984), 231.

39. The story appears in Elaine Pagels, *The Gnostic Gospels* (New York: Vintage Books, 1979), 78–79.

40. See Clément's discussion in Hélène Cixous and Catherine Clément, *The Newly Born Woman*, 32–33.

5. Embodying the Text: Boisterous Tears and Privileged Readings

> Study, then, O man, to know Christ: get to know your Saviour. His body, hanging on the cross, is a book, open for your perusal. The words of this book are Christ's actions, as well as his sufferings and passion, for everything that he did serves for our instruction. His wounds are the letters or characters, the five chief wounds being the five vowels and the others the consonants of your book. Learn how to read the lamentations—and alas! too, the reproaches, outrages, insults and humiliations which are written therein.
>
> The Monk of Farne

The medieval practice of imitating Christ, as chapter 1 made clear, was not confined to the reenactment and self-infliction of his suffering. *Imitatio Christi* began in the semiotic pilgrimage of the memory and the imagination through the signs of narrative and pictorial representation to the stirring of the mystic's affections and meditation. Imitating Christ was conceived of as a kind of reading and remembrance. Whether one embarked on an actual pilgrimage to the Holy Land, heard a sermon on Christ's Passion, viewed a retable or cycle play about the Crucifixion, or read a devotional treatise, one engaged in a reading of the signs, a "following of the signposts," as Geoffrey de Vinsauf phrased it, along the "sure path" of meditation to the body of Christ itself.

It is at the site of Christ's body that the central act of reading takes place. In fact, as the above quotation from the Monk of Farne suggests, the body of Christ was constructed as an open book within which the mystic must learn to read the Passion of Christ. His body is the torn and bleeding parchment, his wounds the vowels and consonants composing the words of the corporeal text. The instruction of his body exists in anagramic form. Words emerge from wounds only if the mystic is able to piece together the eviscerated vowels and consonants into the morphemes and syntax of

Christ's Passion. Without the conventional medieval configurations of the book that enable reading, including margins, rubrication, and glosses, the text of Christ's body is a cryptogram requiring the mystic's decoding. The body of Christ offers itself as a fantastic spectacle to the mystic's desire, but it does not surrender its meaning so easily. It demands a different kind of reading than was available to the literate medieval reader.

The Monk of Farne draws upon the angel's advice to John in Apoc. 10:9–10 to render this new reading: "eat this book which in your mouth and understanding shall be sweet, but which shall make your belly bitter."[1] Like receiving the eucharist, ingesting the book of Christ is an act of remembrance.[2] The bitterness of the reading/eating is directly proportional to the increased knowledge gained from it. Sorrow attends the knowledge produced by this reading, causing the reader to be seized with compassion for the crucified Christ. At the same time, as we saw in chapter 1, such a reading "fills up in his [the reader's] flesh the sufferings which are wanting."[3] The reader's desire makes possible this sorrowful, suffering reading by creating the place for the transference of Christ's pain. Reading proceeds from the place of rupture—Christ's wounded body—to the mystic's flesh, and it is replicated in reading the mystic text. A new desire guides and directs the mystic text, a desire to impress itself on the hearts of its readers, thereby completing the trajectory of mystical contemplation: from inscription on Christ's body to reading of the wounds to inscription on the mystic's body to inscription in the mystic text, and finally, in the readers' hearts. Readers of Margery Kempe's book, then, must search for the rupture which enables reading and rapture at the same time.

A triple reading occurs in and around the mystic text. In addition to the reader's reading of the book, there is the continual presence of the mystic's Passion lection, her reading of Christ's body and displacement of that reading on her own body. Thus when the medieval or twentieth-century reader endeavors to read, she is confronted not only with the materiality of the book, but with the bodily codices inscribed in it. In turn, the reader must bring her own body to bear on this reading by fixing its tortured words and disjointed grammar in her heart. Mystic and reader join in a kind of "lectio corporis" which occurs in the midst of the mystic text.

The body of Christ and corporeal readings of it are never far from Margery Kempe's meditations and experiences as she describes them in her book. The narrative itself can be traced to her desire for suffering: "it was to her a great solace and comfort when she was chided and rebuked for the love of Jesus" (29). As we have seen, this desire for suffering impels her *via mystica*, bringing her into dangerous conflict with her fellow townspeople and with the clerics who endeavor to silence her. Yet her desire is not aimed merely at imitating the shame and reproof endured by Christ in his life. Rather, it represents a desire for reading as well, for it is only through the mystic's ability to read the crucified body of Christ that she is able to "fill up in [her] flesh the sufferings which are wanting." Kempe's *Book* constitutes a series of such readings of Christ's body, beginning with her vision on Mount Calvary.

The scene of her first roarings is also the scene of her first readings of Christ's body. Her vision on Mount Calvary represents a turning point in her narrative. Before the pilgrimage to the Holy Land, the visions she reports consist mostly of "holy speeches and dalliance with our Lord Jesus Christ." Her dialogues with Christ up to this point confirm her ability to hear the divine word, a prerequisite to mystical discourse. In addition, the previous narrative is devoted to her prophetic visions, including her warnings to the priest who wrote the book about two men who try to deceive him, and her prediction of several deaths and recoveries from illness.[4] While she mentions dallying in Christ's Passion early in the narrative, she does not reveal the nature or content of this dalliance. Instead, she concentrates on the effects of her meditation—the fire of love, the wondrous melody, the uncontrollable weeping. Her reason for doing this is that she is seeking confirmation of the truth of her visions from holy learned men. In conjunction with Christ's own assurances of her grace, these clerical confirmations and her prophesies seem to make up a pretext for her vision on Calvary. The narrative clearly divides these earlier revelations and experiences from her trip to the Holy Land that culminates in her vision on Calvary. In this way the narrative prepares for her readings of Christ's body by first authorizing her ability to receive the divine Word.

Except for her vision of Christ's birth, there is no earlier vision as clearly depicted as this one of his Crucifixion on Calvary. It is vastly different from the earlier colloquies between Christ and her soul in that Christ is silent. The vision proceeds as a kind of enumeration of the physical sufferings of Christ to which Kempe is spectator and reader:

> &, whan thorw dispensacyon of þe hy mercy of owyr Souereyn Savyowr Crist Ihesu it was grawntyd þis creatur to beholdyn so verily hys precyows tendyr body, alto-rent & toryn wyth scorgys, mor ful of wowndys þan euyr was duffehows of holys, hangyng vp-on þe cros wyth þe corown of thorn up-on hys heuyd, hys blysful handys, hys tendyr fete nayled to þe hard tre, þe reuerys of blood flowyng owt plentevowsly of euery membre, þe gresly & grevows

wownde in hys precyows syde schedyng owt blood & watyr for hir lofe and hir
saluacyon, þan sche fel down & cryed wyth lowde voys, wondyrfully turnyng
& wrestyng hir body on euery syde, spredyng hir armys a-brode as ȝyf sche
xulde a deyd, & not cowde kepyn hir fro crying,—and þese bodily mevyngys
for þe fyer of lofe þat brent so feruently in hir sowle wyth pur pyte &
compassyon. (70)

(And when through dispensation of the high mercy of our sovereign savior,
Christ Jesus, it was granted this creature to behold so truly his precious tender
body, all rent and torn with scourges, more full of wounds than ever was a
dovehouse of holes, hanging upon the cross with the crown of thorns upon his
head, his blessed hands, his tender feet nailed to the hard tree, the rivers of
blood flowing out plenteously from every member, the grisly and grievous
wound in his precious side shedding out blood and water for her love and her
salvation, then she fell down and cried with a loud voice, wondrously turning
and twisting her body on every side, spreading her arms outstretched as if she
would have died, and could not keep herself from crying,—and these bodily
movements because of the fire of love that burned so fervently in her soul with
pure pity and compassion.)

Kempe's reading takes the form of an enumeration of Christ's wounds and
a visual reckoning with his broken and bleeding body. The striking analogy
between his wounded body and a dovecote full of holes is probably derived
from Rolle's *Meditations on the Passion*, in which he generates this comparison among others as aids to meditation.[5] It is significant that, in the
same series of analogies containing the dovecote image, Rolle also compares Christ's body to a book and prays for the grace to read it:

More yit, swet Jhesu, þy body is lyke a boke written al with rede ynke; so is þy
body al written with rede woundes. Now, swete Jhesu, graunt me to rede
upon þy boke, and somewhate to undrestond þe swetnes of þat writynge, and
to have likynge in studious abydynge of þat redynge. . . . And, swete Jhesu,
graunt me þis study in euche tyde of þe day, and let me upon þis boke study at
my matyns and hours and evynsonge and complyne, and evyre to be my
meditacion, my speche, and my dalyaunce.[6]

(Moreover, sweet Jesus, your body is like a book written entirely with red ink;
so is your body entirely written with red wounds. Now, sweet Jesus, grant me
to read upon your book, and to understand somewhat the sweetness of that
writing, and to take delight in the studious consideration of that reading. . . .
And, sweet Jesus, grant me this study in each time of the day, and let me upon
this book study at my matins and hours and evensong and compline, and
always to be my meditation, my speech, and my dalliance.)

If Kempe was familiar with the dovecote analogy through Rolle's *Medita-tions*, she would also have known this plea of his to be able to read the Christic body. As a subtext to her vision, this analogy between body and book suggests the true end of her desire to suffer for Christ's love. As lover of Christ, she must be able to read the "sweet writing" of his body, to make it her meditation, her speech, and her dalliance, in the words of Rolle. Her reading of the visible tokens of Christ's suffering stirs remembrance in her memory and compassion in her heart. Ultimately, it incites the bodily movements and roarings for which she will become notorious.

The crucified body of Christ becomes Margery Kempe's mystical primer, teaching her how to read his love, mercy, and grace in his humiliation and dis-figurement. Reading Christ's Passion-text resembles the child's experience with his first reader, according to "An ABC Poem on the Passion of Christ," which is among the verse lyrics in John of Grimestone's preaching book:

[I]n place as man may se,
Quan a chyld to scole xal set be,
A bok hym is browt,
Naylyd on a brede of tre,
Þat man callyt an abece,
Pratylych i-wrout;
Wrout is on þe bok with-oute,
.V. paraffys grete & stroute
Bolyd in rose red;
Þat is set with-outyn doute,
In tokenyng of cristis ded.
Red letter in parchemyn
Makyth a chyld good & fyn
Lettrys to loke & se,
Be þis boke men may dyuyne
Þat cristis body was ful of þyne
Þat deyid on rode tre.
On tre he was don ful blythe
With grete paraffys, þat be wondis.V.
As þe mou vunder-stonde.⁷

(In place, as men may see, when a child is seated at school, a book is brought to him nailed on a board. Men call it the ABC, and it is skillfully made. On the outside of the book are fixed five large letters decorated in rose red. This signifies Christ's death, no doubt. The red letter in parchment allows a good child to look and see, [for] by this book men can understand that Christ's body which died on the rood was full of pain. On the tree he was marked very splendidly with great letters, that is the five wounds, as you may understand.)

This primer is nailed, like the body of Christ, to a board. The red ink of the medieval manuscript is compared with the red wounds/letters of Christ's Passion. In this version of the bodily text of Christ, the five wounds serve as the rubric for reading. Much like Rolle, the speaker of the poem further prays that "I might these letters read / Without any difficulty." The one who meditates thus becomes the child struggling to understand the strange and marvelous letters on the pages of his alphabet primer.

Like the child learning the alphabet, Kempe returns again and again to the body of Christ to read its pain and its excess of love. Her own narrative practices what Rolle counsels, namely, that meditation on Christ's body be a continuous and concerted one. While such repetition of her meditations may bore or irritate the modern reader, it serves as a rubric to her mystical and experiential narratives. We cannot read the narrative of her life and visions without being able to read the "sweet writing" of the Christic text inscribed within it.

The frequency of Kempe's outbursts of boisterous weeping such as that on Calvary suggests a continual engagement in meditation on Christ's crucified body. Likewise, Christ's familiar expression of gratitude and praise for her visions and willingness to suffer for his sake alludes to meditations not reported in the narrative. Thus, readers may have the sense that there are more meditations on the Passion in Kempe's text than there actually are. In fact, extended meditation on Christ's Passion is found in only two places in her narrative: during her visit to Mount Calvary and near the end of Book I. Discounting mere references to her Passion meditations, the reader does not find another extended meditation on Christ's suffering and death after the Calvary vision in chapter 28 until chapter 79. Before considering the significance of these two visions together, let us look at this second one.

Kempe's second Passion "reading" begins with the buffeting and scourging of Christ and ends with Christ's appearance to the Virgin and Mary Magdalene. Chapter 80 recounts in great detail Christ's forty lashes, his carrying of the Cross to Calvary, and his mother's distress. Christ's body is stripped, stretched on the Cross, nailed into place, and raised and dropped into a mortise. The rest of this chapter is devoted to the Virgin's grief, the deposition from the cross, and burial of Christ.

Within this broad outline of the Passion sequence we may find Kempe's readings. Kempe's vision of the buffeting, for example, prepares for the central reading of Christ's body in the Crucifixion vision. It departs from the usual accounts of the buffeting in a very interesting way: it multiplies the number of scourgers from one or two to sixteen, the number of whips from one or two to sixteen, and the number of lashes affixed to each whip from three to eight.[8] This multiplication renders the buffeting difficult, even ludicrous, to imagine. Sixteen men holding sixteen lashes with eight metal-tipped strands each would be in serious danger to each other and themselves. Clearly, this multiplication is a reading-effect of the reading of Christ's wounds as letters in a book. The proliferation of wounds requires the proliferation of instruments of wounding, the pens and styluses of Christ's pain.[9]

Kempe reads the buffeting and journey to Calvary in a very specific way:

> Whan sche herd þe wordys & sey þe compassyon þat þe Modyr had of þe Sone & þe Sone of hys Modyr, þan sche wept, sobbyd, & criyd as þow sche xulde a deyid for pite & compassyon þat sche had of þat petows syght.(191)

> (When she heard the words and saw the compassion that the Mother had for the Son and the Son for his Mother, then she wept, sobbed, and cried as though she would have died for the pity and compassion she had of that piteous sight.)

Kempe is reading from the Virgin's offer to bear Christ's Cross and Christ's attempt to "comfort her as he could with many sweet words." Her interpretation is significant because it extends the maternal narrative of compassion beyond the Crucifixion scene, where it is usually found.[10] Her reading here represents an interpolation on the usual Passion narrative.

The reading of Christ's body begins with the scourging and is given its fullest rendering in the Crucifixion. Kempe begins with the stripping of Christ, in which the clothes are seen to rip the skin where the fresh wounds have stuck to the material: "Then that precious body appeared to her sight as raw as something newly flayed out of its skin, very piteous and rueful to behold" (192). In this account and in her narrative of the Crucifixion, Kempe dwells on the details of the dislocation of Christ's body from its perfect wholeness to a disjointed, punctured, and disfigured spectacle:

& a-non aftyr sche beheld how þe cruel Iewys leydyn hys precyows body to þe Crosse & sithyn tokyn a long nayle, a row & a boistews, & sett to hys on hand & wyth gret violens & cruelnes þei dreuyn it thorw hys hande. Hys blisful Modyr beheldyng & þis creatur how hys precyows body schrynkyd & drow to-gedyr wyth alle senwys & veynys in þat precyows body for peyne þat it suffyrd & felt, þei sorwyd and mornyd & syhyd ful sor. Than sey sche wyth hyr gostly eye how þe Iewys festenyd ropis on þe oþer hand, for þe senwys & veynys wer so schrynkyn wyth peyne þat it myth not come to þe hole þat þei had morkyn þerfor, & drowyn þeron to makyn it mete wyth þe hole. . . . & a-non sche sey hem takyn vp þe Crosse wyth owr Lordys body hangyng þer-on & madyn gret noyse & gret crye & lyftyd it vp fro þe erthe a certeyn distawnce & sithyn letyn þe Crosse fallyn down in-to þe morteys. & þan owr Lordys body schakyd & schoderyd, & alle þe joyntys of þat blisful body brostyn & wentyn a-sundyr, and hys precyows wowndys ronnyn down wyth reuerys of blood on eurey syde. (192)

(And soon afterwards she beheld how the cruel Jews laid his precious body on the Cross and then took a long and rough nail, and set it on one of his hands and with great violence and cruelness, they drove it through his hand. His blessed mother watching, and this creature, too, how his precious body shrank and drew together with all the sinews and veins in that precious body for the pain that it suffered and felt, they sorrowed and mourned and sighed full grievously. Then she saw with her spiritual eye how the Jews fastened ropes on the other hand, for the sinews and veins were so shrunken with pain that the hand would not come to the hole that they had made for it, and they pulled on it to make it meet the hole. . . . And soon she saw them take up the Cross with our Lord's body hanging on it and make a great noise and cry and lift it up from the earth a certain distance and afterwards let the Cross fall down into the mortise. And then our Lord's body shook and shuddered, and all the joints of that blessed body burst and broke apart, and his precious wounds ran down with rivers of blood on every side.)

The wracking of Christ's body, the shrinking of his sinews, and the bursting of his joints tear the blessed body apart, causing Kempe to weep and sorrow even more. At this point, the spectacle of Christ's body becomes transferred to Kempe's, as she weeps and roars so that "the church wondered at her body." Her reading of the damaged body of Christ produces a bodily wounding of her own.

Bodily rupture, as we saw in chapter 2, leads to mystical rapture. With the gradual bursting, shaking, and shuddering of the Christic text comes the same rupturing of the mystic text and language itself. The Virgin Mary swoons and Kempe goes mad with sorrow. We can observe how reading the Christic text chokes off language, finally silencing it. Kempe's own body becomes a spectacle of wonder and a marvelous language of "lamentabyl desyr" for the body of Christ. The burial of Christ's body produces a crisis in

Kempe's reading and a rupture in her desire. Its absence becomes displaced in the Virgin's sorrow and her own marvelous body with its wresting, writhing, turning blue as lead, and loud roars. The body which the Marys seek at the tomb has already reappeared elsewhere—both in Kempe's body and in the mystic text that we are reading.

It is highly significant that Kempe's Passion narrative ends with the vigil of Mary and Mary Magdalene at Christ's tomb, and Christ's appearance to them. The vision stops short of Christ's appearance to the apostles, ending instead with the risen Christ's warning to Mary Magdalene to "towche me not." Kempe's distress at Christ's warning has been interpreted to mean that she is too focused on the manhood of Christ. However, in the realm of mystical discourse, this distress at the loss of the Christic body is the necessary precondition for the embodying of her discourse. It provides the point of departure for creating a "body of love" in language and in the text.

These two readings of Christ's crucified body frame Kempe's invention of her narrative. Elsewhere in her *Book* she creates this body through divine speech in her soul—in the form of dalliances, colloquies, and visions. The body of Christ is thus displaced in the mystic's body and text where it demands a reading.

At the same time, the relationship of Christic body/text to book is not a unidirectional one; that is, if Christ's body is inscribed into the mystic text, so is the mystic's body and life inscribed in Christ. Kempe's dictation of her book to her scribe consigns her own experience to the body of Christ in the sense of a sacrifice or a "delivering over." In an early vision in the *Book*, Kempe desires to die for Christ's sake. Because she fears death, she chooses the least fearful kind of death, a swift beheading for "God's love." After thanking her for the thought, Christ assures her of his protection in spite of her desire:

> & ȝet schal no man sle the, ne fyer bren þe, ne watyr drynch þe, ne wynd deryn þe, for I may not for-ȝetyn þe how þow art wretyn in myn handys & my fete; it lykyn me wel þe peynes þat I haue sufferyd for þe." (30)

> (And yet no man shall slay you, nor fire burn you, nor water drown you, nor wind harm you, because I cannot forget you and how you are written in my hands and my feet; I am well pleased with the pains that I have suffered for you.)

The notion of being inscribed in Christ's wounds occurs elsewhere in the *Ancrene Wisse* and the revelations of Mechthild of Magdeburg.[11] In Kempe's version of this idea, Christ suggests that her love and compassion are inscribed in his wounds and in his own remembrance. His body is a virtual text of his recollection of her. As an act of devotion and love, her *Book* likewise becomes written into his wounds, so that readers of it are returned to the Christic body as the primary text.

Like the Christic book where we may read his suffering and passion for our instruction, according to the Monk of Farne, *The Book of Margery Kempe* offers the life of Margery Kempe inscribed in the body of Christ "for our example and instruction." By concluding Book I with her extended vision of Christ's Passion, Kempe inscribes her own life into his wounds, in effect. Wounds and words join in the experience of that which suffers in the soul, although the words are finally inadequate to express this suffering. Only our own reading of the silent, cryptic text of Christ's body enables us finally to be instructed.

Instruction carries a very physical and affective force in such a reading. Through the image of ingesting the book, the Monk of Farne implies a eucharistic act of internalizing that which is inscribed in the body of Christ. Along these same lines, John Lydgate's "The Fifteen Ooes of Christ" invokes the affective power of the Christic text to wound its readers so that they will become lettered in his pain:

> Mercyful Iesu! of grace do adverte
> With thilke lycour wich þou dedyst bleede,
> By remembraunce to write hem in myn herte
> Ech day onys that I may hem reede,
> Close þe capytallys vnder þi purpil weede
> With offte thynkyng on thi bloody fface,
> Thorugh my entraylles let þi passioun sprede,
> Marked tho karectys whan I shal hens pass.[12]

> (Merciful Jesus! of your grace do consider
> With the blood which you did bleed,
> To write them [the wounds] through remembrance in my heart
> That I may read them once each day,
> Comprehend the writing under your purple garment
> With often thinking on your bloody face,
> Through my entrails let your passion spread,
> That I may be marked with those wounds when I shall pass hence.)

The poet's plea for Christ to write the blood of his wounds in his heart recalls the Monk of Farne's frustrated wish that his longing would imprint itself on the hearts of them that hear. The chief effect of this inscription on the reader's heart is an infusion of his Passion. Further, the poet suggests that his very meditation on Christ's bloody face completes the inscription of his suffering with the requisite understanding of the text hidden under the "purple garment," of his wounds. Reading produces this simultaneous inscription on the bodies of both reader and text of Christ. In a sense, the reader participates in the act of crucifying Christ through the act of reading. There can be no reading of the Christic text without such complicity in Christ's suffering, as Lydgate suggests.

Behind the desire to read and understand the Christic text lies the desire for a wounding so that, in Lydgate's words, Christ's Passion may pass through the reader's entrails. One could hardly expect the reader's response to be composed. In fact, it remains to be seen what the reader's affective response should be to the reading of the Christic text. What did Rolle have in mind, for example, when he desired a continuous reading of the Christic text? What type of "reader response" does Lydgate construct with his desire for the passage of Christ's Passion through his entrails?

Returning to the second vision of the Crucifixion in *The Book of Margery Kempe*, we can find Kempe's answer to Lydgate and Rolle. Her *exemplum* of the reader of the Christic text is the Virgin Mary, whose excessive grief and compassion drive her nearly mad. She cries out at the Jews, offers her own body in Christ's place, and finally faints from grief. It is her grief that Kempe assumes in her own fits of roaring and crying. She makes this explicit when, after running about in a fit of madness over the Virgin's swoon, Kempe says to her: "I pray you, Lady, cease your sorrowing, because your Son is dead and out of pain, for it seems to me that you have sorrowed enough. And, Lady, I will sorrow for you, for your sorrow is my sorrow" (193). Kempe is not merely commiserating with the Virgin in this speech to her: she is actively assuming the Virgin's sorrow. This sorrow is, in turn, the sign of the Virgin's reading of Christ's suffering. She is the primary reader at the Crucifixion and the model for all subsequent mystical readings of the Christic body.

It is significant that Kempe's bouts of roaring and "bodily movings" date from her visit to Mount Calvary. Here she becomes a reader of the Christic body along with the Virgin Mary. Her imitation of the Virgin's response is clearly elaborated in the second vision toward the end of Book I, where she places herself among the mourning women at the foot of the Cross. Again and again, Kempe takes her own cues from the Virgin's grief—when Mary and she witness Christ's journey to Calvary, his cruel treatment at the hands of the Jews, and finally, his death. Their parallel descents into despair and temporary madness are simultaneous, and they culminate in Kempe's declaration that she will take on the Virgin's sorrow.

The Virgin, as a boisterous reader of Christ's body, does not issue from the Gospel accounts of the Crucifixion. The only mention of her participation occurs in John 19:25, where she is listed along with Mary Cleophas and the Magdalene as witnessing the Crucifixion. Early patristic commentators invested this silence with meaning, attributing it to the Virgin's patient stoicism which was rooted in her assurance of Christ's Resurrection. Ambrose, Richard of St.-Victor, and Alanus de Insulis, to name a few, envisioned a calm Virgin who silently watched "with pious attention" "quia exspectabat non pignoris mortem sed mundi salutem" (because she awaited not the death of her child, but the salvation of the world).[13]

Patristic interpretations of the Virgin's behavior focused on Simeon's prophecy to Mary during Christ's infancy that her soul would be pierced by a sword (Luke 2:35). This sword was usually interpreted as a sword of sorrow which Mary would experience at Christ's death. Simeon's prophecy, however, raised questions about Mary's perfection, which was demonstrated by her virginity *in partu* and her obedience.[14] Origen interpreted the sword as a sign of Mary's doubt about Christ's Resurrection and redemption of mankind. Hence, the sword which pierces her soul, by Origen's account, reveals a Mary whose humanity causes her to waver in spite of her knowledge of Christ's redemption of mankind,

> then Mary, too, was scandalized at that time. Therefore Simeon prophesies also about the holy Virgin Mary herself; for standing beside the Cross and seeing what is happening and hearing the voices of the killers—even after Gabriel's witness, after the ineffable knowledge of the divine conception, after the great showing forth of miracles, even you, who were taught from above the things of the Lord, will be perplexed and touched by dissension—that is the sword.[15]

Other commentators follow Origen's lead in viewing the sword of sorrow as a crisis of doubt when Mary temporarily forgot Gabriel's witness.[16]

Augustine, by contrast, argues that Mary experienced grief at the Crucifixion in the form of the sword of sorrow, but that she never doubted.[17] Ambrose reconciles this sword with his own version of Mary's stoicism, arguing that she did not grieve at the foot of the Cross. He reads the sword as a sword of foreknowledge rather than one of sorrow.[18] This image of the Virgin found its way into medieval devotional texts and artistic representations as well. It is, perhaps, the Virgin with whom we are most familiar even today.

In the Eastern Church of the Middle Ages, however, the sword of sorrow was viewed in connection with the Virgin's perfect maternity. The sword of sorrow, far from casting doubt on Mary's perfection, became the focus of her veneration in the East. As early as the fourth century A.D., a feast was devoted to Simeon's prophecy to Mary, the feast of *Hypapante*. This feast celebrated Mary's maternity through her sorrow at the Crucifixion. It is this understanding of the sword of sorrow that informed the Eastern development of Mary's role in Christ's suffering. The *mater dolorosa* theme was developed more fully through the writings of Ephraim the Syriac and the Syriac poet, James of Sarug. It is elaborated in the same detailing of the instruments of torture which we find in Kempe's visions and in such devotional guides as the *Meditations on the Life of Christ*. In one such elaboration by Ephraim the Syriac, *Lamentationes gloriosissimae Virginis Mariae super Passione Domini*, the Virgin addresses the instruments of Christ's torture as the visible attributes of her own affective passion:

> Stans juxta Crucem pura et immaculata virgo, Salvatoremque in ea suspensum cernens, dirissimas plagas perpendens, et clavos, querimonias, alapas, flagellaque prospiciens, magno cum planctu, lamentisque dolore plenis exclamabat, dicens: Mi fili dulcissime, fili mi carissime, quo modo Crucem istam portas? Mi fili, et mi Deus, quo pacto sputa, clavos, et lanceam suffers? quo pacto colaphos, irrisiones, injurias, ac contumelias pateris? quo pacto coronam spineam, vestemque purpuream, spongiam, arundinem, fel et acetum sustines? . . . Quid fecisti: aut in quo Hebraeorum gentem, fili mi, offendere potuisti? Et cur scelerati simul atque ingrati illi, te in ligno Crucis suspenderunt? . . . Deficit mihi animus, dum te Cruci suffixum intueor, conclavatumque ac plagis plenum, amantissime fili. . . .[19]

> (Standing next to the Cross and gazing at the Savior suspended before her, the pure and immaculate Virgin pondered the direst of wounds and nails, lamentations, blows, and scourges. With a great wailing and with lamentation full of distress, she cried out, saying: 'My sweetest son, my most precious son, how do you bear this Cross? My son and my God, how do you suffer the spittle, nails, and the lance? How do you bear the blows, the mimickings, the insults, and abuses? How do you endure the crown of thorns and bloody garment, the sponge, the spear, the gall, and the vinegar? . . . What have you done: how could you offend the Hebrew people, my son? And why did those wicked and ungrateful ones hang you on the wooden Cross? My mind fails me, as I look upon you fastened to the Cross and full of wounds and nails, my most beloved son. . . .)

The agents of Christ's suffering—the whips, lance, nails, crown of thorns—
provide the hermeneutic to the Virgin's reading of the wounded body of
Christ. In it she reads her own suffering, as well as her temporary madness:
"My mind fails me." In Ephraim's account her temporary madness and her
excessive display of grief do not, as they do in discussions by Western
Fathers of the Church, diminish the Virgin's purity or her immaculateness.
Ephraim's account of the Virgin's hysterical grief dramatically depicts her
"sword of sorrow." As she reads Christ's wounds and the instruments of his
suffering, she participates in that suffering excessively and boisterously.
Indeed, the signs of Christ's suffering themselves elicit her grief unto
madness. The Virgin's heart and mind undergo a simultaneous rending or
piercing in the course of her meditation upon Christ's body.

The image of the noisy, boisterous, hysterical virgin in medieval culture is derived from the East particularly following the Crusades. The
sorrowing mother, or *mater dolorosa*, of Eastern tradition is neither calm,
patient, nor silent. In the Eastern redaction of the apocryphal *Gesta Pilati*,
for example, the Virgin is unmeasured in her sorrow. She shrieks with grief
and demands of Christ to know how she can endure such suffering. Finally,
she takes her sorrow out on her own body, tearing her face with her
fingernails and beating her breast.[20]

The connection made between Mary's sorrow and her maternity is often
derived from the contrast between the Virgin's joyful and painless giving birth
and her grief at Christ's Passion. The themes of childbirth and grief became
inextricably linked through this contrast. In his commentary on the Gospel
of John, Rupert of Deutz transfers Christ's words to his apostles in John
16:21 to his mother, so that she says, "A woman, when she is in labour, hath
sorrow, because her hour is come." He concludes that Mary suffered birth
pangs at her Son's death, and thereby experienced her dual motherhood of
Christ and all humanity: "Because there were truly 'pains as of a woman in
labour' [Ps. 47:7] and in the Passion of the only begotten Son the blessed
Virgin brought forth the salvation of us all, she is obviously mother of us
all."[21] By Rupert of Deutz's account, the Virgin's motherhood—her labor
in childbirth—is subsumed, or rather displaced, in her grief at his death. She
undergoes the pains of a woman in labor in her own labor of sorrow.

Such a theology underlies the increasingly vehement renderings of the
Virgin's grief in medieval theology, devotion, and even art. Yet this theology implies the Virgin's full participation in Christ's Passion, blurring the
lines between his suffering and her own. Albertus Magnus attempted to
differentiate between the types of suffering sustained by the Virgin and
Christ in order to restrict her role as it was prophesied by Simeon:

Et tuam ipsius animam pertransibit gladius. Passionem enim quam Filius in corpore pertulit, intus in anima sustinuit mater, dum in cruciatu corporis Filii maternus affectus contorquetur.[22]

(And your own soul a sword shall pierce. For the Passion which the son suffered in body, the mother sustained within her soul, when in the Crucifixion of the Son's body the mother's state of mind was affected.)

Albert the Great's distinction between a corporeal and a spiritual passion maintains their equivalence. Devotional treatises such as Pseudo-Bonaventure's *Meditations on the Life of Christ* would view the Virgin's compassion as enlarging on Christ's Passion.[23] The question of how the Virgin could have suffered if she had had faith in Christ's redemption of mankind persists well into the sixteenth century, even though Bonaventure resolved this problem by assigning her experience of the Passion to her "higher" and "lower" faculties. Thus, the Virgin suffered compassion in the lower part of her being through a kind of labor of grief, while in the higher part of her soul, she was secure in her faith in Christ's redemption of mankind.[24] This resolution proves awkward to maintain, however. Although Bonaventure grants the Virgin her grief, he elsewhere maintains that she bore her grief with "perfect virility" and dignity.[25] Clearly, the spectacle itself of Mary's compassion was as much at issue as her experience of suffering. The Virgin's sheer corporeal grief threatened to overwhelm Christ's own Passion and to undermine the Virgin's perfect faith. In spite of numerous representations of the swooning Virgin at the foot of the cross in late medieval and Renaissance painting, her corporeal labor of compassion remained an issue because it conflicted with her perfection.[26]

Nevertheless, the corporeal compassion of the Virgin can be found in medieval hymns as well as in lyrics, drama, and art. One Latin hymn, "Stabat iuxta crucem Cristi," makes explicit the physical nature of Mary's grief through the displacement of her labor, attributing her groans of grief to the long-withheld pains of childbirth.[27] Medieval devotional texts and lyrics, too, represent the Virgin's vehement passion. Pseudo-Bonaventure describes the unconsolable grief of the Virgin, Mary Magdalene, and the rest of the witnesses of Christ's death:

Near the cross, with the Lady, there were also John and the Magdalen, and the Lady's two sisters, that is Mary Iacobi and Salome, and perhaps others as well, all of whom, especially the Magdalen, beloved disciple of Jesus, wept vehemently, nor could they be comforted by their beloved Lord and Master.[28]

Robert Manning's meditation on the Virgin's grief is more detailed than is Pseudo-Bonaventure's, implying that she experienced more than a swoon or pang of grief:

> For whan she say hym drawe to ende
> Y leue she wax out of here mynde;
> She swouned, she pyned, she wax half dede,
> She fylle to þe ground, and bette here hede.[29]

> (For when she saw his life draw to an end
> I believe she went out of her mind;
> She swooned, she pined, she became half dead,
> She fell to the ground, and beat her head.)

In his "Meditations on the Passion," Richard Rolle joins Manning's description of the Virgin, attributing to her matchless love and lack of concern for the world's shame the sorrow which rendered her "as a woman out of herself."[30]

One of the most disturbing images of the Virgin's grief appears in a fifteenth-century English lyric, "Filius Regis Mortuus Est." In this lyric, the Virgin's grief turns to self-injury:

> I met a mayde at þe citeys ende,
> snobbynge & syȝynge sche wes ny schente,
> a fayrer foode had y not kende.
> hurre herre, hure face, sche all to-rente.
> She tuggyd & tere with gret turment;
> sche brake hure skynne boþe body & breste,
> and saide þese wordys euer as sche wente,
> 'filius Regis mortuus est.'[31]

> (I met a maid at the city's end,
> she was almost overcome with sobbing and sighing,
> a fairer creature I knew not.
> her hair, her face, she had entirely rent.
> She tugged and tore with great torment;
> She broke her skin both body and breast,
> and said these words ever as she went,
> 'filius Regis mortuus est.')

While Rolle uses the Virgin's madness as a metaphor, the fifteenth-century lyric passes beyond metaphor to depict the Virgin as "out of herself" with grief. The Virgin's grief more resembles Margery Kempe's own postpartum madness following the birth of her first child than it does Bonaventure's vision of the mother who balances the reactions of the higher and lower parts of her soul.

In medieval drama, the Virgin joins the Magdalene in vehement displays of grief precipitated by the sight of the crucified body of Christ. In the *Chester* play, she ignores the advice of John and Christ to measure her grief, declaring that her "sorrow of this sight/marrs my mynd, mayne, and might."[32] Yet this declaration is tame compared to one in an earlier drama of the Passion. One of the earliest Passion plays in Western drama, the twelfth-century *Montecassino Passion*, culminates in a very moving gesture and speech by the Virgin. Amidst the wailing women at the foot of the Cross, the Virgin exhibits to the surrounding crowd the womb in which she carried Christ and declares with a "powerful cry":

te portai nillu meu ventre
Quando te beio [mo]ro presente
Nillu teu regnu agi me a mmente.

(Why did I carry you in my womb
When I see you dying now.
Remember me in your kingdom.)[33]

The Virgin's speech is provoked by Christ's speech to the thief on the cross in which he promises that they shall meet in the heavenly kingdom. The Virgin calls out in distress at her own exclusion from Christ's promise. Her gesture to her womb links her plea for remembrance with her own labor of compassion and suffering.

In the late medieval *Digby* cycle, the Magdalene and Virgin share in similar boisterous episodes of grief. In her distraction, the Virgin rails against the angel Gabriel for not telling her that her son would die before she faints for a third time. Both the Magdalene and John beg her to "leave your lamentation." After asking her not to mourn so much, John advises her to call to mind the Resurrection in order to put aside her painful affliction, as if to resolve the debate once and for all about Mary's perfection versus her maternal sorrow.[34] Mary continues to lament her "woeful mother's sorrow," which is ultimately inexpressible.[35] She finally scolds

Joseph and the other Marys who try to usher her away from the painful sight of her son:

> What meyn ye, frendes? What is your mynd?
> Towardes me be not so vnkinde!
> His moder am not I?
> Wold ye haue the moder depart hym fro?
> To lefe hym thus I wille not so,
> But bide and sitt hym bye.
> Therefore, gud Joseph, be content!36

> (What do you mean, friends? What is your intention?
> Be not so unkind towards me!
> Am I not his mother?
> Would you have his mother depart from him?
> I do not wish to leave him thus,
> But I will wait and sit by him.
> Therefore, good Joseph, be content!)

Mary implies that her maternity justifies her grief and privileges her own compassion over the grief of her companions.37 In addition to the suffering she experiences at the sight of her son's crucified body, she suffers the indignities of being reprimanded for her sorrow. Her suffering, then, is a dual one which stems from the rending of her heart and the recriminations of those closest to her.

Representation of the Virgin's extravagant grief was not confined to medieval drama. Scenes from the Crucifixion, Deposition, and Entombment in late medieval books of hours often recall the dramatic renderings of the Virgin's sword of sorrow through typical "gestures of despair," including self-injury, throwing up of the arms, and swooning.38 The Virgin is not alone in her vehement mourning in many of these representations: her grief is often shared and expressed by the other female mourners at the Crucifixion or Deposition. *Les Belles Heures du Jean Duc de Berry* dramatizes what some would call hysteria in one of the mourning women of the "Lamentation" and the Magdalene at the "Entombment" (See figures 1 and 2). Such depictions of passionate lamentation must have derived in part from medieval practices of mourning. John Chrysostom and others condemn the habits of widows who tear their hair, bare their arms, and scratch their cheeks in a "vain display" of emotion. The excessive gestures of grief portrayed in *Les Belles Heures* and other books of hours, like those found in

Figure 1. Lamentation. Vespers. *The Belles Heures of Jean, Duke of Berry,* fol. 149v. Reproduced by courtesy of the Metropolitan Museum of Art, the Cloisters Collection, New York.

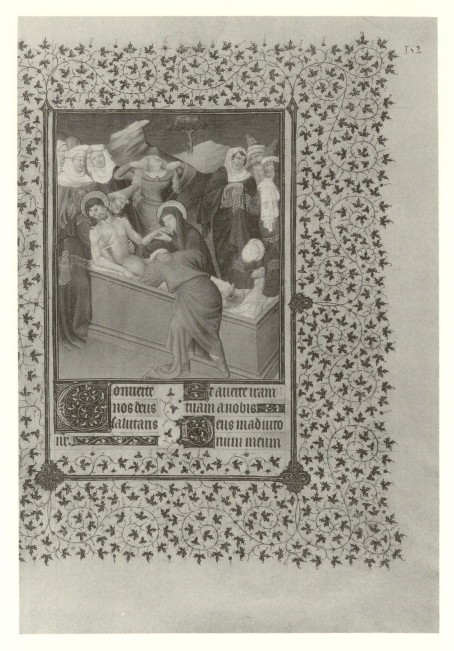

Figure 2. Entombment. *The Belles Heures of Jean, Duke of Berry,* fol. 152r. Reproduced by courtesy of the Metropolitan Museum of Art, the Cloisters Collection, New York.

Kempe's own visions, need to be placed within the context of this condemnation of a medieval practice explicitly associated with women. The figures of the mourning woman and Magdalene depicted in the "Lamentation" and "Entombment" elevate an already unpopular practice into an object of meditation and a model for mystical devotion directed at women. A sixteenth-century reaction to such depictions reveals Church frustration with the convergence of medieval representations of the Virgin and female practices of mourning:

> We also do not excuse those who portray in pictures or writings how the mother of God fainted upon the earth at the cross, overwhelmed and senseless from pain, similar to those women who, caught up in their sorrow, cry aloud, beat their breasts with their fists, pluck out their hair, scratch up their cheeks with their nails and proclaim loudly their misery. . . .[39]

Representations such as those in *Les Belles Heures* threatened to valorize not only female mourning practices but female mystical practices as well.

In spite of such condemnations, some of the most shocking representations of the sorrow of the female mourners may be found in fifteenth-and sixteenth-century sculpture beginning with Donatello.[40] As merely one example of this Italian school of sculpture, Niccolo dell'Arca's *Pietà* (figure 3) strikes out at the viewer with a "berserker frenzy."[41] The Virgin's face is disfigured with grief, while the paroxysms of Mary Cleophas and Mary Magdalene overwhelm the entire tableau (figure 4, detail). The still, silent body of Christ seems threatened by the sheer movement of the figures around it. The suffering of the Virgin and the women mourners largely replaces that of Christ in this tableau, as though his suffering had been displaced onto their bodies. Their displays of grief are contrasted with the calm central figure of John, who gazes with concern out of the tableau.

The women, by contrast, are all focused on the body of Christ. A reading, of sorts, is responsible for the frenzy depicted in the women surrounding Christ's body. In the *Digby* play of "Christ's Burial," the Magdalene articulates the source of her inordinate grief. The burial begins with the weeping of the three Marys and Joseph's advice to the Magdalene to "be of good cheer." The Magdalene invites Joseph to look closely at the body of Christ in order to see his "manifold pains":

> Josephe, luk bettere, behold and see,
> In how litille space how many woundes bee!
> Here was no mercee, her was no pitee,
> But cruelle delinge paynfully![42]

(Joseph, look closer, behold and see,
In how little space how many wounds there be!
Here was no mercy, here was no pity,
Only cruel dealings painfully!)

The Magdalene then goes on to enumerate the Virgin's woes which surpass those of all other mothers. When Joseph asks whether Christ was mindful of her in his Passion, the Magdalene describes Christ's compassion for his mother and his assurance to her that she is "ever in my remembrance." She then recounts his agony and his words, "I am thirsty." Joseph wonders whether Christ desired drink, but the Magdalene says that he was thirsty for charity. Finally, she laments her own contribution as a sinner to Christ's torment, wishing that she, too, could die. The two other Marys caution her to measure her tears, but she is unconsolable.

Finally, turning to the body of Christ, the Magdalene exclaims to Joseph:

Cum hithere, Joseph, beholde and looke,
How many bludy letters beyn written in þis buke—
Smalle margente her is![43]

(Come here, Joseph, behold and look,
How many bloody letters are written in this book—
This is a small margin!)

The Magdalene here invites Joseph to read the Christic body as she has done in her preceding speech. He has yet to read the letters in the bloody text, and so has yet to understand either the Virgin's suffering or the Magdalene's remorse. He responds with alarm, "Yea, this parchment is stretched out of size!" Suddenly, Joseph, too, begins to become lettered in Christ's suffering, just as the Virgin and the Magdalene have already done. He invites "all people who pass hereby" to behold Christ's body with their inward eye and "remember well" the generous drops of blood, the intolerable pains, the torn flesh, the thorns "thrust in his brains," the bones broken by nails.

In essence, Joseph offers a way of reading the Christic body, while the Magdalene and Virgin offer spectacles of that reading. Their readings are privileged ones, for it is they who experience the rending of their own bodies, one through a maternal labor of compassion, the other, through a

Figure 3: Lamentation Group. Niccolo dell'Arca, Bologna, S. Maria della Vita, c. 1464. Photograph reproduced by courtesy of Conway Library, Courtauld Institute of Art, London.

Figure 4. Detail. Lamentation Group. Niccolo dell'Arca, Bologna, S. Maria della
Vita, c. 1464. Photograph reproduced by courtesy of Conway Library, Courtauld
Institute of Art, London.

lover's grief. Although Joseph learns to read Christ's suffering and instructs others to join in his reading, he does not share in the boisterous tears of the Virgin and Magdalene. He continues to rebuke the Magdalene, reminding her of Christ's coming Resurrection and blaming her for lack of faith. He stands apart from the Marys, recalling the promised redemption of mankind. He turns away from the disfigured body to recall Christ's words. The Magdalene is recalled to the words inscribed in his body, words and letters which recall her as well as all sinners. Her reading takes no solace in the margins of his Resurrection.

The *Digby* play of Christ's Burial thus offers two readings of the Christic text. One reads the bleeding body of Christ as a pretext for Resurrection and redemption; the other reads the Christic body as a text for living in the world: "No exalted loftiness toward the beyond. Nothing but the sober difficulty of standing here below."[44] While there is nothing sober about the Virgin or Magdalene's weeping, they refuse to take solace in Christ's Resurrection. Instead, they seek to decipher their own thoughts, words, and deeds in his body. Their reading necessarily produces a rending of their own hearts and an inscription of suffering in their bodies. Against Joseph's warning to consider the "finale cause and conclusion" of Christ's death, the Marys insist upon reading the body of his suffering. Faints, cries, gesticulations of despair, and tears together recollect Christ's Passion even as they are produced by reading his body. From their excess of desire for the Christic text proceeds this immeasurable and alarming expression of suffering, one which cannot be silenced or solaced by Christ's promise of his Resurrection.

Margery Kempe's boisterous tears must be viewed, then, in the context of the Christic text and the Virgin's "reader-response" to it. The "sweet writing" that Rolle seeks to read in Christ's inscribed wounds requires nothing less than a sword of sorrow such as that experienced by the Virgin. In some of the dramatic texts and pictorial representations of the Virgin's grief reviewed so far, we have seen how the Virgin and often the Magdalene become privileged readers of the crucified body of Christ. Only they are able to decode the cryptogram of Christ's suffering, and this decoding invests their own bodies with his suffering, returning language to that which suffers in the soul and body.

Kempe seeks her own privileged reading of the Christic body in her visions of the Crucifixion at the same time that she longs for inscription of her own life in Christ's body and, hence, his remembrance. By reading his body into the narrative of her life, in turn, Kempe bases her text on that privileged reading of the Christic text. She achieves a visionary company with the Virgin and Mary Magdalene, and she devotes her own life to their readings of immeasurable sorrow. Like the Virgin in the *Digby* play, Kempe is scolded and reprimanded for her excessive weeping. In fact, her suffering of shame and reproof for her weeping is modeled on the Virgin's, as the Virgin makes clear in a visionary address to Kempe soon after her visit to Calvary:

> & þerfore, my derworthy dowtyr, be not aschamyd of hym þat is þi God, þi Lord, & þi lofe, no more þan I was whan I say hym hangyn on þe Cros, my swete Sone, Ihesu, for to cryen & to wepyn for þe peyn of my swete Sone, Ihesu Crist; ne Mary Mawdelyn was not aschamyd to cryen & wepyn for my Sonys lofe. And þerfore, dowtyr, ȝyf þu wylt be partabyl in owyr joye, þu must be partabil in owyr sorwe. (73)

> (And therefore, my dear daughter, do not be ashamed of him who is your God, your Lord, and your love, any more than I was when I saw him hang on the Cross, my sweet Son, Jesus, to cry and weep for the pain of my sweet Son, Jesus Christ; nor was Mary Magdalene ashamed to cry and weep for my Son's love. And therefore, daughter, if you wish to be a partaker in our joy, you must be a partaker in our sorrow.)

The Virgin's labor of compassion offers Kempe a clear precedent for escaping the censure of her contemporaries, at the same time that it privileges her ability to read and comprehend "the pain of my sweet Son."[45]

So, too, does the example of Marie d'Oignies, whose weeping convinces Kempe's second scribe to believe in her tears. In the Middle English version of Marie's *vita*, she is described as being "constrained to cry loud in the manner of a woman travailing of child."[46] The maternal labor of compassion becomes associated with the Virgin's reading of the Christic text. Even in her own time, Kempe was not the only one whose boisterous tears could have reminded one of a woman in labor or invited censure. A contemporary of hers, Felix Fabri, documents that female visitors to Jerusalem often "cried out, roared, and wept, as though giving birth."[47] Kempe's own boisterous tears, in spite of the marvel, wonder, and exasperation they induce in her fellow townspeople and pilgrims, participate in a cultural model of compassion based on the Virgin's example by which "vnspekabyl lofe" is translated into "gostly labowr," in Kempe's words.

The purpose of Kempe's roaring is to induce a reading, one which will unsettle the reader's security by reminding him or her of the Virgin's compassion. Christ elaborates five separate tokens or signficances of

Kempe's tears, including her mere weeping and her violent roaring. Fear and remembrance are among the tokens of the "great cries" he visits on Kempe:

> & sum-tyme I ȝeue þe gret cryis and roryngys for to makyn þe pepil a-ferd wyth þe grace þat I putte in þe in-to a tokyn þat I wil þat my Modrys sorwe be knowyn by þe þat men and women myth haue þe mor compassyon of hir sorwe þat sche suffyrd for me. (183)

> (and sometimes I give you great cries and roarings in order to make the people afraid for the grace that I put in you as a token that I wish that my mother's sorrow be known through you, so that men and women might have the more compassion of her sorrow which she suffered for me.)

Kempe's roarings make known the Virgin's sorrow and instill fear at the violence of God's grace. If one reads Kempe's great cries, one comes to know something of the Virgin's sorrow and the text of that sorrow: the crucified body of Christ. At the same time, readers of Kempe's body and book will be reminded of their own intractable hearts.

Like the Christic text, Kempe's own body is subject to misreadings. Her loud cries, her turning the color of lead, and her writhing on the ground, invite various interpretations by clerics and other witnesses of her bodily spectacle:

> For summe seyd it was a wikkyd spiryt vexid hir; sum seyd it was a sekenes; sum seyd sche had dronkyn to mech wyn; sum bannyd hir; sum wisshed sche had ben in þe hauyn; sum wolde sche had ben in þe se in a bottumles boyt; and so ich man as hym thowte. (69)

> (For some said it was a wicked spirit that vexed her; some said it was a sickness; some said she had drunk too much wine; some banned her; some wished she were in the harbor; some wished she were in the sea in a bottomless boat; and so each man as he thought.)

Kempe's companions seek medical and practical explanations for her noisy, unruly behavior: possession, epilepsy, drunkenness.[48] From their various readings of her bodily performances of meditation on Christ's Passion come their banishment of her and their desire for her death. The clerics are skeptical of her crying in particular, saying that "neither our Lady nor any saint in heaven ever cried as you do." (69). Yet Kempe is undeterred, because "they knew very little what she felt." The clerics' misreading of her bodily contortions derives from their presumed knowledge of the Virgin's grief.

They are unable to know what she felt because they rely on a closed reading of the gospel account of the Virgin's grief, one which is circumscribed by selected patristic commentaries, as we have seen. They are not themselves privy to the "unspeakable love" which permits a reading of the Christic text within Kempe's "bodily mevyngys."

Kempe's bodily movings and boisterous tears, then, are not only imitations or assumptions of the Virgin's sorrow: they are proclamations of her own privileged reading of Christ's body. It is in these demonstrations—these spectacles of unspeakable love—that Kempe asserts and lays claim to what she calls "þe secret thyngys of reuelacyonys" and God's "preuyteys" (secrets). In Christ's crucified body is inscribed the secret which Kempe reads and reinscribes in her own bodily revelations. She also becomes the secretary of Christ's body, a guardian of its secrets.[49] The unspeakable love itself authorizes Kempe's access to divine secrets and separates her access from that of the Church and its clerics. Her readings of the Christic text, therefore, are the source of her own bold speech as well as of her written text. They proceed from love and proclaim that love which inspires bodily movings.

The boisterous text of Kempe's body does not, however, reveal God's secret. It merely signifies the ineffable love with which she is endued, just as the "sweet writing" of the crucified body of Christ may not be read without a special grace. Lydgate's desire for reading Christ's bloody face and understanding the text under his wounded flesh is a desire for the experience of Christ's Passion in his own "entrails." No reading is possible without the reader's desire and the experience of that unspeakable love which inspires bodily movings. Kempe's bodily movements both reveal and conceal the secrets of God's speech in her soul by signifying inestimable love and suffering, but no identifiable body of knowledge or doctrine. As God's secretary, Kempe's body preserves the text of his suffering without disclosing the secret knowledge that comes with the suffering.

The "preuyteys" of God are not capable of being transmitted by means of written records of their occurrence and significance. In fact, language itself is choked by these secrets, by that "marvelous communication" which exceeds it.[50] As Kempe's scribe humbly acknowledges toward the end of Book I about her holy meditations,

Wyth swech maner thowtys & many mo þan I cowde euyr writyn sche worschepyd & magnifyed owr Lord Ihesu Crist for hys holy visitacyon & hys comfort. And in swech maner visitacyons & holy contemplacyonis as arn beforn-wretyn, mech mor sotyl & more hy wythowtyn comparison þan be

wretyn, þe sayd creature had continuyd hir lyfe þorw þe preseruyng of owr
Sauyowr Crist Ihesu mor þan xxv ȝer when þis tretys was wretyn. (214)

(With such manner of thoughts and many more than I could ever write she
worshipped and magnified our Lord Jesus Christ for his holy visitation and his
comfort. And in such manner of visitations and holy contemplations as are
written before, [though] much more subtle and higher without comparison
than are written, the said creature had continued her life, through the preserving of our Savior Jesus Christ, for more than 25 years when this treatise was
written.)

The writing of Kempe's book fails to capture the number and tenor of her
meditations because the marvelous communication remains a secret one.

It is this very failure of eventual language, of that which is written
compared with that which has been visited upon and uttered in the soul,
that provides the place in the text for rapture. Each of the occasions of
Kempe's boisterous tears establishes a place of plenteousness, of abundance—two words used by Kempe again and again to describe her roarings.
This plenteousness, in turn, exceeds the power of her scribe to express or
compose. The disjuncture between her high thoughts and meditations and
the language of the text we read offers a crisis in our reading. This crisis, in
turn, enables mystical rapture provided the reader searches for the body of
Christ in the mystic text. Like her boisterous tears, the crisis between oral
and written texts sends the reader elsewhere, to that loss which induces
mystical rapture in the first place.

Kempe's numerous roarings and bodily movings are the result of
mystical love and desire for the absent body of Christ. They provide that
"principal of travel" by which the excess of love passes through language to
those "preuyteys" of private dalliance with God. As readers, we are merely
witnesses of the bodily signs of rapture which recall the body of Christ. Yet
these signs are also occasions for rapture, for excess, rather than merely
spectacles of some divine logic.

The written body of her life, *The Book of Margery Kempe*, is her own act
of love created from the surplus of mystical desire. It is designed to imitate
the body of Christ in its capacity for reminding readers of his love and their
sins. Her own life and mystical journey are continually inscribed in Christ's
remembrance—in the wounds of his hands and feet—as he tells her. So,
too, is her book. Recalling as it does the primary text of the crucified body
with its "sweet writing" for our example and instruction, Kempe's book
offers a reading of her own life inscribed in the body of Christ. *Her* life is for

our example and instruction, as Christ tells her, "for by this book many a man shall be turned to me and believe in it" (216). In order to be able to read this instruction, readers must be able to read the displaced, rapturous mystical body and its exemplar, the body of Christ. The success of her inscription is confirmed in a vision toward the end of Book I in which she reads her name in the Book of Life.[51]

In the context of her own struggles with clerical authority, Kempe's boisterous tears are also significant. As we have seen, through her tears and bodily movings she claims a privileged reading of the Christic text which she uses to found her own text of her visions and experience. At the same time, her tears intrude upon the clerical prerogatives of reading and interpreting the word of God. She arrogates to herself these prerogatives while remaining outside the sites of their practice: the cloister, the pulpit, the anchorage. Further, clerics and other holy men are excluded from her reading "for they knew full little what she felt." Her method of reading depends upon the feelings of compassion, humility, and sorrow, rather than upon privileged access to the Text of Scripture protected by the medieval institution of the Church. In recalling the absent body to language through her narrative, she also recalls the absent Text of medieval culture, circulating it anew through her visions.[52] In effect, she displaces the secret text of ecclesiastical culture with her own bodily reading of Christ's Passion.

It is true that tears and compassion are not new to Christian theology and mysticism. Julian of Norwich outlines a system of "tokens" for testing the visitation of tears in the soul.[53] Clearly, holy tears are supported by a long and respectable tradition in private meditational practice. The difference between what Julian of Norwich describes and what Kempe practices is that Kempe removes tears from the domain of private devotion. Her insistence on the publicity of her tears militates against the very tradition she enlists for her own support. When she takes her tears on the road and into parish churches, she radically alters a tradition which had been previously confined to the oratory and to private prayer.[54] Holy tears in the public marketplace and parish church are quite different from private weeping, insofar as the context for that weeping changes. Kempe's tears become a public spectacle by which others may be reminded of Christ's Passion and their own sins. It is significant that the Grey Friar who banishes Kempe from his church does so not because he opposes her weeping but because he opposes her weeping in his church during his sermons. "I'd prefer this woman were out of the church; she annoys the people," exclaims the friar (149). What offends him is the publicity of her weeping and its capacity for silencing him. Likewise, when two priests begin to doubt whether Kempe's weeping is deceitful or not, they take her out of town to a church in a field. There they are satisfied that she weeps as well in private as she does in public.

Kempe herself expresses doubts about why she should weep in public, since it causes so much peril to herself and others. She begs Christ to relieve her of her public weepings so that she may hear sermons and not alienate her fellow parishoners:

> Lord, þe worlde may not suffyr me to do thy wil ne to folwyn aftyr þi steryng, & þerfor I prey þe, ȝyf it be thy wil, take þes cryingys fro me in þe tyme of sermownys þat I cry not at þin holy prechyng & late me hauyn hem be my-self alone so þat I be not putt fro heryng of þin holy prechyng & of þin holy wordys, for grettar peyn may I not suffyr in þis worlde þan be put fro þi holy worde heryng. (181)

> (Lord, the world cannot suffer me to do your will nor to follow after your stirring, and therefore I pray you, if it be your will, take these cryings from me during sermons so that I do not cry at your holy preaching and let me have them by myself alone so that I am not barred from hearing your holy preaching and your holy words, for I cannot suffer any greater pain in this world than to be barred from hearing your holy word.)

Christ refuses to give her more acceptable private weepings because her roars make others dread his grace and their own sins. Yet some clerics and priests approve of her weeping and endeavor to spare her the annoyance of others by administering the sacrament to her in private (138).

In spite of their efforts, Kempe's weeping never retreats to private prayer. Christ tells Kempe that she is a "mirror" among men, a spectacular *exemplum* in which they may witness God's violent grace and their own recalcitrant hearts. At the same time, her roaring inserts her bodily movings and loud voice into a discourse which would like to exclude her. Yet her discourse of roars is not designed to compete with that of clerks or parish priests; hers is a language with a different purpose altogether. Her discourse of tears cuts through language and silences it, leaving only the surplus of body and voice for people to marvel at—and the possibility of rapture.

Even if language is silenced in Kempe's spectacle of tears, her written text is, in part, a product of her tears. In the course of the dictating and transcribing of it, both she and her scribe experienced bouts of weeping, she tells us (219). In spite of the inadequacy of language to express the abundance and the private communications she has in her visions, she must somehow embody the Christic body in the body of her book. One way she does this is by reading her own life into Christ's. Another path follows the trajectory of mystical desire from love for the absent body to the desire for dialogue in the soul to the incarnation of discourse in the written text. More than a testimony to the truth of her visions or her integrity as a mystic, Margery Kempe's book represents the final stage of the mystic's desire, the manifestation of the crucified body and her own life in language, even though that language is bound to fail her.

Notes

1. Hugh Farmer, ed., *The Monk of Farne: The Meditations of a Fourteenth Century Monk*, trans. by a Benedictine of Stanbrook (London: Darton, Longman, and Todd, 1961), 76. See my discussion of this passage in chapter 1.

2. According to Hugh of St. Cher and Pierre Bersuire, eating the book meant recalling the events of the life of Christ. See Hugh of St. Cher, *Opera Omnia* (Venice, 1732), vol. 7, p. 397, and Pierre Bersuire, *Repertorium morale, Opera Omnia*, quoted in Jesse M. Gellrich, *The Idea of the Book in the Middle Ages: Language Theory, Mythology, and Fiction* (Ithaca, NY: Cornell University Press, 1985), 17.

3. *Monk of Farne*, 76. See my discussion of this passage in chapter 1.

4. *The Book of Margery Kempe*, 53–60. She also prophesies the outcome of a dispute over granting parish privileges to the Chapel of St. Nicholas in Lynn, 58–60.

5. See *The English Writings of Richard Rolle, Hermit of Hampole*, ed. Hope Emily Allen (Oxford: Clarendon Press, 1931), 35–36. Wolfgang Riehle discusses this image in Rolle and Kempe, *The Middle English Mystics*, trans. Bernard Standring (London: Routledge and Kegan Paul, 1981), 45–46.

6. Rolle, *English Writings*, ed. H. E. Allen, 36. All translations are my own unless otherwise indicated.

7. In F. J. Furnivall, ed., *Political, Religious, and Love Poems* EETS, o.s. 15 (London, 1866), 244–45. For the same poem in John of Grimestone's preaching book, see Edward Wilson, *A Descriptive Index of the English Lyrics of John of Grimestone's Preaching Book* (Oxford: Basil Blackwell, 1973), 70–71.

8. In his commentary, Meech remarks on the unusual number of scourgers, whips, and branches in Kempe's vision, attributing this multiplication to her own invention. He notes the retable at Norwich in which only two scourges appear, 334n.

9. This proliferation of wounds is found in Rolle's metaphors for Christ's wounds as stars in the sky, holes in a dovecot, and letters in a book: see "Meditations on the Passion" in *English Writings*, ed. H. E. Allen, 35–36. The medieval practice of numbering the wounds of Christ in conjunction with prayers counts them variously at 5475, 4732, and 4600, see Meech's note, 335n.

10. Mary does not usually ask to bear Christ's cross; the exchange found in Kempe's vision does not usually occur. Except in the Wakefield account of the crucifixion, this exchange does not occur in the medieval cycles or in Pseudo-Bonaventure's *Meditations on the Life of Christ*.

11. For references, see Allen's note, *The Book of Margery Kempe*, 271n. There is also a biblical reference to being written in the hands in Isaiah 49:16.

12. John Lydgate, *The Minor Poems of John Lydgate*, ed. Henry Noble Mc-Cracken, EETS, o.s. 107 (London: Oxford University Press, 1911; rpt. 1962), 248.

13. Ambrose, *Epistola LXIII*, PL 16, col. 1271. For an excellent study of the history of the *planctus Mariae* in medieval drama and patristic commentary, see Sandro Sticca, *The Planctus Mariae in the Dramatic Tradition of the Middle Ages*, trans. Joseph R. Berrigan (Athens: University of Georgia Press, 1988).

14. The debate in the early Church about Mary's virginity is discussed in Hilda Graef, *Mary: A History of Doctrine and Devotion*, vol. 1 (New York: Sheed and Ward, 1963), 32–100. It is interesting that, in the *Odes of Solomon* (second century A.D.), Mary's perfection is rendered in her painless giving birth where, because she gave birth openly and of her own will, "she brought forth, as if she were a man." (Graef, 35).

15. *Homily 17 on Luke*. Quoted in Graef, *Mary*, 46.

16. For example, Basil of Caesarea and Hesychius of Jerusalem, see Graef, *Mary*, 63–64 and 114.

17. Augustine, *Epistola CXXI*, par. 17, PL 33, cols. 468–69. See Graef's discussion of Augustine, *Mary*, 96–97.

18. *Expositio Evangelii secundum Lucam*, ed. M. Adriaen, *CCSL* 14 (Turnholti: Brepols, 1957), 61, 57. See Graef's discussion of Ambrose, *Mary*, 81.

19. *Sancti Ephraem Syri Opera Omnia in Sex Tomos Distributa* (Romae, 1747), VI, 574–75. Quoted in Sticca, *Plantus Mariae*, 35–36.

20. Hope Phyllis Weissman documents this display of "hysterical compassion" in the *Acts of Pilate* and elsewhere in medieval *vitae* and poetry, "Margery Kempe in Jerusalem: *Hysterica Compassio* in the Late Middle Ages," in *Acts of Interpretation: The Text in Its Contexts, 700–1600*, ed. Mary J. Carruthers and Elizabeth Kirk (Norman, OK: Pilgrim Books, 1982), 201–17. In addition, Sticca examines the complaint of the Virgin to Christ in the *Acts of Pilate* in *Planctus Mariae*, 34.

21. Rupert of Deutz, *Comm. in Jo.*, 13, PL 169, 789C. Quoted in Graef, *Mary*, 228.

22. M.-M. Desmarais, O.P., trans., *S. Albert le Grand. Docteur de la méditation morale* (Paris and Ottawa, 1935), 71. This passage is discussed in Sticca, *Planctus Mariae*, 25.

23. Pseudo-Bonaventure, *Meditations on the Life of Christ*, trans. Isa Ragusa, ed. Isa Ragusa and Rosalie B. Green (Princeton, NJ: Princeton University Press, 1961), 235.

24. See Bonaventure's *Commentary on the Sentences*, 18. Graef discusses this distinction in Bonaventure, *Mary: A History of Doctrine and Devotion*, 284–85. For an interesting discussion of the Virgin's grief in medieval art as well as in theology, see Harvey E. Hamburgh, "Aspects of the *Descent from the Cross* from Lippi to Cigoli" (Dissertation, University of Iowa, 1978), 2 vols. The motif of the Virgin's grief in non-dramatic works is discussed by George C. Taylor, "The English 'Planctus Mariae,'" *MP* 4 (1907): 606–37; in the Middle English lyrics, by Theodor Wolpers, "Englische Marienlyrik im Mittelalter," *Anglia* 69 (1950): 7–88, and by Douglas

Gray, *Themes and Images in the Medieval English Lyric* (London: Routledge and Kegan Paul, 1972), 31–71.

25. Bonaventure, *Sermon on the Annunciation*, 6. See Graef, *Mary*, 287.

26. For a very interesting account of the late fifteenth-century Italian debate between the stoic and swooning virgins—*lo spasimo*, as the latter was called—see Hamburgh, "Aspects of the *Descent from the Cross*," vol. 2, p. 752. See also Hamburgh, "The Problem of *Lo Spasimo* of the Virgin in *Cinquecento* Paintings of the *Descent from the Cross*," *Sixteenth Century Journal* 12 (1981): 45–76.

27. "Nunc extorquet cum usura / Gemitus, quos paritura / Natura detinuit." Clemens Blume and Guido Maria Dreves, eds., *Analecta Hymnica Medii Aevi* (New York, 1961), vol. 8, p. 58bC. Quoted in Weissman, "Margery Kempe in Jerusalem," 214n. For other examples, see vol. 32, pp. 152 and 153.

28. Ragusa and Green, *Meditations on the Life of Christ*, 335. Mary's sorrow is detailed in the lancing of Christ's side and in the deposition from the cross, 338–45. Aelred of Rievaulx advises imitation of the Virgin's grief, "Seest thou not how oure Lady wepith? What eyleth the that thou maist not wepe?" *Aelred of Rievaulx's De Institutione Inclusarum*, ed. John Ayto and Alexandra Barratt, EETS, o.s. 287 (London: Oxford University Press, 1984), 21.

29. Robert Manning, *Meditations on the Supper of Our Lord, and the Hours of the Passion*, ed. J. Meadows Cowper, EETS, o.s., 60 (London, 1875), ll. 783–86.

30. Rolle, *English Writings*, ed. H. E. Allen, 22.

31. Carleton Brown, ed., *Religious Lyrics of the Fifteenth Century* (Oxford: Clarendon Press, 1939), 9. Marina Warner discusses this poem in the context of the *mater dolorosa* tradition, *Alone of All Her Sex: The Myth and the Cult of the Virgin Mary* (New York: Vintage, 1976), 206–23. Rosemary Woolf is critical of fifteenth-century lyrics such as this one, which seem to her to whip up emotion for its own sake: see *The English Religious Lyric in the Middle Ages* (Oxford: Clarendon Press, 1968), 259–73. See also Douglas Gray's discussion of the Virgin's grief in the Middle English lyric, *Themes and Images in the Medieval Religious Lyric* (London: Routledge and Kegan Paul, 1972), 135–42.

32. R.M. Lumiansky and David Mills, eds., *The Chester Mystery Cycle*, EETS, s.s. 3, vol. 1 (London: Oxford University Press, 1974), 395. In the York and N-Town cycles, Mary gives more extensive vent to her madness, see Richard Beadle and Pamela L. King, eds., *York Mystery Plays* (Oxford: Clarendon Press, 1984), 227–31, and K. S. Block, ed., *Ludus Coventriae, or the Plaie called Corpus Christi*, EETS, e.s. 120 (London: Oxford University Press, 1922; rpt. 1960, 1974), 294–312.

33. Quoted in Sandro Sticca, *The Latin Passion Play: Its Origins and Development* (Albany: State University of New York Press, 1970), 104. The translation is that of Robert Edwards, *The Montecassino Passion and the Poetics of Medieval Drama* (Berkeley: University of California Press, 1977), 21.

34. Donald C. Baker, John L. Murphy, and Louis B. Hall, Jr., eds., *Late Medieval Religious Plays of Bodleian Mss Digby 133 and E Museo 160*, EETS, o.s. 283 (London: Oxford University Press, 1982), 155–57. In fact, devotional guides urged the one who meditated to join Joseph and John in cautioning the Magdalene to contain her grief, see Rosemary Woolf, "English Imitations of the *Homelia Origenis De Maria Magdalena*" in *Chaucer and the Middle English: Studies in Honour of Russell*

Hope Robbins, ed. Beryl Rowland (Kent, OH: Kent State University Press, 1974), 384–91. Kempe follows this practice in her second vision of the Crucifixion, as we have seen.

35. Baker, Murphy, and Hall, *Late Medieval Religious Plays*, 155–57.

36. Baker, Murphy, and Hall, *Late Medieval Religious Plays*, 158.

37. In fact, this justification of her grief is made in other medieval texts, such as the *Cursor Mundi*, in which the Virgin claims that there is no man so wise in learning that he may know the sorrow of the woman who has borne a child, Richard Morris, ed., *Cursor Mundi*, EETS, o.s. 68 (London, 1878), 1394.

38. Moshe Barasche examines these "gestures of despair" in medieval conventions of mourning and in Italian art; *Gestures of Despair in Medieval and Early Renaissance Art* (New York: New York University Press, 1976).

39. Quoted in Hamburgh, "The Problem of *Lo Spasimo* of the Virgin," 47. For Chrysostom's criticism, see John Chrysostom, *In Joan. hom. 62*, quoted and translated in Barasche, *Gestures of Despair in Medieval and Early Renaissance Art*, 36. As Barasch points out, Chrysostom was not alone in condemning the female practice of extravagant grief: it was the subject of medieval satire and legal prohibition as well, see 139n. In addition, other books of hours depict scenes of mourning similar to that of *Les Belles Heures*, including Jean Pucelle's *Hours of Jeanne d'Evreux* (Entombment), the *Petites Heures du Duc de Berry* (Lamentation), the *Grandes Heures du Duc de Berry* (Lamentation), and the *Hours of Etienne Chevalier* (Pietà).

40. For an overview of the "school" of violent self-injury and gesticulation, see Barasche, *Gestures of Despair*, 103–15.

41. Bernard Moeller uses this phrase to describe German piety in "Piety in Germany Around 1500" in *The Reformation in Medieval Perspective*, ed. Stephen Ozment (Chicago: University of Chicago Press, 1971), 54. For a study of this kind of representation in Italian art, see Timothy Verdon, "The Art of Guido Mazzoni" (Dissertation, Yale University, 1975).

42. Baker, Murphy, and Hall, *Late Medieval Religious Plays*, 144.

43. Baker, Murphy, and Hall, *Late Medieval Religious Plays*, 149.

44. I am borrowing Kristeva's analysis of Hans Holbein the Younger's "The Body of the Dead Christ in the Tomb" in "Holbein's Dead Christ," *Fragments for a History of the Human Body*, Part 1, ed. Michel Feher, Ramona Nadaff, and Nadia Tazi (New York: Urzone, 1989), 265. Kristeva would probably consider Kempe and the Digby Marys examples of the "Gothic eroticism of paroxistic pain," rather than those in the company of Holbein's figures.

45. Hope Phyllis Weissman also notes the importance of Mary's assurance in establishing a pattern of redemption through shame in Kempe's own life, "Margery Kempe in Jerusalem," 210.

46. Quoted in Meech and Allen's notes, *The Book of Margery Kempe*, 323n.

47. The passage from his *Evagatorum in Terrae Sanctae, Arabiae et Egypti Peregrinationem* is quoted in Weissman, "Margery Kempe in Jerusalem," 215.

48. Elsewhere in her *Book*, her companions suspect that she has the "fallyng euyl," or epilepsy, and they spit on her out of disgust, 105. I suspect that is the same sickness referred to here.

49. As H.E. Allen notes, Dorothea of Montau also uses the word to suggest

one who is a repository of divine secrets, while Nicholas Love applies the term to Christ's apostles, since they knew the Lord on earth, *The Book of Margery Kempe*, 292n.

50. I am using Foucault's formulation of the mystic's "secret language of prayer," in *Language, Counter-Memory, Practice: Selected Essays and Interviews*, trans. Donald F. Bouchard and Sherry Simon (Ithaca, NY: Cornell University Press, 1977), 48.

51. For the Book of Life as body of Christ, see Gellrich's discussion of the *liber occultorum* in Dante, *Idea of the Book*, 160–61.

52. Janet Coleman comments on this longstanding irony of Christian tradition, pointing out that the Scripture that informs medieval culture is nevertheless absent from it: "Adherents of a religion based on a text, the word as written by God, fourteenth-century English men and women were none the less never confronted directly with The Word," in *Medieval Readers and Writers: 1350–1400* (New York: Columbia University Press, 1981), 170. This is not to say, however, that lay audiences and readers were not familiar with Scriptures. Vernacular sermons and translations of the Bible made access to Scriptures more common in the fifteenth century than it had been. Nevertheless, knowledge of Scriptures gleaned from medieval sermons and handbooks for preachers was necessarily a fragmented and mediated one, see *Medieval Readers*, 158–221. Margaret Aston also points out that the image of Christ as book reflects the "textual consciousness of the age" in *Lollards and Reformers: Images and Literacy in Late Medieval Religion* (London: Hambledon Press, 1984), 105.

53. *The Book of Margery Kempe*, 42–43. As Allen points out, Julian follows other medieval theologians who had determined the signs or tokens by which the discernment of spirits was tested and proved, 279. Christ, too, gives Kempe five tokens for her tears, 183.

54. Susan Dickman has also argued that "the traditional ideal of compassion which had fostered meditative modes of devotion within the cloister for at least two centuries, once transferred to the world and practiced by ordinary lay folk, was subject to radically different pressures," in "Margery Kempe and the English Devotional Tradition," in *The Medieval Mystical Tradition*, ed. Marion Glasscoe (Exeter, 1980), 168.

6. The Disembodied Text

Margery Kempe concludes the first version of her book with an appeal to the "trewe sentens" shown in the experience she narrates. In fact, as she is careful to explain, she never trusted her revelation until "she knew by means of experience whether it was true or not" (220). By testing her feelings against her experience—and against the text, since the mystic text is always engaged in the act of self-verification—Kempe firmly positions truth in that experience, rather than behind, beyond, or above it. This is consistent with her expressed purpose of writing a treatise which would demonstrate Christ's merciful workings, stirrings, and movings in her own life. As we have seen, her own voice also finds its vindication in the same experience, both textual and worldly. She clearly does not have in mind a treatise modeled on Hilton's *Scala Perfectionis* or *The Cloud of Unknowing*. Although she does claim to dictate her book "for our example and instruction," she does so in the form of dialogue and narrative, rather than as a guide to meditation or contemplation. Her "truth" is thus one which cannot be separated from the format and "experience" of her treatise. The corporeal aspect of Kempe's narrative—the Christic and mystic bodies figured in her language—is never far from the reader's experience of reading her treatise.

Yet Margery Kempe could not control the experiences of readers in the centuries that followed the dictation of her book; nor could she ensure that her truths would remain embodied in the text, the "sentence" in the "experiens," in future editions which were made of her book. She could not prevent the displacement of her own dictated text by the two severely abridged texts which would survive into the twentieth century. Until Hope Emily Allen identified the lost manuscript copy of *The Book of Margery Kempe* from William Butler-Bowdon's library in 1934, and the manuscript was edited in 1940 by the Early English Text Society, modern readers had access to only two versions of the book, in which the experience had been expunged, leaving only disjointed bits of "trewe sentens," in the words of George R. Keiser, "the Dicts and Sayings of Christ to Margerie Kempe."[1]

At first these printed fragments did not entirely replace the book itself. As we saw in chapter 3, a sixteenth-century reader left notes in the margins of the manuscript. This indicates a readership of the manuscript version of Kempe's book at least one century after her death.[2]

The marginalia in the manuscript, along with the published extracts of Kempe's book, suggest both a readership and a reading of *The Book of Margery Kempe*. Yet studies of Kempe tend to view her work in isolation from its readership and the culture which read it in the fifteenth and sixteenth centuries. Her book is mined for the influences on it, the historical context which accounts for it, and its indices to historical figures and life of the late Middle Ages. In the mystical canon, her treatise is generally regarded as the culmination of late medieval spiritual trends, rather than as a work which generated trends of its own.[3] While scholars carefully examine Chaucer's audience and his self-conscious relationship to past and future literary traditions, few treat Kempe's book as anything but a product (anomalous or not) of late medieval spiritual traditions. In this way, scholarship effectively isolates Kempe's book from its immediate and secondary readerships, much as her own contemporaries ostracized her from their communities. In effect, this amounts to denying Kempe an influence and allowing her a capacity only for being influenced.

I do not wish to argue, however, for Kempe's influence either. As I have already shown, Kempe herself qualifies (if she does not outright reject) the very genealogy of influences she cites in her book. She confounds the reader's desire for an authoritative tradition founding her text by privileging her own voice—and the oral/aural text of her dialogues with Christ— over the textual witness of her *auctoritees*. For the feminist project of delineating the position of woman's writing, the paradigm of influence itself is suspect, since it is based on a male tradition of cultural patrilineage. This model already excludes women except as receptors or mediums of male culture. Like the Aristotelian model of sexuality, this model of cultural transmission privileges the active male author over the passive female author, whose nature it is to receive and pass along a tradition to which she nevertheless cannot contribute. She is wax to the seal of patriarchal tradition, an impression of a male culture of letters, to adapt the analogy used in the *Anatomia vivorum* for describing the relationship between male and female sexual anatomies.

Indeed, just as the sexual anatomies paradigm is used to fault the female anatomy for its inferior symmetry and energy, the influence paradigm is pressed into service to limit the female author's authorship. Thus,

Kempe never measures up to the other English mystics because she fails to found a readership or a mystical following.[4] That she is never cited in the mystical texts of later writers is proof of her limitations as an author and a mystic, according to most influence-based arguments. The fact that her work is generally considered to be the first autobiography in the English language does not salvage her reputation, for even as autobiography *The Book of Margery Kempe* fails to inspire imitation. It merely survives as an instance of autobiography which then disappears, only to re-emerge long after other autobiographies have taken credit for originating and defining the characteristics of the genre.

I do not wish to press the influence paradigm into service here merely to reverse our assessment of Kempe's place in medieval culture or the "tradition" of women writing. Nor am I satisfied with classifying her as a "maverick" who remained on the margins of a society under the influence of the monolithic institution of the medieval Church.[5] This type of endorsement of Kempe merely reaffirms the principles by which she has previously been excluded in scholarship. It celebrates her difference and even monologizes it at the cost of considering a place for that difference *within* rather than without medieval culture. Worse, it allows scholarship to retain intact and unquestioned its own patriarchal paradigms.

Michel Foucault has already outlined the ideological workings of the influence paradigm. The search for a "principle of coherence," particularly one which affirms the "sovereignty of collective consciousness" as a method of explanation, always underlies the project of determining influence. In fact, as Foucault makes clear, such a project relies on the mundane criteria of resemblance and repetition, rather than on any proof of an essential unity in the subject of study.[6] A further assumption underlying the study of influence is that there exists a "tradition," or a discernible mainstream in any historical period with respect to which any person, idea, or work may be positioned.[7] If we wish to determine Kempe's influence, then, we are forced to accept these other paradigms, which are patriarchal, and as I have argued, we must ultimately acknowledge her failure. Clearly, some other paradigm—though no less ideological—is called for to avoid the foregone conclusions of the influence paradigm.

To begin with, I want to turn to three sets of notes left in the margins of the manuscript version of *The Book of Margery Kempe* to get some idea of early readings of her book. By reading the readers' marginal comments, we can discern the fragments and traces of early readings of her book. In turn, a comparison of these marginal annotations with the early printed editions of the *Book of Margery Kempe* will reveal distinctly different registers of reading which occurred in the century after her death. The marginalia and the printed editions together suggest a wide readership for her book, one which crossed lay/monastic lines. If her influence cannot be attested, the circulation of her book can be, and it allows us to track the course of our own contemporary response to the book—a response which, as we shall see, was partly created by Wynkyn de Worde and Henry Pepwell.

Three Readings

Having looked at the relationship between Kempe's experience and her book, I would like to turn to the experience of her book after her death in order to compare my own reading of it in the last few chapters with a cultural reading of it. The purpose of such a study is to be able to examine the ideology informing both modern and early modern readings of *The Book of Margery Kempe*. In turn, I hope to establish the need for a feminist reformulation of the way in which we read Margery Kempe and the Middle Ages as well.

We do not know what happened to the version of Kempe's book that she dictated to her second scribe between 1436 and 1438. The only surviving manuscript of her book is one which was copied by the scribe who signed it, "Salthows," probably soon after Kempe dictated her book.[8] As early as the late fifteenth century, this manuscript copy belonged to the Carthusian monastery of Mount Grace in Yorkshire. The marginal notation described in chapter 3 represents the comments of one sixteenth-century reader, most likely a monk at Mount Grace, and an earlier reader.[9] In addition, there are three other sets of comments, two of which call attention to what the reader thought were important places in the text, and one which made a few emendations in the manuscript. It has not been determined where or when these annotations were made, but since they came before the red annotations, they were probably made sometime during the late fifteenth and early sixteenth centuries.

Before looking at these annotations further, one important conclusion needs to be drawn. The fact that the manuscript copy of *The Book of Margery Kempe* belonged to the Mount Grace library suggests that there was *at least* a monastic audience for her book. One could also speculate that Mount Grace might have even commissioned the copy of Kempe's book for its library. Yet Kempe seemed to pitch her treatise at a lay audience, since it is meant as an instructive example of a manner of living after the life of Christ. H. S. Bennett has documented the rather extensive reading public for works of devotion and religious instruction in the fifteenth century even before the printing press made such works cheap and accessible.[10] It is more surprising that a monastic audience was interested in reading her book than that a lay audience might have been.

The series of annotations give us a clue to Kempe's fifteenth- and sixteenth-century audiences, even if we cannot determine whether three of the four were lay or religious. I am not proposing, however, that it is possible to derive a coherent picture of their readings. The annotations are simply too cryptic in some cases; nor can they be regarded either as the sum of the reader's interest and commentary on the text. All that may be concluded from examining these annotations is what *some* of the interests and emphases of these readers were, as well as how they judged Kempe's mystical experiences.

Of the four sets of annotations, one set may be disregarded because it consists mainly of stylistic emendations in the text.[11] Two sets written in brown ink may be treated together, since they are rather sketchy and much less frequent than those of the third set. For the purposes of discussion, I will label these two sets as "Reader 1" and "Reader 2."[12] Reader 1 takes an interest in aspects of Kempe's experience that neither of the other two readers comments on. For example, Reader 1 places *nota* ("note well") signs to the side of Kempe's temptation by the man who propositions her in St. Margaret's early in her book (15). This reader also singles out her husband's faithful companionship during her difficult travels in England (32). The significance of spiritual experiences, such as Kempe's first roaring on Mt. Calvary (105), is also annotated by Reader 1. In addition to such reading signals, the reader often repeats words from the text, keying his/her reading into themes in the book. The most persistent marginal note is the word "loue" or "lof," in each case referring to an instance of divine love manifesting itself to Kempe.[13] Since Reader 1's comments are limited to about half the manuscript, amounting to only twenty notes, this recurrence is emphatic. Before drawing any conclusions, I want to compare this set of comments to those of the second reader.

Reader 2 writes only eleven comments, but they are more elaborate than Reader 1's one-word notes. "Nota de clamore," for example, reveals that this reader, like the first, considered Kempe's first roaring on Calvary significant. Unlike the first reader, this one remarks mainly on Kempe's spiritual experiences, such as her marriage to Christ, her visionary confession to John the Baptist, and Christ's speeches to her. Finally, the reader singles out Kempe's story of the bear and the pear tree with a "narracio," and remarks on the miraculous ability of Kempe's German confessor to understand her English (88 and 126).

The only overlap in these comments is the references to Kempe's roaring and to her visionary confession to John the Baptist. Otherwise, these two fifteenth-century readers responded differently to Kempe's book. While the theme of love emerges from Reader 1's marginal notes, no discernible theme—or trace of the reader's desire—is apparent in the second reader's notes. What is more interesting about the second reader's comments is that they treat with reverence and seriousness those very aspects of Kempe's mysticism most controverted by modern mystical scholars. An obvious example is her marriage to Christ, which the reader labels, "de desponsa[cio]ne eius ad deum patrem," while modern scholars see Kempe's marriage as a literalization of the mystical concept.[14] In addition, Reader 2's note about her roaring, which is called "clamore," aligns what many consider to be Kempe's most excessive practice with Rolle's third stage of mystical ecstasy, *canor*, "song," as I pointed out in chapter 3.[15]

In different registers, both readers take Kempe's treatise as a document concerned with various "trewths," including truths about divine love, human love expressed through tears, and the effects of divine revelation in the world. While the first reader takes it more as a "comfort and solaas" to sinners in the world, the second reader finds mystical guidance in Kempe's text apart from her worldly experiences. It is, perhaps, important to acknowledge what these readers do not note, as well as what they do, in order to compare them to modern readers. First, there is no suggestion in any of the marginal comments of any criticism of either Kempe or her mysticism. Only selections of key passages for the reader's spiritual development are attended to. Second, nowhere is Kempe compared to Julian of Norwich. Even the third reader, who recognizes the anchoress in a marginal note, never compares Kempe's revelations to hers. This is significant, considering the persistent tendency in modern scholarship to compare the two women and to find Kempe wanting.[16] Although Julian's *Showings* enjoyed only "limited circulation" until the seventeenth century, a copy of her short text dates from c. 1450. More significantly, it was probably a Carthusian manuscript, just as Kempe's was.[17] These annotators could very well have been familiar with the short text of the *Showings*, yet they never refer to it in their marginal comments on Kempe's book. Fifteenth-century readers, whether lay or religious, apparently did not compare these two mystics merely for the fact that both were women who had mystical visions and that they lived at about the same time in the same geographical area.

The third reader, reading a bit later than the first two, from the early sixteenth century, leaves many more annotations, and hence, a much fuller account of his reading. Because this reader compares Kempe's habit of weeping to that of Richard Methley (c. 1451/2–1528), he is presumed to have written his annotations sometime in the early sixteenth century.[18] In addition, his references to Methley, who was a Carthusian at Mount Grace, suggest that he, too, might have been a monk at the same monastery where Margery Kempe's book was housed. In addition to stylistic emendations, this reader inscribed copious commentary and summary of Kempe's text, including a few line drawings of hearts, hands, a pillar, and "our Lady's smock" all keyed in to passages.[19]

Sue Ellen Holbrook has examined the third reader's annotations for the purpose of comparing them with later extractions of Kempe's text by Wynkyn de Worde. She sums up the overall insights represented by this reader's annotations:

> [The annotator] responds not only to love, thinking, compassion, charity, mourning, detraction, reward, the acceptance of tribulation, patience, the right way to heaven and so forth, but also to the problem of being a mystic when one is also a wife, the passionate quality and marital form of her spiritual relationship to the Lord, and, notably, the visions, the cries, the feelings of weakness and of fire burning—i.e., the sensory manifestations of communion with God, and the similarity between Kempe's experiences and those of Methley, Norton and Rolle.[20]

This sweeping coverage of what amounts to over seventy-two comments reveals the reader's simultaneous interest in the "trewth" and the "experiens," as Kempe had articulated it.[21] I would like to single out a few of the notations to map out some of Reader 3's commentary.

The first kind of commentary, which I have already partially addressed, is that which identifies specific ideas and practices in Kempe's narrative with those of Rolle, Methley, and Norton. Methley and Norton are particularly significant, since they lived after Margery Kempe. Both were monks at Mount Grace, Norton achieving the status of prior, while Methley was a vicar until his death in 1528.[22] Reader 3 refers to them in five different places in the text, in each case next to Kempe's roaring during her visions of Christ's Passion. The reader writes, "father M. was wont so to doo," next to a passage in which Kempe falls down and roars in response to a vision of the parting of Mary and Christ. After Kempe's first bout of roaring on Calvary, she explains that she had these fits often and "they made her very weak in her bodily might, and especially if she heard of our Lord's Passion" (68–69). The reader notes, "so fa[ther] RM & f[ather] Norton & of Wakenes of þe passyon" (68). Elsewhere Kempe describes how, when she is seized by her compassion for Christ's Passion, "she with the crying twisted her body turning from one side to the other and turned entirely blue as the color of lead" (105). Reader 3 comments matter-of-factly, "so dyd prior Nort[on] in hys excesse."

These comments together point to one disturbing conclusion, that two Carthusian monks engaged in the same mystical practice of falling down and crying loudly—what some have called "morbid enthusiasm" and hysteria—that Kempe describes. Hope Emily Allen comments that Methley was known to have been an "extreme exponent of 'sensory devotion,'" as was another Carthusian, Nicholas Love, author of the Middle English translation of the *Meditationes Vitae Christi*. She then attempts to isolate these two from the order as a whole in a telling defense of Carthusian spirituality:

> The ecstatic *marginalia* apparently emanating from the Charterhouse of Mountgrace c. 1500 (though expressing a type of devotion found in other English Charterhouses at that period, . . .) may not represent the point of view of all English Carthusians, since earlier there was clearly a division of opinion in the order. The Carthusians were of course an international organisation, and though the English Carthusians were great propagandists of English mystical writings . . . , various signs give evidence of piety in English Charterhouses not in the tradition of those writings.[23]

Considering that Allen was so knowledgeable about these ecstatic experiences in the writings of women mystics, it is somewhat surprising that she is so clearly uncomfortable with the references to possible Carthusian affinities with Kempe's ecstatic experiences. She attempts to dissociate the reader and the two monks alluded to from the larger and more representative "tradition" of Carthusian spirituality in order to preserve it from contamination by what amounts to a lunatic fringe, in her formulation.

Allen is not alone in her desire to preserve the "tradition" of Carthusian piety described by David Knowles as embracing the "primitive spirit of austerity and seclusion."[24] Knowles, too, singles out Methley and Mount Grace priory, along with Nicholas Love and the London Charterhouse, for diluting the "spirit of the English mystics" enjoyed by the "spiritual *élite*" with a "somewhat different and more pietistic atmosphere."[25] Scholars would prefer to associate the spirit of late Carthusian spirituality with a treatise such as *The Chastising of God's Children*, a text which explicitly condemns religious enthusiasm, or with a particular Carthusian's criticism of Rolle's mysticism.[26] In addition, the Carthusians' role in importing, copying, and circulating spiritual treatises in late medieval England is emphasized as the highest form of occupation for those committed to strict solitude. The words of Dom Guigo, fifth prior of the Grande Chartreuse, are often cited in this regard: "Surely we ought to preserve books most carefully, as immortal food for our souls, and to make volumes assiduously, that, because we cannot preach the word of God by mouth, we may with our hands."[27] The fact that the two major Carthusian writers in England, Nicholas Love and Richard Methley, were "religious enthusiasts" seems to embarrass the austere image of Carthusian spirituality represented by Guigo.[28] While modern scholarship is concerned with preserving Guigo's image of Carthusian interest in spiritual texts over the examples of Methley and Norton, the third reader shows no such concern.

For our purposes of observing the cultural context for Kempe's book, Reader 3's notes are important. He clearly found Kempe's roaring to be a legitimate expression of religious devotion and one with which he was familiar. His notes suggest an alternative tradition to the one which is used by modern scholars to define a spiritual élite. Although he mentions Prior Norton's "excesse," nowhere either in this comment or elsewhere does he hint that this behavior is aberrant or inappropriate. In fact, his other comments implicate this behavior in a theology which never defends, condemns, or rationalizes such behavior. In order to contextualize this reader's comments, I need to sketch the contours of Methley's work. I cannot adequately summarize all of Methley's work here, but I can select portions of his work which will be useful to understanding this reader's comments. This is admittedly a selection of key concepts from Methley and not a comprehensive study, although I hope that it will provide direction for a future, full-length study of Methley.

In chapter 3, we saw how this third reader recognized in Kempe's sensory mystical experiences, particularly of the fire of love, certain resemblances to Richard Rolle. References to "ignis divini amoris," "feruent loue," and "langor amoris" link Kempe's experiences of tears and burning love to Rolle's. However, these comments could also allude to Richard Methley's mystical experiences. It is Methley who elaborates the idea of "languor" in connection with his sensory mystical experiences. Like

Kempe, Methley has been accused of being a "spiritual exhibitionist," primarily because of his "sensory devotion." Behind such evaluations of Methley and Kempe lie fears that such mystics are unaware of the "spiritual dangers risked by the unlearned enthusiast."[29] Among those dangers are heresy and misuse of metaphorical sensual language to denote actual physical experiences.

Yet these fears are modern—not medieval or early modern—ones. The sixteenth-century reader exhibits none of them. Even the fifteenth-century treatise which discourages religious enthusiasm, *The Chastising of God's Children*, recognizes the bodily signs as legitimate ones, as long as they are not sought as ends in themselves. Describing the heavenly sweetness visited by Christ on his lovers, the *Chastising* author says it is "more delightful (to the body and soul) than all the mirth and enjoyment that all the world could give at one time." The spiritual drunkenness which attends such visitations is a bodily spectacle, according to the author:

> Þis maner drunkennesse makiþ sum men to synge, and worshippe god for fulfillyng of gladnesse. Sum men in þat tyme bien plenteuouse of teeris; sum men in that tyme bien stired wiþ al þe membris of her bodi, so þat þei muste skippe, ren or daunce: summe for ioie bete her handis togidre: summe crien aloude wiþ an hiȝ uoice: summe bien stille and mow nat speke.[30]

> (This kind of drunkenness makes some men sing and worship God for filling them full of gladness. Some men at that time are full of tears; some men at that time are stirred in all the members of their body, so that they must skip, run, or dance: some for joy beat their hands together: some cry aloud with a high voice: some are still and cannot speak.)

Rolle's *canor* and *clamor* are here understood as bodily practices, just as Kempe and Methley understand them. Reader 3 clearly reads the body in the text out of this tradition when he links Kempe's tears and cries to those of Methley and Norton.

Richard Methley and Margery Kempe

As a way of fleshing out the reader's understanding of Kempe's text, I would like to focus briefly on some of the works of Richard Methley.[31] Described by one scholar as "probably, the most influential writer at Mount Grace after Nicholas Love," Methley leaves three autobiographical treatises, a partial treatise on the discernment of spirits, and two Latin translations of other mystical works. The three autobiographical treatises, *Scola amoris languidi*, *Dormitorium dilecti dilecti*, and *Refectorium salutis*, are most relevant to the reader's comments on Kempe's text, since they recount Methley's own mystical experiences.[32] The unedited treatises survive together in a manuscript whose copious marginal glosses indicate frequent use and study.[33]

The three treatises were written over a period of three years. The earliest, the *Scola amoris languidi*, was written in 1484. It was followed by the *Dormitorium dilecti dilecti* in 1485 and the *Refectorium salutis* in 1487. Methley apparently wrote all three treatises for the purpose of imparting his spiritual experiences to the other monks at Mount Grace. He claims in the *Scola amoris languidi* to write in "new tongues" infused with the grace of Christ's spiritual visitations:

> In nomine iesu linguis loquor nouis, vt dicunt alicui [sic] de me, qui audierunt aut libros quos per graciam scripsi, legerunt. Nouis (inquam) quia de noua vita in christo iesu, . . .[34]

> (In the name of Jesus I speak in new tongues, so they say about me who hear or read the books which I have written by means of grace. I say "with new tongues" because of the new life I lead in Christ Jesus, . . .)

Like Kempe, Methley construes his treatise as an example for the instruction of others, and he claims a voice which comes only from grace.[35]

Using his newfound speech, Methley instructs his readers in his range of experiences of *amor sensibilis*, "sensory love." It is this theme running throughout his treatises which prompted Hope Emily Allen to label Methley "an extreme exponent of 'sensory devotion.'" Others have pointed to this same characteristic of sensory mystical experience to charge Methley with "a *naiveté* which suggests that [he], at least at this period of his life, had not yet attained to the wisdom of the saints."[36] Criticisms of Methley bear a striking resemblance to those of Kempe which single out her morbid literalism, her excessive sensuality, and her hysterical behavior. The consistency of scholarship here is instructive, in that it suggests broader affiliations between Kempe and Methley than between Kempe and Julian of Norwich.

Methley clearly establishes the importance of *amor sensibilis* to his mystical project in the beginning of his first treatise, the *Scola amoris languidi*:

> Omnium creaturarum summum studium est amare et amari. . . . Hinc est enim quod, quia deum diligo actuali deuocione gracias illi ago in secula seculorum,

omnes ad amandum deum prouocare studeo. Et quia amor est causa tocius vniuersitatis, nichil melius quam amorem ponere potest propter remedium, vt ad amorem sensibilem tandem attingere valeat omnis qui diligere cupit.[37]

(The highest study of all creatures is to love and to be loved. . . . Hence it is also that, because I love God with active devotion, I give thanks to him forever by attempting to provoke others to love God. And because love is the cause of the entire universe, nothing is better capable than love of bringing one to the remedy, so that all who desire to love may finally succeed in attaining sensory love.)

Methley sums up his own experience of this sensory love in the re-peated exclamation from the Song of Songs, *amore langueo*. Methley's account of this languishing with love resembles Rolle's description of the same mystical fervor described in chapter 3. Excess of love for the beloved one who is absent precipitates this languishing, or love-longing. In turn, this languor attends the material sensation of fire in the mystic's mind and heart. Kempe, too, draws on Rolle's notion of languor in her desire to be rid of the world and united with Christ, while the sixteenth-century reader labels her weeping fits *langor amoris*. Clearly, Methley, Kempe, and the reader are familiar with a kind of sensory expression of mystical love associated with—but not limited to—the fire of love.

In the second chapter of his *Scola amoris languidi*, Methley acknowl-edges that sensory languor is not pleasant for the lover: in fact, it is the most odious thing of all, for it "ravishes the lover from his delight." And yet, the experience of divine love is inseparable from this most difficult feeling of languor. Love and languor are, Methley claims, "inseparable companions because love is the cause of languor and languor is the cause of love."[38] This languor is also the cause of tears and heavenly song, as Methley later points out. The fervor which accompanies the mystical lover's languor, in turn, produces that fire of love felt in the senses. Both sensations seize the lover with incredible vehemence.[39]

In the same treatise, Methley demonstrates the vehemence of this languor, and its power to seize him in the midst of his monastic duties. After warning that "he who has not experienced [*languor amoris*] should not impugn it out of envy for the solitary," Methley attempts to convey what he has already acknowledged to be inexpressible:

In festo sancti petri ad vincula in monte gracie corporaliter fui in ecclesia. Et dum peracta quam celebraui missa deo gracias reddere curarem, per medita-cionis modum et oracionem nimis valde visitauit me deus. Nam in tantum amore langvi quod fere expiraui. Quomodo autem hoc fieri potuit sicut possum per graciam dei dicam vobis freres mei. Amor et desiderium dilecti susceperunt me spiritualiter in celum, ut praeter mortem nil me deesset (inquantum sapio) de gloria dei qui sedet in trono et hoc pro parte mea. Denique omnem penam et timorem et omnem meditacionem alicuius rei vel [et] creatoris studium deliberatam consideracionem oblitus eram. . . . Sed inualescente languore amoris vix cogitare potui formans in spiritu hec verba, "Amor, amor, amor!" Et tandem deficiens ab hac forma exspeceam quem totaliter spiritum exspirare possem, "A, a, a!" tummodo aut consimili modo canens pocius quam clamans in spiritu per gaudio.[40]

(On the feast of St. Peter in Chains I was bodily in the church at Mount Grace. After I had finished celebrating Mass, I was engaged in giving thanks when God visited me with exceeding vehemence in meditation and prayer, and I yearned with such love that I nearly died. How this could be done I will tell you as best I can, my brothers. Love and desire for the Beloved raised me spiritually into heaven, so that nothing of the glory of God who sits on the throne would have been lacking to me except for death (so far as I know). Then I completely forgot all pain and fear and all meditation of any thing, even deliberate thought about my desire for the Creator. . . . But as the languor of love grew stronger I was scarcely able to think, forming these words in my spirit, "Love! Love! Love!" And at last ceasing from this behavior, I desired that I would give up my spirit totally in a manner more like singing than shouting in spirit out of joy, Ah! Ah! Ah!")

Methley's mystical raptures, like Kempe's, begin in an abundance of love leading to languor and to the choking of all language in the cries and song of spiritual joy. At other times, his joy reduces him to repeating the name of Jesus over and over again.[41] Sometimes tears also accompany Methley's sensory languor, although he is not always aware of them during his raptures.[42]

The sensuality of Methley's mystical raptures is expressed in language familiar to those acquainted with affective spirituality: inebriation, liquefaction of the heart, heavenly song, and the burning fire of love. His devotion, like his love, is experienced through a sudden and violent ravishment of the senses: "subito languor rapuit me in sensibilem dulcedinem deuocionis" (suddenly languor ravished me into the sensual sweetness of devotion).[43] The main danger of this sensory devotion for Methley is that it interrupts and interferes with his duties as a monk, including his reading of a passage from Ecclesiastes to the other monks in the refectory.[44] Unlike Kempe's, his mystical raptures are not usually public ones, nor does he report that they arouse the hostility that hers do.

In spite of the influence Richard Rolle has had on Methley's mystical discourse, he is careful to distinguish his own experiences of languor from Rolle's experience of the heat of love:

> vita mea consistit in amore languore, dulcore, feruore, canore, rarius tamen in sensibili feruore quia dilectus michi promisit quod frequencius in languore sicut et ille almus Ricardus dictus de hampol frequencius in calore de quo non legi quod tam frequens fuerit in languore.[45]

> (my life consists of the yearning [languor] of love, sweetness, fervor, and song; less often it consists of sensory fervor because my beloved promised me that I would be more frequently in a state of languor, just as Richard of Hampole was more frequently in a state of heat, since I did not read that he was in a state of languor very frequently.)

Methley's distinction between Rolle's sensory devotion and his own consists in the affective mode that devotion assumes. Although Methley speaks elsewhere of the sensual fire of love, he considers his experience of languor to be the more significant. Rolle, too, speaks of this languor in his *Incendium amoris*, but it represents only one aspect of his larger concern with the three stages of mystical rapture: fire, sweetness, and song.

While Methley clearly conceives of his mystical experience in sensual terms, his own understanding of *amor sensibilis* is not quite as simple as it appears. For Methley elsewhere recounts how this sensual love exceeds all senses, claiming that mystical languor "ravishes the mind above all corporeal senses."[46] In his numerological interpretation of the name "Jesus," Methley discovers the number five, which suggests to him the five senses and reminds him that the lover of Christ must close off his senses if he is to open up his heart.[47] Finally, Methley defines the solitude of monastic life not as a physical withdrawal from the world but as control over the senses.[48]

What may appear to be a paradox according to our own often simplistic distinction between the physical and the spiritual does not appear to have bothered Methley. His visions, like his language, abound in the "physical." "Vehemence," "sensation," "excess," "ravishment," "languor," "inebriation," "clamor," "tears," and "liquefaction" are among the most often used terms for Methley's sudden and violent inductions into mystical rapture. His sensual love leads to his extravagant desire to die "in some special miraculous way" after the example of the saints.[49] Yet, he also writes about the way to purest contemplation, something which seems inconsistent with his "naive" experience of sensory devotion.[50] In fact, Methley's later works are not about this sensory devotion at all, but about methods for the discernment of spirits, the difficulty of determining truth amidst the disagreement of learned men, and controversy over contemporary prophets and evangelists.[51] His letter on the solitary life written to Hugh the Hermit is occupied with the monastic virtues of obedience, chastity, poverty, and silence, and with the five practices of the solitary: good prayer, meditation, reading "holy englisshe bokes," contemplation, and chores.[52]

Clearly, for Methley, there is no incompatibility between his monastic vocation and his "excessive sensory devotion," or between that devotion and "pure contemplation." This distinction is created and preserved in modern scholarship, not among even the most learned and devout of medieval mystics, such as Richard Methley was.[53] Neither does Methley feel compelled, as the author of the *Cloud of Unknowing* did, to insist upon the metaphoricity of his language to deter the "spiritually obtuse" from "false experience."[54] In his comparison of his mystical languor and Rolle's fire Methley is concerned in his comparison of his mystical languor and Rolle's fire with identifying the different registers of *amor sensibilis*; he does not feel called upon to warn against the "disobedience of the imagination" or the dangers of enthusiasm, as do some of his predecessors and modern scholars. Love experienced through and beyond the senses is, as Methley states in the beginning of the *Scola amoris languidi*, the highest calling to which a person can be drawn.

Reading Kempe in terms of Methley's *amor sensibilis*, the sixteenth-century reader highlights what he sees as an example of her languor, namely, her weeping. Her inability to suppress her boisterous tears and her writhing are read as tokens of her longing. This connection is made explicit in the reader's comment, "langyng loue," next to Kempe's plea to Christ, "Alas, Lord, how long shall I thus weep and mourn for your love and for desire of your presence?" (176) It is the absence of the beloved which inspires the longing and its manifestations in her roaring and writhing, just as for Methley, this same longing inspires a "sweet sensation of devotion" and a desire for death.[55] The reader's specific references to Methley's practice of weeping are further suggestive of this association among love, languor, and "sensible" devotion. He attributes Kempe's own excesses to the "feruent love" which runs as a theme throughout Methley's work.[56] Reader 3 annotates Christ's speech to Kempe in which he asks what better token there is of love than weeping for Christ's love (158). One other kind of love is noted by the reader, *amor impaciens*, next to Kempe's roaring and cries "I die, I die," while she observes a sacramental procession in Bristol during the Feast of Corpus Christi. The very same marginal annotation appears at the end of Methley's *Scola amoris languidi* by another reader (presumably), who responds to Methley's desire to die.[57]

In these notations, the reader attends to the bodily text, or what Methley would have called Kempe's "sensible love." That he is also aware of the excessiveness of her ardor, with all its bodily manifestations, is apparent in his comment that another Carthusian, John Norton, also fell down and roared at the Passion "in hys excesse." Yet there is nothing to indicate that this reader regarded either Kempe or Norton critically. Instead, he seems to have read the excesses of both as gestures of that "sensible love" which Methley documented in his own autobiographical treatises. Using Methley's texts as a gloss of Kempe's book, the reader would have had no reason to be critical of this excess; instead, as my summary of Methley's works indicates, a familiarity with Methley would have drawn the reader's attention to those physical tokens of mystical revelation which modern readers call naive. The reader attends to this aspect of Kempe's text as though he took Methley's opening lines to the *Scola amoris languidi* as his rubric: "the highest study of all creatures is to love and be loved."

In addition to his responses to the "sensible text" of Kempe's narrative, the sixteenth-century reader demonstrates his engagement with the "experience" of the text. Kempe's pilgrimage to the Holy Land, her various consultations with clerics and Julian of Norwich about her revelations, her interrogations by the Church, and her criticism at the hands of her fellow townspeople are all subjects of interest to the reader. He expresses admiration for her "meek answer" (*meke hanswer*) to the priest who accuses her of being deceived by the devil. He regards her interrogation on the Articles of Faith by a Leicester abbot as a "difficult examination" (*examinatio dura*, 115). He notes another interrogation at York in which Kempe is asked to explain the biblical command to "increase and multiply." He also makes note of the "good clerks" who defend her against the Grey Friar who banishes her from his church, the "good priest" who reads to Kempe, and the "devout doctor" who tolerates her weeping (167, 143, and 166).

Of Kempe herself, the reader singles out three times her "discrecion," that is, her verification of her revelations by telling them to priests and holy men. He notes her doubt about God's grace when she refuses to believe that a vision of the damned comes from Him (144). He also pays attention to her early trials, such as her temptation to sleep with the man who propositioned her in St. Margaret's and her attempt to persuade her husband to release her from her marriage obligations to him (14 and 23–24). He comments approvingly on her "charity" (*nota charitatem eius*) when she prays to God to have mercy on other sinners (141). Perhaps the most revealing comment about Kempe's meditational practices appears next to a passage in which Kempe claims that God was continually in her thoughts, and that she beheld Him in all creatures: "nota bene eius perfeccionem" (note well her perfection) writes the reader. Together, these comments reflect a reading of the subject of Kempe's narrative which would be considered naive today because they fail to see beyond her sincerity and piety to the limitations of her mysticism.

The sixteenth-century reader's comments provide more than a gloss to *The Book of Margery Kempe* and an index to themes of interest to the monastic order responsible for the preservation and transmission of spiritual texts in late medieval England. I am more interested in these annotations for what they can reveal about the textual community in which it was read in the sixteenth century.[58] In other words, I would like to consider what this reader's annotations reveal about the community in which Kempe's book was read, that is, the Carthusian monastery at Mount Grace. This will allow us to examine how that community (and Kempe's book) changes in the succeeding centuries in its printed incarnations.

Reading Margery Kempe in terms of Richard Methley, as the sixteenth-century reader has done, suggests that he (like Methley) sees little contradiction between the life devoted to strict seclusion and contemplation and the life engaged in the kind of "excessive sensory devotion" we have observed in both Kempe and Methley. Neither does he seem to be troubled by the daring literalness or sensuality of her visions. In addition, he reads her visions and meditations, in conjunction with her experience, as tokens of her perfection. The numerous repetitions of the text, along with pious exclamations in response to it, indicate that the reader takes seriously Christ's designation of Kempe as a mirror, or example, for others, even monks.[59] He is interested both in her trials and struggles with her contemporaries as well as in her visions. In a sense, he reads the experience and truth together, as Kempe wanted her readers to do, even if his reading redefines her truth at the same time. His sympathy with Kempe's narrative does not necessarily mean that he reads her as she wished to be read or that he understands her: it merely means that he had a context for understanding her, a community of spiritual texts in which Kempe's book was understood, including works by Methley, Rolle, the *Cloud* author, Hilton, and Nicholas Love that were housed in his own library at Mount Grace.[60] In spite of his very different vocation, the reader is able to participate in the visionary and experiential realms of Kempe's text.

Such a reading would be rendered impossible by the two printed editions of extracts from Kempe's book in the early sixteenth century.

The Disembodied Text

"Here begynneth a shorte treatyse of contemplacyon taught by our lorde Ihesu cryste, or taken out of the boke of Margerie kempe of lynn." So begins the first printed edition (1501) of *The Book of Margery Kempe* by the printer Wynkyn de Worde, successor to William Caxton. Representing one of only four mystical texts in the vernacular which were published by an early English printer, Kempe's book achieved a certain distinction after her death.[61] The incipit reveals the changes which Kempe's text underwent in de Worde's printing. From a self-styled "schort tretys" about the experience and "felyngys" of Margery Kempe, *The Book of Margery Kempe* became a short treatise of contemplation taught by "our Lord Jesus Christ." No longer a narrative exploring the intersections of truth and experience, Kempe's book was transformed into an instructional handbook for devotion. In the process of this transformation, her voice was almost entirely expunged from the text.

Wynkyn de Worde's edition is largely a compilation of extracts—twenty-eight, to be exact—from the Salthouse manuscript edited by Meech and Allen. These extracts are quite short (ranging from two to seventeen lines long). They are also rearranged from the sequence found in the complete manuscript, jumping back and forth in places and skipping many chapters at a time. The short passages are presented as a series of discreet units without any indication that they are drawn from different contexts in her book. Thus, Christ's speech to Kempe in one vision is elided with a completely different speech in another, and the narrative voice shifts throughout the excerpts. The result is that the narrative of Kempe's text is lost in favor of a series of short sayings, mostly of Christ to Kempe.

In fact, Kempe's own voice is heard in only four of the twenty-eight extracts. While the narration indirectly refers to her, direct utterance is reserved for Christ.[62] Where Kempe does speak, she prays for mourning and weeping for her love; she desires to be publicly scorned for her love; she begs for mercy; and finally, she protests that Christ should show his grace to priests instead of to her. Nothing of her weeping and roaring, her stories, her early ordeals of conversion and chastity, or her encounters with hostile pilgrims or religious men survives in de Worde's edition. Her visions of the

Passion are reduced to one brief account which is devoid of her usual detail. Where her voice does appear, it is humble, muted, effectively erased, except as it seems to express her meek compliance with Christ's instructions.

Holbrook charts the repression of Kempe's text at the hands of the excerptor and the creation of a new devotional text for women. This new text consists of a series of Christ's instructions to Kempe, beginning with his steering her away from wrong modes of devotion, such as public penance and martyrdom, to his counselling her to endure weeping, suffering, and rebuke with patience, to his promise of her reward in heaven.[63] In order to create this text, the excerptor has omitted all that was controversial in Kempe's life and text:

> In sum, the extractor has searched for passages that commend the patient, invisible toleration of scorn and the private, inaudible, mental practice of good will in meditation rather than public or physical acts or sensory signs of communion with God and has left behind all that is radical, enthusiastic, feminist, particular, potentially heretical and historical.[64]

Voice and body, which are so intrusive in Kempe's narrative, are noticeably absent from Wynkyn de Worde's text. The very publicity of Kempe's speech and her visions is converted into private acts of prayer. De Worde's text bears none of the traces of the boisterous body or speech of Kempe's narrative.

One feature of de Worde's text, however, is striking. He concludes it with an exchange between Kempe and Christ in which she says that Christ should "show these graces" to religious men and priests instead of to her. He responds,

> . . . nay nay doughter, for þat I loue best þat they loue not, & þat is shames, repreues, scornes, & despytes of þe people, & therfore they shall not haue this grace, for doughter he that dredeth þe shames of this worlde may not parfyghtly loue god." (357)

> (. . . no, daughter, for that which I love best they love not at all—that is, shame, reproofs, scorn, and spite from the people—and therefore they shall not have this grace, for daughter, he that dreads the shame of this world cannot love God perfectly.)

This anti-clerical statement achieves a powerful emphasis by its position at the end of the quarto volume of selections. While this serves to reinforce the direction of the volume toward private devotion, it also exposes the implicit critique in all mystical texts of the ministers and institution of the Church.

Norman Blake has argued that Wynkyn de Worde's printing of this and other devotional works was due to his lack of skill as a translator (unlike Caxton) and to his "strong religious convictions."[65] More recently, however, George Keiser has challenged this analysis with the view that de Worde "was determinedly catering to an audience whose interests he understood very well."[66] This audience included noblewomen, such as Lady Margaret Beaufort, mother of King Henry VII, the merchant class, and clerics from Syon, Sheen, and London monasteries in particular.[67] De Worde depended not only on an audience for his devotional works but on the patronage of the nobility and the availability of manuscripts from Syon monastery and the assistance of Syon monks as translators.[68]

This audience may have been responsible for establishing a taste for "exemplary narrative," which guided the publishing decisions of Caxton as well as de Worde. The author of one of de Worde's devotional works, *Contemplacion of synners* (1499), sums up this taste: "now a dayes it lyketh best a man to here or rede compylacyons whiche ben compendyous, pleasaunt & prouffytable/short in sayenge & large in sentence."[69] This desire for concentrated, concise, and pithy sayings can be seen in such works as *The fruytfull sayings of Dauyd*, published by de Worde in 1508, or two compilations made at Syon monastery, *The Directory of conscience* (1527) and *A deuout epystle. . . for them that be timorous. . . in conscience* (1535?).

Such a taste in publishing, reflecting the piety and patronage of a large readership, may be responsible for the transformation of Kempe's book into a series of extracts which are "short in saying and large in sentence." Wynkyn de Worde himself is probably not responsible for the abridgement of the manuscript version of *The Book of Margery Kempe*; it is more likely that the excerpts were already compiled before de Worde decided to publish them.[70] In the context of other works, such as the *Contemplacion of synners* published by de Worde, the excerpts of Kempe's book seem tailored to the demand for compendious, pleasant, and profitable compilations which offered devotional guidance to religious and laypersons. It is possible to speculate that Syon monastery might have played a role in the printing of this edition, given its practice of funding de Worde's press with manuscript editions of devotional texts. Kempe herself visited Syon monastery in 1434 to receive a pardon, and there inspired a young man to become a monk. It is conceivable that this monastery, which was familiar with her book, might have encouraged de Worde to print the extracts for the education of laypeople.

Whatever the genealogy of de Worde's printed edition, it was produced in the company of other devotional works, including saint's lives, service books, and especially, practical guides for contemplation. In addition to Hilton's *Scale of Perfection*, de Worde published the *Lyf of Saint Katherin of senis* (1493), *Lyf of saynt Ursula* (n.d.), and *the reuelacions of Saynt Elysabeth the kynges doughter of hungarye*. His books of devotional guidance include a compilation of "dyvers wrytyngs of holy men" for religious men (1500; *STC* 1978), and a book dedicated "to all maner of people necessary and comfortable" for the edification of soul and body, called *The myrrour of the chyrche* (1521; *STC* 965). Among mystical and devotional texts, he published *The Chastising of God's Children* (1494), *The meditations of saint Bernard* (1499; *STC* 1917), *Speculum vitae Christi* (1486; *STC* 3277), *The Pylgrimage of perfection* (1526; *STC* 3325), and *The passyon of our lorde Jesu cryst* (1521; *STC* 14558). In 1519 de Worde published the Middle English work of Catherine of Siena, the *Orchard of Syon* (*STC* 4815), from a manuscript found in Syon monastery. Richard Sutton, a steward of Syon, had de Worde publish the work "that many relygyous and devoute soules myght be releved and have conforte therby . . ."[71] Kempe would, no doubt, have approved of this visionary and devotional company even if she would not have approved of the drastically reduced form her treatise had taken.

De Worde's "edition" of *The Book of Margery Kempe* was anthologized by Henry Pepwell in 1521. This anthology of mystical writings includes portions of six works, including Richard of St. Victor's *Benjamin Minor*, *The Divers Doctrines of Saint Katherin of Seenes*, Hilton's *Song of Angels*, and three works associated with *The Cloud of Unknowing*, namely, the *Epistle of Prayer*, *Epistle of Discretion in Stirrings of the Soul*, and the *Treatise of Discerning of Spirits*.[72] As I have shown in chapter 2, the last two works are devoted to cautionary measures against false visions and thoughts. Hilton's work, too, is thought to be a treatise against the "excessive use of imagery."[73] Richard of St. Victor's work is devoted to the description of ravishment, ending in Pepwell's selection with an account of that *mentis excessus* I have alluded to in chapter 4. The excerpts from Catherine of Siena's *Orchard of Syon* consist, like those from *The Book of Margery Kempe*, of "divers doctrines" taught by Christ and Catherine.

It is ironic that the "compendious" Kempe inhabits such illustrious company, half of which is critical of the kind of mysticism she describes in her book. A further irony is the often cited reference to her as "a deuoute ancres" in the explicit of the selection. This designation in Pepwell's edition seems to complete the process of revision which began in de Worde's edition. With the experience and voice of Margery Kempe expunged from the 1501 edition, all that remains in Pepwell's edition is for the woman herself to be revised. It is, nevertheless, an appropriate emendation of the "egregious" Kempe into the "deuoute ancres," since it signals the suppression of the very condition of Kempe's voice and experience: her publicity. The cost of her inclusion in Pepwell's anthology is not only the internment of her public voice and bodily movings into a text which she occasions by her very silence, but the erasure of her experience which is so critical to the "trewth" of her book.

It is important to remember that, while the patronage and readership of sixteenth-century England enjoyed the type of piety rendered in the editions of de Worde and Pepwell, the monks of Mount Grace were reading and commenting on the more ecstatic and boisterous text of Margery Kempe. Perhaps the greatest irony is that Kempe, who was designated to be a mirror among sinners, should find her readership not among the lay population to whom she appealed but within an order of monks dedicated to strict seclusion and austerity.

Because modern scholarship had no access to the Carthusian manuscript of Kempe's book until 1934, it was dependent on the heavily edited excerpts of the de Worde and Pepwell editions. That dependence has shaped the subsequent readings of Kempe's book more than most scholars acknowledge. The discovery of her book aroused excitement based initially on the expectations produced by the excerpted editions of her book. In his introduction to the modern edition of Pepwell's anthology, Edmund Gardner, writing before 1925, speculates about Kempe and her book:

> The revelations show that she was (or had been) a woman of some wealth and social position, who had abandoned the world to become an ancress, following the life prescribed in that gem of early English devotional literature, the *Ancren Riwle*. It is clearly only a fragment of her complete book (whatever that may have been); but it is enough to show that she was a worthy precursor of that other great woman mystic of East Anglia: Juliana of Norwich.[74]

Gardner's comparison of Kempe and Julian is based on the fact that both were thought to be anchoresses living in East Anglia. Pepwell's edition inspires this comparison with Julian even before it was known that Kempe visited the anchoress during her lifetime. In addition, Kempe was often compared to Catherine of Siena, a comparison which Pepwell's edition sets up.

The surprise and subsequent disappointment with which the Salthouse manuscript was greeted arose, in part, from these expectations.

Kempe was not Julian of Norwich or Catherine of Siena, a point which has been made more than once.[75] It was Pepwell's edition which anticipated a comparison between Catherine and Kempe. The availability of Julian's *Showings* in modern English editions and the fact that she was a woman set her up as an arbitrary standard of comparison for Kempe. The disappointment of scholars in *The Book of Margery Kempe* is derived from editions of her work based on sixteenth-century piety and patronage and on the circumstantial availability of other mystical texts. The "trewth" and the "experiens" Kempe sought to authorize in her text were subjected to the criteria of Pepwell's text. She became discredited by the editions of de Worde and Pepwell and their readership's taste for "compendious" devotional works, short in saying and large in sentence. Had she really been an anchoress, she might have been excused for what we have trouble accepting. As Herbert Thurston wrote in an early review of the Butler-Bowdon modern English translation,

> If she had really been an ancress, living secluded in her cell, these peculiarities would not have mattered. But she insisted on going everywhere, following, as she believed, the special call of God.[76]

As Clarissa Atkinson comments, this reaction differs little from that of the Canterbury monk who wished Kempe were "enclosed in a house of stone" so that no one could speak with her.[77]

We can observe from the reactions in Kempe's own lifetime to the efforts of modern scholarship to come to terms with her book the persistent effects of a cultural desire exhibited in its efforts to suppress the female body and voice by privileging the so-called spiritual and aescetic realms of experience. Yet, as we have also observed, Carthusian monks such as Methley and the readers who left their comments in the margins of Kempe's book read her book in a way that we cannot. The excesses which we would like to attribute to hysteria and repressed sexuality found acceptance under the rubric of *amor sensibilis* in the fifteenth and sixteenth centuries.

In spite of the evidence of this readership, all that can be said about *The Book of Margery Kempe* is that it enjoyed a fairly wide circulation among diverse populations. Wynkyn de Worde is largely responsible for this wide circulation even if he had the book drastically reduced to ensure its marketability. Although this circulation may not satisfy our own desires for clearly delineated lines of influence, it is nevertheless significant. Scholars cannot assume that because Kempe did not establish a cult of followers or an influence on later mystics, she "simply ceased to speak" with the completion of her book.[78] Our own assumption of Kempe's isolation from her culture except where she was influenced by other mystics is partly the result of our experience of her book. The loss of her book, until recently, from circulation meant that scholars constructed the story of medieval mysticism and culture without her. With her book's recovery, we are now faced with fitting her in or isolating her out. Kempe might have been amused by the fact that it is the experience of modern scholars, not her own, which ultimately has determined the fate of her book.

There is, I think, another observable factor in the isolation of Kempe's book by modern scholars, and that is its autobiographical aspect. Kempe's explicit detail about her life and experiences, her travels, and her contemporaries is used to limit the vision of her book. Its merit lies mainly in its reflection of her times and its insights into her own character, but not much more. Where this autobiographical element is seen as excessive, Kempe's book becomes merely a testimony to her self-preoccupation. Where it is not, it tends to absorb the focus of scholarly attention. She may be credited with an eye for detail and some interesting experiences, but this contributes nothing to her credit as a mystic or author. As Barry Windeatt, the translator of the modern edition of Kempe's book, makes explicit, "By comparison with the recollected revelations of the great mystics, Margery's *Book* is almost too autobiographical, too concerned with the mundane difficulties and obstacles that confronted Margery in life."[79] This type of prejudice underlies much of Kempe criticism, and I suggest that it derives from an issue of gender. In its simplest formulation, this issue returns to the old Aristotelian distinction between masculine and feminine realms of experience as corresponding to the spiritual and the physical. The spiritual and mundane, and by analogy, the mystical treatise and autobiography, are viewed as incompatibile. The basis for both distinctions, I suggest, is a gendered one which associates masculinity with the spirit and authority, and femininity with experience. Scholars are more likely to focus on the autobiographical (and hence mundane) when the subject is a woman. It is as though the Wife of Bath had set women's agenda for times to come by asserting her experience (and autobiography) over authority. The narrow interpretation of autobiography and experience as mundane and untranscendent permits scholars to isolate Kempe and other women writers, praising them only for their ability to write about that which they know best.

I am not suggesting, as an alternative, that we adopt the views of a sixteenth-century Carthusian reader, nor that his reading is necessarily better than that of the excerptor for de Worde's edition or than our own reading. What I do suggest is that we begin to become aware of the reception of books like Kempe's in order to observe how our own readings are constructed by the circumstances of publication and transmission of texts and by our own cultural investment in issues embracing the body, gender, theology, and reading. Any analysis of *The Book of Margery Kempe*, or any other medieval text, needs to take stock of its own cultural positioning.[80]

I have been arguing for the interrelationship of bodies, speech, discourse, and books in mystical texts, particularly *The Book of Margery Kempe*. Their interrelationship depends upon the ideological framework of medieval culture, from its theory of the complicity of the feminine and the flesh, to its prescriptions for the female religious, to its modes of literary and theological discourse. Mystical texts are usually read apart from this ideological framework, because their subject is assumed to be, in the words of the famous scholar of mysticism, Evelyn Underhill, "the deepest mysteries of the transcendental life."[81] Yet even these texts inhabit the societies, ideologies, and politics of their cultures. Indeed, Stephen Ozment has already argued that mystical theology is a dissent ideology, and one feminist scholar has asserted the connections between mystical theology and power.[82] *The Book of Margery Kempe* insists upon this connection between mystical texts and the ideologies of medieval culture as well as its social and institutional structures. While other mystical texts might not inhabit the material world so fundamentally or explicitly, they nevertheless engage the world they inhabit by their very position outside the institution of the Church. As long as the discourse of mysticism is dependent on divine revelation in the world and in the human heart, the realm of experience authorizes it. We cannot ignore the fundamental importance of that experience in all its institutional, ideological, and material complexity when we read mystical texts unless we wish to adopt Wynkyn de Worde's vision of mystical texts as "short in saying and large in sentence."[83]

Taking this ideology into account, we have to be more careful when we collapse the practices of male and female mystics into one and the same phenomenon. We cannot simply point to the fact that male mystics used female imagery, imitated a feminized body of Christ, or adopted a sensual mystical language as evidence that men and women were doing the same things in the late Middle Ages. My own comparison of Richard Methley and Margery Kempe is not meant to suggest that men practiced the same spirituality that women did. There are similarities, and these similarities help us to understand a context for reading Kempe's book, but they do not suggest that the experiences and writings of these two people amounted to the same thing. The ideology of the flesh and the text prohibits our seeing the two as practicing essentially the same thing. Gender intervenes. In a culture which defines and makes taboo women and the flesh, the excesses of men and women in their spiritual practices are simply not equivalent. It means something quite different for Methley to fall to the ground, scream out, and weep during Mass or in private prayer than it does for Kempe to do the same in church or on Mount Calvary. Likewise, Kempe's use of material language and emotional attachment to Christ cannot be explained simply by reference to the practices of Cistercians and Franciscans before her nor to Methley after her. While these practices reveal general historical contexts for Kempe's life and book, they cannot tell us what they *meant* for their own culture, nor what Kempe's life meant for her own. Neither can we say what these same practices mean without investigating the complicity of scholarship in its own ideologies, as well.

Jean Gerson tried to articulate that ideology when he remarked that there was "something else" to women's spirituality which made it different. I have tried to pursue that "something else" in the medieval body, mystical discourse, and *The Book of Margery Kempe* in all its complexity and calamity. Kempe's book challenges teachers and readers by always pointing us to this something else of medieval culture which Gerson sought to define and control, and which we must continue to explore.

Notes

1. "The Mystics and the Early English Printers; The Economics of Devotionalism," in *The Medieval Mystical Tradition in England: Papers Read at Dartington Hall, July 1987,*Exeter Symposium IV, ed. Marion Glasscoe (London: D. S. Brewer, 1987), 17. I am indebted to Keiser's analysis of fifteenth-century readership in this chapter.

2. It is probably the case that the manuscript, which was housed at the Carthusian monastery of Mount Grace, came into the the possession of the Butler-Bowdon family at the time of the dissolution of the monasteries. However, we have no direct evidence of this, only two bookplates of Henry Bowdon (b. 1754). See Meech and Allen, xxxii; Butler-Bowdon speculated soon after the manuscript's discovery that it came into his family at some time during the dissolution of the monasteries, *The Times* (London), September 30, 1936, 13.

3. In particular, Richard Kieckhefer ends his study of fourteenth-century saints and definitions of sanctity with Margery Kempe, who "sums up conveniently the spirituality of the era," *Unquiet Souls: Fourteenth-Century Saints and Their Religious*

Milieu (Chicago: University of Chicago Press, 1984), 183. As I have noted elsewhere, Wolfgang Riehle views Kempe as a distortion of late medieval trends, although she and Julian of Norwich together "[fit] the pattern of the late medieval female mystic as this pattern developed on the continent," *The Middle English Mystics*, trans. Bernard Standring (London: Routledge and Kegan Paul, 1981), 11 and 27. Clarissa W. Atkinson is primarily interested in Kempe as a mirror of her times in her book-length study, *Mystic and Pilgrim: The Book and the World of Margery Kempe* (Ithaca, NY: Cornell University Press, 1983). I do not wish to fault any of these studies for what they do not do, but merely to point out how such studies have shaped our readings of Kempe and considerations of her "place" in late medieval culture.

4. An interesting variation on this paradigm is the paradigm of sainthood, which requires veneration of both the saint and her *vita*. Dorothy of Montau and Catherine of Siena were promoted posthumously by their scribes, John Marienwerder and Raymond of Capua. Because Kempe's scribe did not do this, she is sometimes seen as a failed saint; see Kieckhefer, *Unquiet Souls*, 188–89.

5. Nevertheless, some of the more sympathetic and illuminating studies of Kempe have taken just this view, including Atkinson's and Kieckhefer's, as well as that of Maureen Fries, "Margery Kempe," in *An Introduction to the Medieval Mystics of Europe*, ed. Paul E. Szarmach (Albany: State University of New York Press, 1988), 217–35.

6. I am drawing upon his analysis in *The Archaeology of Knowledge and the Discourse on Language*, trans. A. M. Sheridan Smith (New York: Pantheon Books, 1972), 21–22.

7. Foucault, *Archaeology of Knowledge*, 21.

8. The evidence for this early dating is that the hand has been attributed to the mid-fifteenth century and that the watermarks suggest that the paper was probably from Holland around 1440–50, see Meech and Allen, xxxiii–iv.

9. The notation of at least four readers is given in the Meech and Allen edition where it occurs, and it is discussed in Meech's introduction, xxxiii–xliv.

10. *English Books and Readers 1475 to 1557* (Cambridge: Cambridge University Press, 1952), 8–9.

11. Meech identifies this set by the black ink used in all the annotations, xliii.

12. Reader 1 corresponds to the notes in large letters, Reader 2, to the writer of small brown letters, according to Meech's description, xliii.

13. The marginalia appear on pp. 39, 46, and 49. In the first case, Kempe is informed in her soul of God's love for her; in the second, she is assured by an anchorite that her tears signify that love; and in the third, Christ himself assures her that he loves her as well as any virgin.

14. For example, see Riehle's analysis, *Middle English Mystics*, 37. Carolyn Walker Bynum attributes such literal renderings of mystical concepts to the medieval woman mystic's insistence on the physical, *Holy Feast and Holy Fast: The Religious Significance of Food to Medieval Women* (Berkeley: University of California Press, 1987), 246 and 248.

15. This marginal association of Kempe's cries with *clamore* suggests that the reader also reads Kempe's activity in terms of Marie d'Oignies's "loud cries," which

are reported by Kempe's scribe (153). Meech and Allen think the scribe has mistranslated the Latin account of Marie's behavior, taking "clam" (secretly) for "clamore," 322–23n. Even if this is true, the second reader clearly reinforces this mistake.

16. David Knowles gives Kempe credit for being a better wife than the Wife of Bath, but concedes that neither "in depth of perception or wisdom of spiritual doctrine, nor as a personality can she challenge comparison with Julian of Norwich," in *The English Mystical Tradition* (London: Burns and Oates, 1961), 139. Even though this was the general assessment, Kempe continued to be compared with Julian. See also Robert K. Stone, *Middle English Prose Style* (The Hague and Paris: Mouton, 1970), 155–56; T. W. Coleman, *English Mystics of the Fourteenth Century* (Westport,CT: Greenwood Press, 1971), 175; and Riehle, *Middle English Mystics*, 27–31, 96, 102–3, 112, and 116.

17. See Colledge and Walsh's introduction to their modern English edition of *Showings* (New York: Paulist Press, 1978), 21. The manuscript bears a signature of James Grenehalgh of Sheen Charterhouse around 1500, a place Kempe visited in 1434.

18. The handwriting is that of the late fifteenth or early sixteenth century and reveals dialectal features of Northern Middle English, according to Meech, xxxvi. This makes it possible that the reader was also a monk at the Carthusian priory of Mount Grace.

19. Meech only guesses that these drawings, also in red ink, were made by the red annotator, xxxviii.

20. "Margery Kempe and Wynkyn de Worde," in *The Medieval Mystical Tradition in England: Papers Read at Dartington Hall, July 1987,* ed. Marion Glasscoe, Exeter Symposium IV (Cambridge: D. S. Brewer, 1987), 37. I will be drawing upon Holbrook's very insightful analysis of de Worde's extractions of the book, but my own interests lie in the feminist implications of these different "readings" of Kempe's book for medieval culture.

21. I am not including textual emendations or illustrations in this count, only those comments which summarize, respond to, clarify, or contextualize Kempe's text. I have used Meech's summary of these comments for my count, xli–xlii.

22. James Hogg provides a biography of Methley in his edition of Methley's letter to Hugh the Hermit, "Richard Methley: To Hew Heremyte, A Pystyl of Solytary Lyfe Nowadayes," *Analecta Carthusiana* 31 (1977): 95–99. Information about John Norton may be found in Hogg, 'Mount Grace Charterhouse and Late Medieval English Spirituality,' *Analecta Carthusiana* 82, pt. 3 (1980): 40–43. David Knowles gives a brief introduction to each writer in *The Religious Orders in England,* vol. 2 (Cambridge: Cambridge University Press, 1957–62), 224–26 and 239.

23. Meech and Allen, 330n. Allen attributes the association of Norton and Methley with Kempe's cries to the doctrine of *languor,* as Methley describes it in one of his works, Meech and Allen, 291n. I shall return to this idea in Methley later.

24. *The Religious Orders in England,* 2, 130. I am not denying that such a tradition of piety existed in the Carthusian Charterhouses, for it has been amply described and documented by E. Margaret Thompson, *The Carthusian Order in England* (London, 1930). My point here is that scholars seem intent on seeing the

examples of a different kind of piety as "aberrant," and so, perpetuating a mono-lithic idea about Carthusian spirituality.

25. *The English Mystical Tradition*, 151. This new piety is called *devotio moderna*, and it is characterized by its "direct, loving, almost pietistic approach to Jesus, the crucified lover of the soul," see Knowles, *The Religious Orders in England*, vol. 2, 223.

26. This treatise is based on Ruysbroek's work, *The Spiritual Espousals*, and it is thought that the Carthusians were responsible for bringing it to England, Joyce Bazire and Eric Colledge, eds., *The Chastising of God's Children and the Treatise of Perfection of the Sons of God* (Oxford: Basil Blackwell, 1957), 58. The criticism of Rolle is that his mysticism had misguided the unlearned into a facile belief in sensory experiences, see H. E. Allen, *Writings Ascribed to Richard Rolle, Hermit of Hampole, and Materials for His Biography* (New York: D. C. Heath, 1927), 335 and 529–37.

27. Quoted in Michael G. Sargent, "The Transmission by the English Carthu-sians of Some Late Medieval Spiritual Writings," *Journal of Ecclesiastical History* 27 (1976): 226. The role of the Carthusians in the production and circulation of late medieval spiritual texts is amply documented by Sargent, 225–40; by Thompson, *The Carthusian Order in England*, 313–53; and by Roger Lovatt, "The *Imitation of Christ* in Late Medieval England," *Transactions of the Royal Historical Society*, Fifth Series 18 (1968), 97–121.

28. Hogg notes that writers were "few in number" among the English Carthu-sians, thereby giving prominence to Methley, "Richard Methley: To Hew Here-myte," 95. Hogg acknowledges his own disappointment in the "exaggerated emo-tionalism and a tendency to 'excesses'" suggested by the marginal references to him in Kempe's book, 91–92.

29. Quotations are from Eric Colledge's comments in his introduction to the fifteenth-century English spiritual treatise, *The Chastising of God's Children*, 52. It is only fair to point that Colledge's remarks are made in the context of asserting that Methley proves himself more cautious in his comments on his Latin translation of *The Cloud of Unknowing* and *The Mirror of Simple Souls*.

30. Bazire and Colledge, *The Chastising of God's Children*, 103. The writer goes on to say that this joy draws those who experience it to "goostli lyuenge," so he does not advocate it as an end in itself.

31. Norton also wrote three treatises, *Musica Monachorum*, the *Thesaurus Cordium vere Amacium*, and *Deuota lamentacio deuoti Iohannis Norton prioris*. These have not been edited, but are available in Lincoln Cathedral Library MS. 57 (A.6.8). Hogg has looked at these works, which, he says, are "very untidily written in a sixteenth-century hand after the author's death," "Mount Grace Charterhouse," 40. I have not been able to examine these manuscripts.

32. The partial treatise on the discernment of spirits, *Experimentum Veritatis*, survives in the London Public Record Office Collection SP I/239, including a Middle English letter by Methley to Hugh the Hermit. The two works translated into Latin and glossed by Methley are *The Cloud of Unknowing* and the heretical work by Margaret Porete, *Mirror of Simple Souls*. In addition, Methley refers to other works of his which have not survived. For these, see Hogg, "Mount Grace Charter-house," 30.

33. The manuscript containing the three treatises is Trinity College Cambridge MS. 0.2.56 (1160). *Scola amoris languidi* appears on ff. 1r–24v; *Dormitorium dilecti dilecti* on ff. 25r–48r; and *Refectorium salutis* on ff. 49r–70v. Hogg has edited the *Refectorium salutis*, but it is not generally available, see "A Mystical Diary: The *Refectorium Salutis* of Richard Methley of Mount Grace Charterhouse," *Kartausermystik und -mystiker*, Bd. 2," *Analecta Carthusiana* 55 (1981): 208–88. Glosses and marginal notes attest to the careful attention given the manuscript by the other Carthusians.

34. F. 13v. All abbreviations in the manuscript have been expanded. The translations are my own. For convenience, hereafter the titles of Methley's works will be abbreviated in the notes as follows: *SAL* for *Scola amoris languidi*, *DDD* for *Dormitorium dilecti dilecti*, and *RS* for *Refectorium salutis*.

35. Methley makes a similar statement of his "new mode of speaking" for instruction in the beginning of *DDD*, f. 25v.

36. So says Knowles, *Religious Orders*, 2, 224. Knowles goes on to say that, nevertheless, "it would be wholly unjust to dismiss him as merely an emotional and excitable dreamer." Still others, however, are not so sure. Even James Hogg, who has studied Methley extensively, extends the hope that, in Methley's later life, during which time he was relatively silent, perhaps he "outgrew his early naiveté," "Mount Grace Charterhouse," 31.

37. Ff. 1r–v, and transcribed in Hogg, "Mount Grace Charterhouse," 35. Hogg notes that Augustine's *Confessiones* raises a similar point in the form of a question, "Et quid erat, quod me delectabat, nisi amare et amari?" Bk. 2, ch. 2, quoted in Hogg "Richard Methley," 102n.

38. Methley uses the word *odiosissima* to describe mystical languor. He adds that languor and love are "inseparable companions": "amor et languor inseparabiles comites sunt, quia amor est causa languoris et languor causa amoris" (f. 2r).

39. "Languor enim amoris non sivit languentem lugere, sed cogit amantem canere; languor amoris fletum facit feruescere, et ubi est feruor factoris, ibi interdum est sensibilis ignis amoris" (f. 2v).

40. F. 7r–v.

41. There are many examples of this invocation of Christ's name, including *DDD*, f. 34v–35r, 36r–38r, and *RS*, f. 61v–62v; on the name of Christ as a remedy against temptation, *SAL*, f. 13r–13v and *RS*, 54v–55v; on a numerological interpretation of the letters in Jesus's name, *RS*, f. 62v–63r.

42. See *RS*, f. 59r–v and 63v–64r.

43. *RS*, f. 59r. For examples of the other types of physical experiences mentioned above, see his vision of the crucified Christ in *DD*, f. 45r–v, his experience of the heavenly melody in contrast to earthly melodies, f. 33v, and sensory love, f. 33r–v, 38v, etc.; in *SAL*, see f. 14r–v; on the intoxication of love, see *RS*, f. 49v and 64r–v, on the liquefaction of the heart, f. 54r–v, on the excess of mind, f. 54v–55r, and on spiritual song, f. 60r–v.

44. *RS*, f. 67v.

45. *RS*, f. 56r.

46. *RS* f. 58r: "Cogitarem iterum venit in me sensibilis ille amor et languor qui

exsuperant omnes sensus. Et hoc hic omnibus christianis dico quod quociens cum
vehemencia venit mentem supra sensus corporeos rapit."

47. *RS*, f. 63r.

48. *DDD*, f. 27v–28r.

49. *RS*, f. 66r: "Et opto vt fiat speciali miraculoso modo propter exemplarem
sanctitatem tocius mundi." Knowles and Hogg have singled out this desire for
spectacular death as an example of Methley's "less pleasing" aspects, see *Religious
Orders*, 2, 224, and "Mount Grace Charterhouse," 37. It is important to note that
Kempe, too, desired this kind of extravagant spectacle, although she confessed that
the only kind of death she could imagine without being overcome by fear was to
have herself bound to a pillar and beheaded with an ax (30).

50. For example, see *SAL*, f. 15r–17v. Knowles attempts to resolve the inconsist-
ency by holding out hope that Methley's experiences evolved into "a deeper and
more truly mystical contemplation" in his later life, while the most he can say of his
earlier visions is that they "are at least on the fringe and threshold of the contemplative life," *Religious Orders*, 2, 225. "Without wishing to interpret the enigmatic
evidence of the comparative silence of his later years as a sign of greater spiritual
calm and increasing maturity," Hogg nevertheless points to Methley's later work to
speculate that he "outgrew his early naiveté," "Mount Grace Charterhouse," 31.

51. Since I have not been able to consult his later work, the *Experimentum
Veritatis*, I am relying on Hogg's summary of this text in "Mount Grace Charterhouse," 31.

52. "Richard Methley," 118.

53. Indeed, Methley's "standard of Latinity and his theological competence
might lead one to postulate study at a continental university, if he had not attended
Oxford or Cambridge," Hogg notes, "Richard Methley," 98, although Methley's
silence on this subject suggests that he probably was not educated at a university.

54. *Cloud of Unknowing*, ch. 45. The *Cloud* author argues that mystical language
is always inadequate for expressing spiritual experiences, since it is produced by the
tongue, which is a physical organ, making it, too, physical, ch. 61. Hilton also
warned against the literal understanding of metaphorical language in *Scale of Perfection*, Bk. 1, chs. 7 and 26.

55. For example, *RS*, f. 59r–v.

56. His note appears next to Kempe's "boystows sobbyngys & gret plente of
terys" and exclamations, "I dey" (40). The reader also notes her "feruour of loue" in
conjunction with Kempe's own use of the phrase to describe her behavior as "a dron-
kyn woman" during a vision of Simeon's presentation of Christ at the Temple (198).

57. F. 21r: "Quia amor impaciens, cuncta sibi cedere redit."

58. Brian Stock defines textual communities as "microsocieties organized
around the common understanding of a script" in *Listening for the Text: On the Uses
of the Past* (Baltimore and London: Johns Hopkins University Press, 1990), 23. I am
broadening Stock's definition to include communities of readers, not just religious
communities configured by texts and their interpreters. See also Stock, *The Implications of Literacy: Written Language and Models of Interpretation in the Eleventh and
Twelfth Centuries* (Princeton, NJ: Princeton University Press, 1983), 88–240.

59. Meech classifies one set of his annotations as his "pious ejaculations," and he includes such exclamations as "Amen," and "Iesu helpe me," among others, xlii.

60. Of course, he might also have read some of the more than 150 books and manuscripts housed in other Carthusian libraries in England. For some of these, see Sargent, "The Transmission by the English Carthusians of Some Late Medieval Spiritual Writings," 225–40; Lovatt, "The *Imitation of Christ* in Late Medieval England," 97–121; and Thompson, *The Carthusian Order in England*, 313–34.

61. George Keiser lists the other three works printed, including Walter Hilton's *Scala perfectionis* and *Mixed Life* and Rolle's *Form of Living*, "The Mystics and the Early English Printers: The Economics of Devotionalism" in *The Medieval Mystical Tradition in England: Papers Read at Dartington Hall, July 1987*, ed. Marion Glasscoe, Exeter Symposium IV (London: D. S. Brewer, 1988), 9.

62. I am indebted to Holbrook's study of the excerpts in my analysis of them, "Margery Kempe and Wynkyn de Worde," in *The Medieval Mystical Tradition in England*, 27–46. She finds that Kempe speaks in only 18 percent of the text, while Christ's speech makes up 60. The narration occupies about 22 percent (29).

63. "Margery Kempe and Wynkyn de Worde," 30–33.

64. "Margery Kempe and Wynkyn de Worde," 35.

65. N. F. Blake, *Caxton: England's First Publisher* (New York: Harper and Row, 1976), 189.

66. Keiser, "Mystics and the Early English Printers," 10.

67. Keiser, "Mystics and Printers," 22–23. Keiser points out that we have no evidence of the literary patronage of the merchant class for de Worde's printed books, but he argues that it nevertheless remains a strong possibility. Barbara Belyea attributes Caxton's success to the "urban middle class," "Caxton's Reading Public," *ELN* 19 (1981): 18. Bennett notes that 40% of the output of the two major printers in England in the early sixteenth century, de Worde and Henry Pynson, was religious and devotional, and that it catered to a religious as well as a lay audience, *English Books and Readers 1475–1557*, 65.

68. Blake, *Caxton: England's First Printer*, 191.

69. Quoted in Keiser, "Mystics and Printers," 16. I am indebted to Keiser for my own description of this sixteenth-century taste in devotional literature, 15–20.

70. Blake, *Caxton: England's First Printer*, 189. Holbrook speculates that Kempe's last confessor, Master Robert Springold, a secular and bachelor of law, made the compilation, "Margery Kempe and Wynkyn de Worde," 38–40.

71. Quoted in Blake, *Caxton: England's First Printer*, 90.

72. Pepwell's edition is preserved in the British Museum Library, C. 37. It has been revised and modernized by Edmund G. Gardner, *The Cell of Self-Knowledge* (London: Chatto and Windus, 1925), 51–59.

73. Riehle, *Middle English Mystics*, 10. For this view, see Phyllis Hodgson, *Three 14th-Century English Mystics* (London: Longmans, 1967), 32. The treatise begins: "Dere brother in Cryste I haue vnderstandynge by thyne owne speche / and also by tellynge of another man þat thou yernest and sesyrest gretely for to haue more knowledge and vnderstandynge then thoug hast of aungelles songe / and heuenly sowne / what it is / and on what wyse it is perceyued & felte in a mannes soule / &

howe a man may be syker that it is trewe / and not fayned / & howe it is made by the presence of the good aungell / and not by the in-puttynge of þe euyll aungell." A Middle English version of this work may be found in C. Horstmann, *Yorkshire Writers: Richard Rolle of Hampole* (London and New York, 1895), 175–83.

74. *The Cell of Self-Knowledge*, xx–xxi.

75. I have already cited some of the criticisms of Kempe's book. Only Martin Thornton makes a point of distinguishing (rather than comparing) Kempe's work and those of Catherine or Julian, in the first extended study of Kempe's book, *Margery Kempe: An Example in the English Pastoral Tradition* (London: SPCK, 1960). He tries to remove her from the ascetic tradition in which Pepwell's edition placed her and reconsider her in the pastoral tradition, 14–15.

76. His review appears in the *Tablet*, October 24, 1936, 570.

77. *Mystic and Pilgrim*, 201.

78. I am borrowing Barry A. Windeatt's comment about the inconclusiveness of the ending of Kempe's book in his modern English translation, *The Book of Margery Kempe* (New York: Penguin Books, 1985), 15. To be fair, Windeatt does not make an argument about Kempe's influence, but like other scholars he is mainly interested in the book as it reflects her life. This is the way in which Kempe becomes isolated through the reluctance of scholars to venture beyond her life for her book's cultural significance.

79. Windeatt, *The Book of Margery Kempe*, 23.

80. Nancy Partner pretends to reread Kempe's book, but her conclusions are alarmingly similar to early Freudian assessments of Kempe's sexuality and disturbingly unselfconscious, "Rereading *The Book of Margery Kempe*: Psychohistory, Psychonarrative, and History," a paper presented at the International Congress on Medieval Studies at Kalamazoo, Michigan, 1990. It will be published by *Exemplaria* in Spring 1991.

81. *Mysticism. A Study in the Nature and Development of Man's Spiritual Consciousness* (New York: Dalton, 1961), 454.

82. Stephen E. Ozment, *Mysticism and Dissent: Religious Ideology and Social Protest in the Sixteenth Century* (New Haven, CT: Yale University Press, 1973), 1–13, see ch. 1 above. For feminist arguments for the relationship between ideology and mysticism, see Beckwith, "A Very Material Mysticism," 34–57, and Catherine F. Smith, "Jane Lead: The Feminist Mind and Art of a Seventeenth-Century Protestant Mystic," in *Women of Spirit: Female Leadership in the Jewish and Christian Traditions*, ed. Rosemary Ruether and Eleanor McLaughlin (New York: Simon and Schuster, 1979), 183–203.

83. Ozment makes an even stronger case for the anti-institutional and anti-intellectual aspect of mystical discourse in its reliance on the individual's experience in the world, *Mysticism and Dissent*, 4–13.

Bibliography

PRIMARY SOURCES

Aelred of Rievaulx. *Aelred of Rievaulx's De Institutione Inclusarum*. Ed. John Ayto and Alexandra Barratt. EETS, o.s. 287. London: Oxford University Press, 1984.

Ambrose. *Epistolae. PL* 16, cols. 913–1342.

Ambrose. *Expositio Evangelii Secundum Lucam*. Ed. M. Adriaen. CCSL 14. Turnhout: Brepols, 1957.

Anselm, Saint. *The Prayers and Meditations of St. Anselm*. Trans. Benedicta Ward, S.L.G. Middlesex: Penguin, 1973.

Aristotle. *Peri Hermenias I*. Trans. Harold P. Cooke. Loeb Classical Library. Cambridge, MA: Harvard University Press, 1938.

Augustine. *De civitate Dei*. Ed. Bernardus Dombart and Alphonsus Kalb. CCSL 47–48. Turnhout: Brepols, 1955.

———. *De Genesi ad litteram. PL* 40, cols. 415–75.

———. *De trinitate*. Ed. W. J. Mountain and Fr. Glorie. CCSL 50–50A. Turnhout: Brepols, 1968.

———. *Enarrationes in psalmos*. Ed. D. Eligius Dekkers and Iohannes Fraipont. CCSL 38–40. Turnhout: Brepols, 1956.

Baker, Donald C., John L. Murphy and Louis B. Hall, Jr., eds. *The Late Medieval Religious Plays of Bodleian Mss. Digby 133 and E Museo 160*. EETS, o.s. 283. London: Oxford University Press, 1982.

Barnum, Priscilla Heath, ed. *Dives and Pauper*. EETS, o.s. 275. London: Oxford University Press, 1976.

Bazire, Joyce and Eric Colledge, eds. *The Chastising of God's Children and the Treatise of Perfection of the Sons of God*. Oxford: Basil Blackwell, 1957.

Beadle, Richard and Pamela L. King, eds. *York Mystery Plays*. Oxford: Clarendon Press, 1984.

Benson, Larry D., ed. *The Riverside Chaucer*. New York: Riverside, 1987.

Bernard of Clairvaux. *Sermo de conversione ad clericos*. In *S. Bernardi Opera*. Vol. IV. Ed. J. Leclercq and H. M. Rochais. Rome: Editiones Cistercienses, 1957.

———. *Bernard of Clairvaux: Selected Works*. Trans. G. R. Evans. New York: Paulist Press, 1987.

———. *Sermones de diversis*. Ed. J. Leclercq and H. Rochais. In *S. Bernardi Opera*. Vol. VI, pt. 1. Rome: Editiones Cistercienses, 1970.

———. *Sermones super cantica canticorum*. In *S. Bernardi Opera*. Vol. I. Ed. J. Leclercq, H. M. Rochais, and C. H. Talbot. Rome: Editiones Cistercienses, 1957.

Block, K. S., ed. *Ludus Coventriae, or the Plaie called Corpus Christi*. EETS, e.s. 120. London: Oxford University Press, 1922; rpt. 1960, 1974.

Blume, Clemens and Guido Maria Dreves, eds. *Analecta hymnica Medii Aevi*. New York, 1961.

Bokenham, Osbern. *Legendys of Hooly Wummen*. Ed. Mary S. Sergeantson. EETS, o.s. 206. London: Oxford University Press 1938; rpt. 1971.

Blunt, John Henry. *The Myroure of Oure Ladye*. EETS, e.s. 19. London: Oxford University Press, 1973.

Pseudo-Bonaventure. *Meditations on the Life of Christ*. Trans. Isa Ragusa. Ed. Isa Ragusa and Rosalie B. Green. Princeton, NJ: Princeton University Press, 1961.

Bridget of Sweden. *The Revelations of Saint Birgitta*. Ed. William Patterson Cumming. EETS, o.s. 178. London, 1929; rpt. 1971.

Brown, Carleton, ed. *Religious Lyrics of the Fifteenth Century*. Oxford: Clarendon Press, 1939.

Burchard of Worms. *Decretorum libri XX*. PL 140, cols. 557–1058.

Capes, William W. *The Register of John Trefnant, Bishop of Hereford*. Hereford, 1914.

Catherine of Siena. *The Orcherd of Syon*. Ed. Phyllis Hodgson and Gabriel M. Liegey. EETS, o.s. 258. London: Oxford University Press, 1966.

Chrysostom, John. *Homilies on the Epistle to the Hebrews*. Ed. F. Gardner. *A Select Library of Nicene and Post-Nicene Fathers*. Vol. 14. Grand Rapids, MI: Eerdmans, 1978.

Christine de Pisan. *The Book of the City of Ladies*. Trans. Earl Jeffrey Richards. New York: Persea Books, 1982.

Colledge, Edmund and Bernard McGinn, trans. *Meister Eckhart: The Essential Sermons, Commentaries, Treatises and Defense*. New York: Paulist Press, 1981.

Deanesly, Margaret, ed. *The Incendium Amoris of Richard Rolle of Hampole*. Publications of the University of Manchester, Historical Series, 26. London, 1915.

Desmarais, M.-M., O.P., trans. *S. Albert le Grand. Docteur de la méditation morale*. Paris and Ottawa, 1935.

Dumeige, Gervais, ed. and trans. *Richard de Saint-Victor: Les Quatre degrés de la violente charité*. Paris, 1955.

Farmer, Hugh, ed. *The Monk of Farne: The Meditations of a Fourteenth Century Monk*. Trans. by a Benedictine of Stanbrook. London: Darton, Longman and Todd, 1961.

Ferré, M. J. and L. Baudry, ed. and trans. *Le Livre de l'expérience des vrais fidèles: Texte latin publié d'après le manuscript d'Assise*. Paris: Droz, 1927.

Furnivall, F. J., ed. *Political, Religious, and Love Poems*. EETS, o.s. 15. London, 1866.

Gardner, Edmund G. *The Cell of Self-Knowledge*. New York and London: Chatto and Windus, 1925.

Hodgson, Phyllis, ed. *The Cloud of Unknowing*. EETS 218. London: Oxford University Press, 1944; rpt. 1958, 1973.

———. *Deonise Hid Diuinite*. EETS, o.s. 231. London: Oxford University Press, 1958.

Hogg, James, ed. "A Mystical Diary: The *Refectorium Salutis* of Richard Methley of Mount Grace Charterhouse." *Kartausermystik und -mystiker*, Bd. 2. *Analecta Carthusiana* 55 (1981): 208–38.

————. "Richard Methley: To Hew Heremyte, A Pystyl of Solytary Lyfe Nowa-dayes." *Analecta Carthusiana* 31 (1977): 91–119.

Holmstedt, G., ed. *Speculum Christiani*. EETS, o.s. 182. London: Oxford University Press, 1933; rpt. 1971.

Horstmann, C., ed. *Prosalagenden. Die legenden des Ms. Douce 114. Anglia* 8 (1885): 134–83.

Hugh of St. Victor. *Selected Spiritual Writings*. Trans. A Religious of CSMV London: Faber and Faber, 1962.

Humbert of Romans. *Treatise on Preaching*. Ed. Walter M. Conlon. Trans. The Dominican Students, Province of St. Joseph. Westminster, MD: Newman Press, 1951.

Jacopone da Todi. *Jacopone da Todi: The Lauds*. Ed. Serge and Elizabeth Hughes. New York: Paulist Press, 1982.

John Chrysostom. *Homilies on the Epistle to the Hebrews*. Ed. F. Gardner. *A Select Library of Nicene and Post-Nicene Fathers*. Vol. 14. Grand Rapids, MI: Eerdmans, 1978.

Julian of Norwich. *A Book of Showings to the Anchoress Julian of Norwich*. Ed. Edmund Colledge and James Walsh. 2 vols. Toronto: Pontifical Institute of Mediaeval Studies, 1978.

————. *Showings*. Trans. Edmund Colledge and James Walsh. New York: Paulist Press, 1978.

Kempe, Margery. *The Book of Margery Kempe*. Ed. and trans. William Butler-Bowdon. New York, 1944.

————. *The Book of Margery Kempe*. Ed. Sanford B. Meech and Hope Emily Allen. EETS, o.s. 212. London: Oxford University Press, 1940; rpt. 1961.

————. *The Book of Margery Kempe*. Trans. Barry A. Windeatt. New York: Penguin, 1985.

Kirchberger, Clare, trans. *The Goad of Love*. London, 1952.

Lumiansky, R. M. and David Mills, eds. *The Chester Mystery Cycle*. EETS, s.s. 3, vol. 1. London: Oxford University Press, 1974.

Lydgate, John. *The Minor Poems of John Lydgate*. Ed. Henry Nobel McCracken. EETS, e.s. 107. London: Oxford University Press, 1911; rpt. 1962.

Manning, Robert. *Meditations on the Supper of Our Lord, and the Hours of the Passion*. Ed. J. Meadows Cowper. EETS, o.s. 60. London, 1875.

Mastro, M. L. Del, trans. *The Stairway of Perfection*. Garden City, NY: Image Books, 1979.

Mechtild of Hackeborn. *The Book of Gostlye Grace of Mechtild of Hackeborn*. Ed. Theresa M. Halligan. Studies and Texts 46. Toronto: Pontifical Institute of Medieval Studies, 1979.

Methley, Richard. *Dormitorium dilecti dilecti*. Trinity College, Cambridge MS. O. 2. 56 (1160): ff. 25r–48r.

————. *Refectorium salutis*. Trinity College, Cambridge MS. O. 2. 56 (1160): ff. 49r–70v.

————. *Scola amoris languidi*. Trinity College, Cambridge MS. O. 2. 56 (1160): ff. 1r–24v.

Millett, Bella, ed. *Hali Meiðhad*. EETS, o.s. 284. London: Oxford University Press, 1982.

Morris, Richard, ed. *Cursor Mundi*. EETS 68. London: N. Trubner, 1878.

Muckle, J. T., ed. "The Letter of Heloise on Religious Life and Abelard's First Reply." *Mediaeval Studies* 17 (1955): 241–53.

Noffke, Suzanne, trans. *Catherine of Siena: The Dialogue*. New York: Paulist Press, 1980.

Petroff, Elizabeth Alvilda, ed. *Medieval Women's Visionary Literature*. Oxford: Oxford University Press, 1986.

Rolle, Richard. *The English Writings of Richard Rolle, Hermit of Hampole*. Ed. Hope Emily Allen. Oxford: Clarendon Press, 1931.

———. *The Fire of Love*. Trans. Clifton Wolters. New York: Penguin, 1972.

———. *The Fire of Love, and The Mending of Life or The Rule of Living*. Trans. Richard Misyn. Ed. Ralph Harvey. EETS 106, o.s. London, 1896; rpt. in 1973.

———. *Richard Rolle: The English Writings*. Trans. Rosamund S. Allen. New York: Paulist Press, 1988.

———. *The Melos Amoris of Richard Rolle*. Ed. E. J. F. Arnould. Oxford: Basil Blackwell, 1957.

———. *Writings Ascribed to Richard Rolle, Hermit of Hampole and Materials for His Biography*. Ed. Hope Emily Allen. The Modern Language Association of America, Monograph Series 3. New York: D.C. Heath and Co., 1927.

———. *Yorkshire Writers: Richard Rolle of Hampole: An English Father of the Church, and His Followers*. Ed. C. Horstman. London: Swan Sonnenschein and Co., Vol I, 1895.

Rowland, Beryl, ed. *Medieval Woman's Guide to Health: The First English Gynecological Handbook*. Kent, OH: Kent State University Press, 1981.

Salu, M. D., trans. *The Ancrene Riwle*. London: Burns and Oates, 1955.

Suso, Henry. *The Life of the Servant*. Trans. James M. Clark. London, 1952.

Tanner, Norman C. *Heresy Trials in the Diocese of Norwich, 1428–31*. London, 1977.

Theoderich. *Guide to the Holy Land*. Trans. Aubrey Stewart. 2nd ed. New York: Italica Press, 1986.

Thomas à Kempis. *The Imitation of Christ*. Trans. Leo Sherley-Price. New York: Penguin, 1952.

Tolkien, J.R.R., ed. *Ancrene Wisse: The English Text of the Ancrene Riwle edited from MS. Corpus Christi College Cambridge 402*. EETS 249. London: Oxford University Press, 1962.

Walsh, James, trans. *The Cloud of Unknowing*. New York: Paulist Press, 1981.

Wilson, Edward. *A Descriptive Index of the English Lyrics of John of Grimestone's Preaching Book*. Oxford: Basil Blackwell, 1973.

Wilson, Katharina M., ed. *Medieval Women Writers*. Athens: University of Georgia Press, 1984.

SECONDARY SOURCES

Aers, David. *Community, Gender, and Individual Identity: English Writing 1360–1430*. London: Routledge, 1988.

Allen, Rosamund, "'Singuler Lufe': Richard Rolle and the Grammar of Spiritual Ascent." In *The Medieval Mystical Tradition in England: Papers Read at Dartington Hall, July 1984*. Proceedings of the Third International Exeter Symposium, ed. Marion Glasscoe. Cambridge: D. S. Brewer, 1984. 28–54.

Aston, Margaret. *Lollards and Reformers: Images and Literacy in Late Medieval Religion*. London: Hambledon Press, 1984.

———. "Lollardy and Sedition, 1381–1431." *Past and Present* 17 (1960): 1–44.

Atkinson, Clarissa W. *Mystic and Pilgrim: The Book and the World of Margery Kempe*. Ithaca, NY: Cornell University Press, 1983.

Bakhtin, Mikhail. *Rabelais and His World*. Trans. Helene Iswolsky. Bloomington: Indiana University Press, 1984.

Barasche, Moshe. *Gestures of Despair in Medieval and Early Renaissance Art*. New York: New York University Press, 1976.

Bateson, Mary, ed. *Catalogue of the Library of Syon Monastery*. Cambridge, 1898.

Bäuml, Franz H. "Varieties and Consequences of Medieval Literacy and Illiteracy." *Speculum* 55 (1980): 237–65.

Beckwith, Sarah, "A Very Material Mysticism: The Medieval Mysticism of Margery Kempe." In *Medieval Literature: Criticism, Ideology, and History*. Ed. David Aers. Brighton: Harvester Press, 1986. 34–57.

Belyea, Barbara. "Caxton's Reading Public." *ELN* 19 (1981): 14–19.

Bell, Susan Groag. "Medieval Women Book Owners: Arbiters of Lay Piety and Ambassadors of Culture." In *Women and Power in the Middle Ages*. Ed. Mary Erler and Maryanne Kowaleski. Athens: University of Georgia Press, 1988. 149–87.

Bennett, H. S. *English Books and Readers, 1475–1557*. Cambridge: Cambridge University Press, 1952.

Bennett, Judith M. "Public Power and Authority in the Medieval English Countryside." In *Women and Power in the Middle Ages*. Ed. Mary Erler and Maryanne Kowaleski. Athens: University of Georgia Press, 1988. 18–36.

———. "The Village Ale-Wife: Women and Brewing in Fourteenth-Century England." In *Women and Work in Preindustrial Europe*. Ed. Barbara A. Hanawalt. Bloomington: Indiana University Press, 1986. 20–36.

Blake, N. F. *Caxton: England's First Publisher*. New York: Harper and Row, 1976.

———. "Revelations of St. Matilda." *Notes and Queries* 20 (1973): 323–25.

Brown, Peter. *The Body and Society: Men, Women, and Sexual Renunciation in Early Christianity*. New York: Columbia University Press, 1988.

Bugge, John. *Virginitas: An Essay in the History of a Medieval Ideal*. Archives internationales d'histoire des idées. Series minor 17. The Hague: Martinus Nijhoff, 1975.

Bullough, Vern L. "Medical and Scientific Views of Women." *Viator* 4 (1973): 485–501.

Burrow, J. A. *The Ages of Man: A Study in Medieval Writing and Thought*. Oxford: Clarendon Press, 1986.

Bynum, Carolyn Walker. "The Female Body and Religious Practice in the Later Middle Ages." In *Fragments for a History of the Human Body*, Part 1. Ed. Michel Feher, Ramona Naddaff, and Nadia Tazi. New York: Urzone, 1989. 161–219.

————. *Fragmentation and Redemption: Essays on Gender and the Human Body in Medieval Religion*. New York: Urzone, 1989.

————. *Holy Feast and Holy Fast: The Religious Significance of Food to Medieval Women*. Berkeley: University of California Press, 1987.

————. *Jesus As Mother: Studies in the Spirituality of the High Middle Ages*. Berkeley: University of California Press, 1982.

Camporesi, Piero. *The Incorruptible Flesh: Bodily Mutation and Mortification in Religion and Folklore*. Trans. Tania Croft-Murray. Cambridge: Cambridge University Press, 1988.

Certeau, Michel de. *La fable mystique, XVIᵉ–XVIIᵉ*. Bibliothèque des Histoires. Paris: Éditions Gallimard, 1982.

————. *Heterologies: Discourse on the Other*. Trans. Brian Massumi. Minneapolis: University of Minnesota Press, 1986.

Cixous, Hélène. "The Laugh of the Medusa." In *New French Feminisms*. Ed. Elaine Marks and Isabelle de Courtivron. New York: Schocken Books, 1981. 245–64.

Cixous, Hélène and Catherine Clément. *The Newly Born Woman*. Trans. Betsy Wing. Minneapolis: University of Minnesota Press, 1986.

Clanchy, M. T. *From Memory to Written Record: England, 1066–1307*. Cambridge, MA: Harvard University Press, 1979.

Coleman, Janet. *Medieval Readers and Writers: 1350–1400*. New York: Columbia University Press, 1981.

Coleman, T. W. *English Mystics of the Fourteenth Century*. Westport, CT: Greenwood Press, 1971.

Collis, Louise. *Memoirs of a Medieval Woman: The Life and Times of Margery Kempe*. New York: Crowell, 1964.

Cross, Claire. "'Great Reasoners in Scripture': The Activities of Women Lollards 1380–1530." In *Medieval Women*. Ed. Derek Baker. Oxford: Basil Blackwell, 1978. 359–80.

Delaney, Sheila. "'Mothers to Think Back Through': Who Are They? The Ambiguous Example of Christine de Pizan." In *Medieval Texts and Contemporary Readers*. Ed. Laurie A. Finke and Martin S. Shichtman. Ithaca, NY: Cornell University Press, 1987. Pp. 177–97.

Denise, Mary. "*The Orcherd of Syon*: An Introduction." *Traditio* 14 (1958): 273–81.

Dickman, Susan. "Margery Kempe and the Continental Tradition of the Pious Woman." In *The Medieval Mystical Tradition: Papers Read at Darlington Hall, July 1984*. Proceedings of the Third International Exeter Symposium. Ed. Marion Glasscoe. Woodbridge, Suffolk, 1984. 150–70.

————. "Margery Kempe and the English Devotional Tradition." In *The Medieval Mystical Tradition in England: Papers Read at the Exeter Symposium, July 1980*. Ed. Marion Glasscoe. University of Exeter, 1980. 156–72.

Dinshaw, Carolyn. *Chaucer's Sexual Poetics*. Madison: University of Wisconsin Press, 1989.

Douglas, Mary. *Purity and Danger: An Analysis of the Concepts of Pollution and Taboo*. London: Routledge and Kegan Paul, 1966.

Eco, Umberto. *The Aesthetics of Thomas Aquinas*. Trans. Hugh Bredin. Cambridge, MA: Harvard University Press, 1988.

Edwards, Robert. *The Montecassino Passion and the Poetics of Medieval Drama*. Berkeley: University of California Press, 1977.

Ferrante, Joan M. "The Education of Women in the Middle Ages in Theory, Fact, and Fantasy." In *Beyond Their Sex: Learned Women of the European Past*. Ed. Patricia H. Labalme. New York and London: New York University Press, 1980. 9–42.

Fleischman, Suzanne. "Philology, Linguistics, and the Discourse of the Medieval Text." *Speculum* 65 (1990): 19–37.

Fleming, John V. *An Introduction to the Franciscan Order*. Chicago: Franciscan Herald Press, 1977.

Foucault, Michel. *The Archaeology of Knowledge and the Discourse on Language*. Trans. A. M. Sheridan Smith. New York: Pantheon Books, 1972.

———. *Language, Counter-Memory, Practice: Selected Essays and Interviews*. Trans. Donald F. Bouchard and Sherry Simon. Ithaca, NY: Cornell University Press, 1977.

Fries, Maureen. "Margery Kempe." In *An Introduction to the Medieval Mystics of Europe*. Ed. Paul E. Szarmach. Albany: State University of New York Press, 1984. 217–35.

Gallop, Jane. *Thinking Through the Body*. New York: Columbia University Press, 1988.

Geary, Patrick J. *Furta Sacra: Thefts of Relics in the Central Middle Ages*. Princeton, NJ: Princeton University Press, 1978.

Gellrich, Jesse M. *The Idea of the Book in the Middle Ages: Language Theory, Mythology, and Fiction*. Ithaca, NY: Cornell University Press, 1985.

Gilson, Etienne. *The Mystical Theology of St. Bernard*. Trans. A.H.C. Downes. London, 1940.

Goodman, Anthony E. "The Piety of John Brunham's Daughter, of Lynn." In *Medieval Women*. Ed. Derek Baker. Oxford: Basil Blackwell, 1978. 347–58.

Grabes, Herbert. *The Mutable Glass: Mirror-Imagery in Titles and Texts of the Middle Ages and English Renaissance*. Trans. Gordon Collier. Cambridge: Cambridge University Press, 1989.

Graef, Hilda. *Mary: A History of Doctrine and Devotion*. 2 vols. New York: Sheed and Ward, 1963.

Gray, Douglas. *Themes and Images in the Medieval English Religious Lyric*. London: Routledge and Kegan Paul, 1972.

Grayson, Janet. *Structure and Imagery in Ancrene Wisse*. Hanover, NH: University Press of New England, 1974.

Hamburgh, Harvey E. "Aspects of the *Descent from the Cross from Lippi to Cigoli*." Dissertation: University of Iowa, 1978. 2 vols.

———. "The Problem of *Lo Spasimo* of the Virgin in *Cinquecento* Paintings of the *Descent from the Cross*." *Sixteenth Century Journal* 12 (1981): 45–76.

Hanning, Robert W. "'I Shal Finde It in a Maner Glose': Versions of Textual Harassment in Medieval Literature." In *Medieval Texts and Contemporary Readers*. Ed. Laurie A. Finke and Martin B. Shichtman. Ithaca, NY: Cornell University Press, 1987. 27–50.

Hardison, O. B. *Christian Rite and Christian Drama in the Middle Ages*. Baltimore: Johns Hopkins University Press, 1965.

Hirsh, John C. "Author and Scribe in *The Book of Margery Kempe*." *Medium Aevum* 44 (1975): 145–50.

Hodgson, Phyllis. "*The Orcherd of Syon* and the English Mystical Tradition." *Proceedings of the British Academy* 50 (1964): 229–49.

———. *Three 14th-Century English Mystics*. London: Longmans, 1967.

Hogg, James. "Mount Grace Charterhouse and Late Medieval English Spirituality." *Analecta Carthusiana* 82, pt. 3 (1980): 1–43.

Holbrook, Sue Ellen. "Margery Kempe and Wynkyn de Worde." In *The Medieval Mystical Tradition in England: Papers Read at Dartington Hall, July 1987*. Ed. Marion Glasscoe. Exeter Symposium IV. London: D. S. Brewer, 1987. 27–46.

Huizinga, J. *The Waning of the Middle Ages*. New York: Doubleday, 1954.

Irigaray, Luce. *This Sex Which Is Not One*. Trans. Catherine Porter. Ithaca, NY: Cornell University Press, 1985.

Jacobus, Mary, Evelyn Fox Keller, and Sally Shuttleworth, eds. *Body/Politics: Women and the Discourses of Science*. New York and London: Routledge, 1990.

Jacquart, Danielle and Claude Thomasset. *Sexuality and Medicine in the Middle Ages*. Trans. Matthew Adamson. Princeton, NJ: Princeton University Press, 1988.

Keiser, George R. "The Mystics and the Early English Printers: The Economics of Devotionalism." In *The Medieval Mystical Tradition in England*. Ed. Marion Glasscoe. London: D. S. Brewer, 1987. 9–26.

Kermode, Frank. *The Genesis of Secrecy: On the Interpretation of Narrative*. Cambridge, MA: Harvard University Press, 1979.

Kieckhefer, Richard. *Unquiet Souls: Fourteenth-Century Saints and Their Religious Milieu*. Chicago: University of Chicago Press, 1984.

Knowles, David. *The English Mystical Tradition*. London: Burns and Oates, 1961.

———. *The Religious Orders in England*. 3 vols. Cambridge: Cambridge University Press, 1957–62.

Kolve, V. A. *Chaucer and the Imagery of Narrative: The First Five Canterbury Tales*. Stanford, CA: Stanford University Press, 1984.

Kowaleski, Maryanne. "Women's Work in a Market Town: Exeter in the Late Fourteenth Century." In *Women and Work in Preindustrial Europe*. Ed. Barbara A. Hanawalt. Bloomington: Indiana University Press, 1986.

Kristeva, Julia. *Desire in Language: A Semiotic Approach to Literature and Art*. Ed. Leon S. Roudiez. Trans. Thomas Gora, Alice Jardine, and Leon S. Roudiez. New York: Columbia University Press, 1980.

———. "Holbein's Dead Christ." In *Fragments for a History of the Human Body*. Part 1. Ed. Michel Feher, Ramona Naddaff, and Nadia Tazi. New York: Urzone, 1989. 238–69.

———. *Powers of Horror: An Essay in Abjection*. Trans. Leon S. Roudiez. New York: Columbia University Press, 1982.

———. *Tales of Love*. Trans. Leon S. Roudiez. New York: Columbia University Press, 1987.

Laqueur, Thomas. *Making Sex: Body and Gender from the Greeks to Freud*. Cambridge, MA: Harvard University Press, 1990.

Ladner, Gerhart B. *"Homo Viator*: Medieval Ideas of Alienation and Order." *Speculum* 42 (1967): 239–46.

Lawton, David. "The Voice of Margery Kempe's Book." Paper presented at the Modern Language Association Convention, New Orleans, 1988.

Le Goff, Jacques. *The Medieval Imagination*. Trans. Arthur Goldhammer. Chicago: University of Chicago Press, 1988.

Lochrie, Karma. *"The Book of Margery Kempe*: A Marginal Woman's Quest for Literary Authority." *Journal of Medieval and Renaissance Studies* 16 (1986): 33–56.

Lovatt, Roger. "The *Imitation of Christ* in Late Medieval England." *Transactions of the Royal Historical Society*, Fifth Series 18 (1968): 97–121.

Maclean, Ian. *The Renaissance Notion of Woman: A Study in the Fortunes of Scholasticism and Medical Science in European Intellectual Life*. Cambridge: Cambridge University Press, 1980.

McDonnell, Ernest W. *The Beguines and Beghards in Medieval Culture*. New Brunswick, NJ: Rutgers University Press, 1954.

Maisonneuve, Roland. "Margery Kempe and the Eastern and Western Tradition of the 'perfect fool.'" In *The Medieval Mystical Tradition in England: Papers Read at the Second Exeter Symposium, July 1982*. Ed. Marion Glasscoe. University of Exeter, 1982. 1–17.

Minh-ha, Trinh T. *Woman, Native, Other: Writing Postcoloniality and Feminism*. Bloomington: Indiana University Press, 1989.

Minnis, A. J. *Medieval Theory of Authorship: Scholastic Literary Attitudes in the Later Middle Ages*. London: Scolar Press, 1984; 2nd ed. Philadelphia: University of Pennsylvania Press, 1988.

Moeller, Bernard, "Piety in Germany Around 1500." In *The Reformation in Medieval Perspective*. Ed. Stephen Ozment. Chicago: University of Chicago Press, 1971. 50–75.

Moore, R. I. *The Formation of a Persecuting Society: Power and Deviance in Western Europe, 950–1250*. Oxford: Basil Blackwell, 1987.

Moorman, John. *The History of the Franciscan Order*. Oxford: Clarendon Press, 1968.

Murray, Alexander. *Reason and Society in the Middle Ages*. Oxford: Clarendon Press, 1978.

Newman, Barbara. *Sister of Wisdom: St. Hildegard's Theology of the Feminine*. Berkeley: University of California Press, 1987.

Obrist, Barbara. "The Swedish Visionary Saint Bridget." In *Medieval Women Writers*. Ed. Katharina M. Wilson. Athens: University of Georgia Press, 1984. 227–51.

Olson, Glending. *Literature as Recreation in the Later Middle Ages*. Ithaca, NY: Cornell University Press, 1982.

Ong, Walter J. *Orality and Literacy: The Technologizing of the Word*. New York: Methuen, 1982.

———. "Orality, Literacy, and Medieval Textualization." *New Literary History* 16 (1984): 1–12.

———. *The Presence of the Word: Some Prolegomena for Culture in Religious History*. New Haven, CT: Yale University Press, 1967.

Owst, G. R. *Literature and the Pulpit in Medieval England*. Oxford: Basil Blackwell, 1961.

―――. *Preaching in Medieval England: An Introduction to the Sermon Manuscripts of the Period c. 1350–1450*. New York: Russell and Russell, 1965.

Ozment, Stephen. *Mysticism and Dissent: Religious Ideology and Social Protest in the Sixteenth Century*. New Haven, CT: Yale University Press, 1973.

Pagels, Elaine. *Adam, Eve, and the Serpent*. New York: Random House, 1988.

―――. *The Gnostic Gospels*. New York: Vintage Books, 1979.

Pantin, William Abel. "Instructions for a Devout and Literate Layman." In *Medieval Learning and Literature: Essays presented to Richard William Hunt*. Ed. J. J. G. Alexander and M. T. Gibson. Oxford: Clarendon Press, 1976.

Partner, Nancy. "Rereading *The Book of Margery Kempe*: Psychohistory, Psychonarrative, and History." Paper presented at the International Congress of Medieval Studies, Kalamazoo, MI, 1990.

Patterson, Lee. *Negotiating the Past: The Historical Understanding of Medieval Literature*. Madison: University of Wisconsin Press, 1987.

Peck, George T. *The Fool of God: Jacopone da Todi*. University: University of Alabama Press, 1980.

Riehle, Wolfgang. *The Middle English Mystics*. Trans. Bernard Standring. London: Routledge and Kegan Paul, 1981.

Robertson, D. W., Jr. *A Preface to Chaucer: Studies in Medieval Perspectives*. Princeton, NJ: Princeton University Press, 1962.

Robertson, Elizabeth. *Early English Devotional Prose and the Female Audience*. Knoxville: University of Tennessee Press, 1990.

―――. "The Rule of the Body: The Feminine Spirituality of the *Ancrene Wisse*." In *Seeking the Woman in Late Medieval and Renaissance Writings: Essays in Feminist Contextual Criticism*. Ed. Sheila Fisher and Janet E. Halley. Knoxville: University of Tennessee Press, 1989. 109–34.

Sargent, Michael G. "The Transmission by the English Carthusians of Some Late Medieval Spiritual Writings." *Journal of Ecclesiastical History* 27 (1976): 225–40.

Scarry, Elaine. *The Body in Pain: The Making and Unmaking of the World*. Oxford: Oxford University Press, 1985.

Schaub, Uta Liebmann. "Foucault's Oriental Subtext." *PMLA* 104 (May, 1989): 306–16.

Schulenburg, Jane Tibbetts. "The Heroics of Virginity: 'Brides of Christ and Sacrificial Mutilation.'" In *Women in the Middle Ages and the Renaissance: Literary and Historical Perspectives*. Ed. Mary Beth Rose. Syracuse: Syracuse University Press, 1986.

Smith, Catherine F. "Jane Lead: The Feminist Mind and Art of a Seventeenth-Century Protestant Mystic." In *Women of Spirit: Female Leadership in the Jewish and Christian Traditions*. Ed. Rosemary Ruether and Eleanor McLaughlin. New York: Simon and Schuster, 1979. 183–203.

Stallybrass, Peter. "Patriarchal Territories: The Body Enclosed." In *Rewriting the Renaissance: The Discourses of Sexual Difference in Early Modern Europe*. Ed. Margaret W. Ferguson, Maureen Quilligan, and Nancy J. Vickers. Chicago: University of Chicago Press, 1986. 123–42.

Stallybrass, Peter and Allon White. *The Politics and Poetics of Transgression*. Ithaca, NY: Cornell University Press, 1986.

Stanton, Domna C. "Autobiography: Is the Subject Different?" In *The Female Autograph*. Ed. Domna Stanton. Chicago: University of Chicago Press, 1987.

Stargardt, Ute. "The Beguines of Belgium, the Dominican Nuns of Germany, and Margery Kempe." In *The Popular Literature of Medieval England*. Ed. Thomas J. Heffernan. Tennessee Studies in Literature, vol. 28. Knoxville: University of Tennessee Press, 1985. 277–313.

———. "The Influence of Dorotea von Mantau on the Mysticism of Margery Kempe." Dissertation, University of Tennessee, 1981.

Sticca, Sandro. *The Latin Passion Play: Its Origins and Development*. Albany: State University of New York Press, 1970.

———. *The Planctus Mariae in the Dramatic Tradition of the Middle Ages*. Trans. Joseph R. Berrigan. Athens: University of Georgia Press, 1988.

Stock, Brian. *The Implications of Literacy: Written Language and Models of Interpretation in the Eleventh and Twelfth Centuries*. Princeton, NJ: Princeton University Press, 1983.

———. *Listening for the Text: On the Uses of the Past*. Baltimore: Johns Hopkins University Press, 1990.

Stone, Robert K. *Middle English Prose Style: Margery Kempe and Julian of Norwich*. The Hague and Paris: Mouton, 1970.

Suleiman, Susan Rubin, ed. *The Female Body in Western Culture: Contemporary Perspectives*. Cambridge, MA: Harvard University Press, 1986.

Taylor, George C. "The English "Planctus Mariae,'" *MP* 4 (1907): 606–37.

Thompson, E. Margaret. *The Carthusian Order in England*. London, 1930.

Thornton, Martin. *Margery Kempe: An Example in the English Pastoral Tradition*. London: SPCK, 1960.

Thurston, Herbert. Review. *Tablet*, October 24, 1936: 570.

Underhill, Evelyn. *Mysticism. A Study in the Nature and Development of Man's Spiritual Consciousness*. New York: Dutton, 1961.

Vance, Eugene. *Mervelous Signals: Poetics and Sign Theory in the Middle Ages*. Lincoln: University of Nebraska Press, 1986.

Vauchez, André. *Les laïcs au Moyen Âge: pratiques et expériences religieuses*. Paris: Éditions du Cerf, 1987.

———. *La Sainteté en Occident aux derniers siècles du moyen âge d'après les procès de canonisation et les documents hagiographiques*. Bibliothèque des études françaises d'Athènes et de Rome 241. Rome: École Française de Rome, 1981.

Verdon, Timothy. "The Art of Guido Mazzoni." Dissertation: Yale University, 1975.

Wallace, David. "Mystics and Followers in Siena and East Anglia: A Study in Taxonomy, Class, and Cultural Mediation." In *The Medieval Mystical Tradition in England: Papers Read at Dartington Hall, July 1984*. Ed. Marion Glasscoe. London, D. S. Brewer, 1984.

Ward, Benedicta, *Harlots of the Desert: A Study of Repentance in Early Monastic Sources*. Kalamazoo, MI: Cistercian Publications Inc., 1987.

Warner, Marina. *Alone of All Her Sex: The Myth and the Cult of the Virgin Mary*. New York: Vintage, 1976.

Warren, Ann K. *Anchorites and Their Patrons in Medieval England*. Berkeley: University of California Press, 1985.

Weaver, Elissa. "Spiritual Fun: A Study of Sixteenth-Century Tuscan Convent Theater." In *Women in the Middle Ages and the Renaissance: Literary and Historical Perspectives*. Ed. Mary Beth Rose. Syracuse: Syracuse University Press, 1986.

Weinstein, Donald and Rudolph M. Bell. *Saints and Society: The Two Worlds of Western Christendom, 1000–1700*. Chicago: University of Chicago Press, 1982.

Weissman, Hope Phyllis. "Margery Kempe in Jerusalem: *Hysterica Compassio* in the Late Middle Ages." In *Acts of Interpretation: The Text in Its Contexts, 700–1600*. Ed. Mary J. Carruthers and Elizabeth Kirk. Norman, OK: Pilgrim Books, 1982.

Wolpers, Theodor. "Englische Marienlyrik im Mittelalter." *Anglia* 69 (1950): 7–88.

Woolf, Rosemary Woolf. "English Imitations of the *Homelia Origenis De Maria Magdalena*." In *Chaucer and the Middle English: Studies in Honour of Russell Hope Robbins*. Ed. Beryl Rowland. Kent, OH: Kent State University Press, 1974. 384–91.

———. *The English Mystery Plays*. Berkeley: University of California Press, 1972.

———. *The English Religious Lyric in the Middle Ages*. Oxford: Clarendon Press, 1968.

Yates, Frances A. *The Art of Memory*. London: Routledge and Kegan Paul, 1966.

Index

University of Pennsylvania Press
NEW CULTURAL STUDIES SERIES
Joan DeJean, Carroll Smith-Rosenberg, and Peter Stallybrass, Editors

Barbara J. Eckstein. *The Language of Fiction in a World of Pain: Reading Politics as Paradox.* 1990.

Alex Owen. *The Darkened Room: Women, Power and Spiritualism in Late Victorian England.* 1990.

Jonathan Arac and Harriet Ritvo, editors. *Macropolitics of Nineteenth-Century Literature: Nationalism, Exoticism, Imperialism.* 1991.

Kathryn Gravdal. *Ravishing Maidens: Writing Rape in Medieval French Literature and Law.* 1991.

Karma Lochrie. *Margery Kempe and Translations of the Flesh.* 1991.

This book has been set in Linotron Galliard. Galliard was designed for Mergenthaler in 1978 by Matthew Carter. Galliard retains many of the features of a sixteenth century typeface cut by Robert Granjon but has some modifications that give it a more contemporary look.

Printed on acid-free paper.